*Ancient
Visions*

Ancient
Visions

Petroglyphs and Pictographs from the Wind River and Bighorn Country, Wyoming and Montana

Julie E. Francis
Lawrence L. Loendorf

THE UNIVERSITY OF UTAH PRESS
SALT LAKE CITY

LIBRARY OF CONGRESS CATALOGING-IN-PUBLICATION DATA

Francis, Julie E.
    Ancient visions : petroglyphs and pictographs from the Wind River and
Bighorn country, Wyoming and Montana / Julie E. Francis and Lawrence L.
Loendorf.
        p.   cm.
    Includes bibliographical references and index.
    ISBN 0-87480-692-5 (alk. paper)
        1. Indians of North America—Wyoming—Wind River Basin—Antiquities.
    2. Indians of North America—Bighorn Basin (Mont. and Wyo.)—Antiquities.
    3. Petroglyphs—Wyoming—Wind River Basin.   4. Petroglyphs—Bighorn Basin
    (Mont. and Wyo.)   5. Rock paintings—Wyoming—Wind River Basin.   6. Rock
    paintings—Bighorn Basin (Mont. and Wyo.).   7. Wind River Basin (Wyo.)—
    Antiquities.   8. Bighorn Basin (Mont. and Wyo.)—Antiquities.
    I. Loendorf, Lawrence L.   II. Title.
    E78.W95 F735   2001
    978.7'6—dc21   2001004437

06 05 04 03 02   FRONTISPIECE   Contrasting images from the Wind River and Bighorn Basins.
                   Left: Shield-bearing warrior painted in polychrome from the Pryor Mountain area,
5 4 3 2 1   Montana. *Right:* Startling pecked Dinwoody anthropomorphic figure from the upper
                   Wind River area, Wyoming.

CONTENTS

FIGURES

TABLES

ACKNOWLEDGMENTS

OVER TWO HOT DAYS IN THE SUMMER OF 1991, WE SET
out with Mike Bies and Gary Bingham of the Worland Office of
the Bureau of Land Management and Marvin Rowe of Texas A & M
University to visit pictograph and petroglyph sites in the Bighorn Basin. To
say the least, the number and quality of the sites we visited impressed us
deeply, but never in our wildest dreams did we imagine we would write a
book about some of those sites and dozens of others in the Bighorn and
Wind River Basins.

Mike Bies deserves a great deal of credit for this book. He has continued to find ways to sponsor recording and dating projects in the Worland
BLM District and has volunteered on other recording projects. Furthermore, he has contributed many useful ideas in discussion and debate about
the paintings and engravings of the Bighorn and Wind River Basins.

Ron Dorn and Marvin Rowe, along with their colleagues and students,
have led the world in their efforts to establish chronometric ages for petroglyphs and pictographs. We are extremely fortunate to have been able to
work with such dedicated professionals and are most grateful they have
chosen Wyoming and Montana for some of their pioneering research.

We believe Linda Olson is the most capable and accurate recorder of
petroglyphs and pictographs in the world. Linda produced nearly all the
wonderful illustrations in this book. The same is true for Stu Conner. He is
a superb photographer and mentor who has assisted us with dozens of
requests for help and inspiration.

Sharon Kahin has also been most supportive of this book. Through the
Fremont County Historic Preservation Commission, she was instrumental
in securing a grant from the Wyoming State Historic Preservation Office to

record petroglyphs in the Torrey Valley. We also thank Ring Lake Ranch, the Lucius Birch Center for Western Tradition, the Wind River Historical Center, and the Dubois Museum for their assistance.

Funding for dating studies was provided by the Bureau of Land Management/Wyoming State Office, the Bureau of Reclamation, the National Science Foundation, the Wyoming State Historic Preservation Office, the Wyoming Department of State Parks and Cultural Resources (formerly the Department of Commerce), and the University of North Dakota. The BLM deserves a special note of thanks for funding and logistical support (film, ladders, trailers, GPS units, and other equipment) for many of the recording projects. Additional support was provided by the Office of the Wyoming State Archaeologist and the Wyoming Department of Transportation. Thanks to the Bureau of Land Management, the Shoshone National Forest, the Bureau of Reclamation, Wyoming State Parks (especially Dave Taylor at Medicine Lodge Creek State Park), and the Nature Conservancy for permission to visit and document sites under their jurisdiction. Jim and Beverly Braten, Sam and Phyllis Hampton, Mike and Corky Messenger, Jean Murdock, and Harold Stanton gave permission to enter private lands. Jim Stewart should also be recognized for his efforts to record sites in the Wind River Basin. His site forms and drawings proved a valuable source of additional information.

We owe a special note of thanks to Dave Whitley and Linea Sundstrom for their insightful comments on the manuscript. Ron Dorn reviewed early drafts of the dating chapter and provided several figures. We have benefited immeasurably from many lively discussions about the Bighorn and Wind River Basins with Dave Whitley and David Lewis-Williams. George Frison has been most supportive of our efforts, putting his encyclopedic knowledge of the area at our disposal. Åke Hultkrantz visited several sites with us and shared his ethnographic information and knowledge of Shoshone spiritual practices. Dave Reiss, Berta Newton, and Terry Moody assisted with several of the figures in this book. Artwork for the opening page of each chapter is from Tipps & Schroedl (1985). Their illustrations are outstanding. We are most grateful to Jeff Grathwohl of the University of Utah Press for his support and patience in the production of this book and to Kim Vivier for her wonderful copyediting.

In large measure, this book is the product of many volunteer hours (even when there was some small amount of funding, it was never adequate for fair wages), and we are most grateful to the many who helped with recording, site visits, and site records: Dianne Berrigan, Mike Bies, Evelyn Billo, Jeani Borchert, JoDee Cole, Dee Marcellus Cole, Stuart Conner, Fred Chapman, Deb Dandridge, Claire Dean, Pam Gaulke, Celeste

Havener, Gary Havener, Ishmael Havener, Mary Hopkins, Janet Lever, Bob Mark, Joseph Medicine Crow, Linda McNeal, Peter Nabokov, Lloyd "Mickey" Old Coyote, Ann Phillips, Brady Potts, Bill Puckett, Jessi Steward, Steve Sutter, Russ Tanner, Alice Tratebas, Suzanne Warner, John Whitehurst, Haman Wise, and Courtney Yilk. We hope we have not forgotten anyone.

Finally, a special thanks from both of us to Jim Francis, Paula Loendorf, Bones, Brandy, and Hannah for their understanding during the fieldwork and the writing of this book.

ONE

Ancient Images

Diversity and Complexity

THE BIGHORN AND WIND RIVER BASINS OF NORTH-
central Wyoming and southern Montana are home to one of the
most diverse assemblages of hunter-gatherer petroglyphs and pictographs
in the world. This area has long been known for the spectacular and surreal anthropomorphic images of the Dinwoody tradition (Figure 1.1).
Equally common, however, is a startling array of other human forms, ranging from simple stick figures to elaborate shield-bearing warriors. Bears,
elk, deer, antelope, bighorn sheep, canids, felines, rabbits, birds, amphib-
ians, and reptiles, as well as occasional plants and abstract designs, stand
alongside human images. And to add to the remarkable mixture, all these
figures were executed using almost every imaginable type of manufacturing
technique: petroglyphs were made by pecking, several types of incising,
and abrading, and pictographs were painted with one, two, or many different colors. Some images combine all these techniques.

This diversity is bewildering, but it should not be surprising in view of
the location of the Bighorn and Wind River Basins at the intersection of
three major physiographic and cultural regions of the North American
continent (Figure 1.2). The volcanic Absaroka Range and Yellowstone
Plateau create a formidable barrier between the Bighorn and Wind River
Basins and the Columbia Plateau to the west and northwest. The Pryor
Mountains on the north and the Bighorn Mountains on the east separate
the basins from the vast grasslands of the Great Plains. To the west and
south the Continental Divide follows the crest of the Wind River
Mountains, separating the Wind River Basin from the high deserts of the
Great Divide and Green River Basins, which are ecologically and culturally
similar to the eastern Great Basin. Despite these geographic barriers, the

1.1. *(Opposite)*
Elaborate interior-lined
Dinwoody figure from
central Bighorn Basin.
This petroglyph illus-
trates the frightening
nature of the Dinwoody
tradition, most notice-
ably in the distortions
of the head and arms.
The arms are consider-
ably shortened; on the
figure's left hand, two
fingers are elongated,
giving the appearance
of claws, and the
thumbs of both hands
have a thickened
appearance. The small
figure at the foot of the
largest one appears to
be holding a plant and
has one human foot
and one claw foot. The
largest figure stands
about 1 m in height.
Drawing courtesy of
Linda Olson and the
Bureau of Land Man-
agement, Worland
Field Office.

1

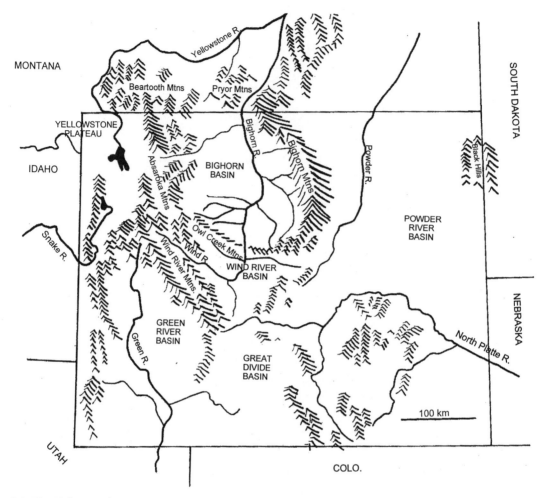

1.2. The Bighorn and Wind River Basins and surrounding physiographic features.

Bighorn and Wind River Basins were home to Native American tribes of both Great Plains and Great Basin cultural and linguistic affiliations, and the area was at least periodically visited or used by Plateau groups. The wide range of imagery reflects the cultural diversity seen during the historic period, and we believe this same diversity characterized much of the prehistoric period.

Native Americans, both past and present, hold traditional knowledge about the images painted and engraved on the caves, cliffs, and outcrops of the region, and this knowledge is central to an understanding of these images. Considerable information can be gleaned from the ethnographic record of the American West as well as from traditional leaders of modern Native American communities. Using Shoshonean and Crow ethnography as a powerful interpretive tool, we offer compelling evidence that these images can be more completely understood through the Native American perspective. It is now clear that religious experience and belief systems form the cultural context for the manufacture and use of the vast majority of petroglyphs and pictographs in the Bighorn and Wind River Basins.

The ancient imagery of the Bighorn and Wind River Basins can and should be integrated with the remainder of the archaeological record of the area. Despite the fact that petroglyphs and pictographs occur at many of the key excavated sites in the region, these images have rarely been reported or studied in relation to the excavations. Such relationships have been one focus of our investigations. Excavating at the base of panels, we have recovered datable materials and tools used in the manufacture of the paintings or engravings. Advances in experimental dating techniques have allowed us to begin the process of incorporating the temporal variation of the imagery with the standard archaeological chronologies of the region. With the support of land-managing agencies, academic institutions, and historic preservation agencies, we have brought specialists to the Bighorn and Wind River Basins, visited numerous sites, and collected countless samples for chronometric analysis. As a result, the ancient imagery of the Bighorn and Wind River Basins is among the best-dated in the world.

As we recorded sites, gathered chronological data, and conducted research for this book, our picture of the ancient history of the Bighorn and Wind River Basins began to diverge from the one offered by traditional archaeological reconstructions. Most archaeological studies have emphasized technology, hunting strategies, subsistence, and climate change. Indeed, these models have been predicated on ethnographic analogies emphasizing the simplicity of hunter-gatherers in the area, assuming a one-to-one correlation of simple technology, simple responses to climate change, and simple ideological systems (e.g., Mulloy 1965). In contrast, we found that the religious ideologies of technologically simple hunter-gatherers exhibit a large measure of complexity hitherto unrecognized and unexplored and that the region had far more diversity than has been suspected.

The questions raised in this book open archaeology, and in particular the archaeology of hunter-gatherers, to entirely new research directions that go beyond the techno-environmental approach characterizing most studies of the past several decades. We hope this book will lead others to appreciate the complexity of hunting and gathering cultures in the Bighorn and Wind River Basins and throughout the world.

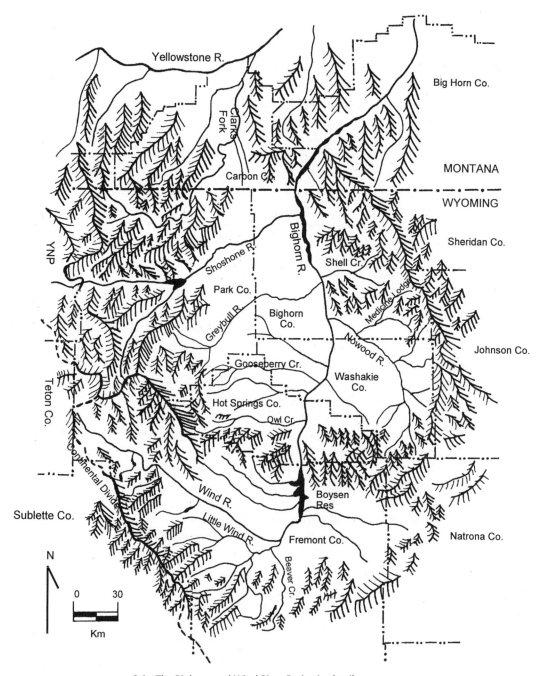

2.1. The Bighorn and Wind River Basins in detail.

TWO

The Bighorn and Wind River Basins

The Physical Environment

THE BIGHORN AND WIND RIVER BASINS, TRADITIONALLY considered part of the Northwestern Plains (see Frison 1978, 1991), form a unique ecological enclave within this larger region (see Frison 1978:90). They lie almost entirely within Wyoming (Figure 2.1), where they include most of Fremont, Hot Springs, Washakie, Bighorn, and Park Counties. The northernmost portion encompasses Carbon County and portions of Big Horn County in Montana. All told, this region measures approximately 360 km north-south and 200 km east-west. Interior basin elevations range from 1,750 m in the Wind River Basin to 1,250 m in the Bighorn Basin. With the exception of the Pryor and Owl Creek ranges, the surrounding mountains have all been glaciated and form the highest peaks in the state of Wyoming. Mountain passes into the basins average around 3,000 m in elevation, and peaks in the Wind Rivers and Bighorns attain elevations of nearly 4,500 m.

The region is quite arid, and from basin to mountaintop, temperature and precipitation vary with elevation. In the northern portion of the Bighorn Basin, precipitation averages 17.5 cm annually (Becker and Alyea 1964) but increases rapidly to around 63.5 cm in the surrounding mountains. Moisture occurs in the form of often violent summer thunderstorms and blinding winter snows. Temperatures are likewise quite variable. In the interior basin, summer highs regularly exceed 38°C and winter lows of −34°C are common; in the mountains, temperatures can range from highs of 32°C in the summer to lows of −46°C in the winter (Hoffman and Alexander 1976:1–2). Wide variations in both seasonal and diurnal temperatures, along with violent summer and winter precipitation, create an environment that is often harsh and unpredictable.

As in the rest of the arid intermountain West, rapidly changing elevation, temperature, and precipitation interact to create a series of stratified vegetation zones. There are six major zones in the region (Porter 1962), beginning with the desert-scrub community that dominates the interior basin floors. As one goes up the mountainsides, desert scrub gives way to a broad band of juniper and pine in the foothills, a narrow strip of sagebrush grasslands, heavily timbered mountain slopes, and alpine communities. Timberline is between 3,000 and 3,330 m. Streamside communities, which also change with elevation, cross-cut these major zones.

The distribution of petroglyph and pictograph sites in the Bighorn and Wind River Basins is directly related to many aspects of the region's geological history, modern topography, and drainage system. The Bighorn, Pryor, and Wind River mountain ranges are all uplifts formed by a major mountain-building episode in the late Cretaceous and Paleocene known as the Laramie Orogeny (King 1977). The uplifts are asymmetrical anticlines, typical of the eastern ranges of the Middle Rocky Mountain province, with a Precambrian core flanked by steeply dipping Paleozoic and Mesozoic rocks (Thornbury 1965). These Paleozoic and Mesozoic formations are the source of cherts and quartzites that were used as raw material for chipped stone tools throughout the region. The Absarokas are the exception to this pattern. Volcanic eruptions beginning about 50 million years ago resulted in the formation of the Yellowstone Plateau and Absaroka Range and buried Paleozoic and Mesozoic rocks on the western side of the Bighorn Basin.

The modern topography of the region is a product of Pleistocene glaciation and increased stream erosion. The Absarokas, Wind Rivers, and Bighorns are spectacular examples of glacial topography (Figure 2.2). Cirques, horns, and vast U-shaped valleys are carved into the bedrock. Terminal and lateral moraines dammed many streams, creating glacial lakes. Increased stream competence led to downcutting and erosion, forming many of the canyons dissecting the mountainsides and exposing Paleozoic and Mesozoic rocks along the margins of the basins.

Many of these Pleistocene features play significant roles in Native American religious and spiritual beliefs. For example, glacial lakes such as Dinwoody Lake and Bull Lake have major importance for the Eastern Shoshone. The massive Tensleep Sandstone, exposed in many of the canyons, was a favorite formation for painting and engraving (Figure 2.3). Similarly, erosion in the interior basins has occasionally exposed outcrops of late Cretaceous sandstones, producing unusual tilting rock surfaces, odd

2.2. The glaciated peaks of the Wind River Mountains. These peaks are among the highest in Wyoming and are the headwaters for the Wind River, east of the Continental Divide, and the Green River, west of the divide.

2.3. The canyon country of the Bighorn Mountain foothills. This photographs looks northeast across Medicine Lodge Creek canyon toward the timbered mountain slopes of the higher elevations. In this area the Triassic Chugwater formation (red beds) over-lie the lighter Tensleep Sandstone. The Medicine Lodge Creek site occurs at the base of the canyon in the left-central portion of the photograph. The Beehive site is at the base of the sandstone butte in the center of the photograph.

2.4. Cretaceous and Late Paleocene rocks exposed in the Castle Gardens area of the interior Wind River Basin. This unique rock outcrop presents an unusual micro-environment. The area contains thousands of incised and painted images and is the type site for the distinctive Castle Gardens shield style.

2.5. The arid, interior Bighorn Basin. Dinwoody tradition figures occur along the sandstone outcrops.

erosional remnants, and badlands (Figures 2.4, 2.5). These hard sand-stones have become heavily varnished and were also frequently used for the manufacture of pecked images.

The Wind River originates at the Continental Divide in the northern Wind River Mountains and flows southeasterly into the Wind River Basin. It abruptly turns north in the central portion of the basin and flows through the steep gorge of Wind River Canyon, which separates the Owl Creek Mountains on the west from the Bighorn Mountains on the east. Once the stream enters the Bighorn Basin at Wedding of the Waters near the mouth of the canyon, it becomes known as the Bighorn River. A major complex of mineral hot springs, the Great Hot Springs, occurs on the east side of the Bighorn River just below the Wedding of the Waters. These springs have central ritual and ceremonial importance for the Eastern Shoshone, who value them in part for their healing waters (see Trenholm and Carley 1964:285–292).

Below the Great Hot Springs, now the site of present-day Thermopolis, the Bighorn River flows north along the east side of the basin. It exits the basin and enters the Great Plains through Bighorn Canyon, which separates the Pryor and Bighorn Mountains. Downstream from Bighorn Canyon the river flows into the Yellowstone River, which drains into the Missouri River.

The Cultural Environment

The archaeological record of the Bighorn and Wind River Basins reflects the diverse ecological settings of the region. Beginning around 1980, archaeologists uniformly applied Northwestern Plains chronologies developed by Frison (1978) to archaeological remains throughout the western half of Wyoming. With the explosion of energy development and the related archaeological projects in the late 1970s through the mid-1980s, researchers realized that Great Basin chronologies and projectile point typologies were also suitable for cultural remains in western Wyoming (Metcalf 1987). Archaeologists are now applying these terms to prehistoric remains in north-central Wyoming (McNees et al. 1995).

The Bighorn and Wind River Basins have been occupied for a minimum of 11,000 years. Although there is some evidence for communal game hunting during the Paleoindian period, the archaeological record reflects occupation by hunters and gatherers who used a wide variety of plants and animals. On the Plains, in contrast, prehistoric groups relied more extensively on communal bison hunting. Only one communal bison kill, the Horner site, is known from the study area, and bison (*Bison bison*) bone occurs only occasionally in archaeological sites until the Late Archaic and Late Prehistoric periods (Frison 1978:348). Mule deer (*Odocoileus hemionus*), mountain sheep (*Ovis canadensis*), and antelope (*Antilocapra americana*) dominate faunal assemblages (Frison 1978:348).

Small animals also had great importance. Wood rat (*Neotoma cinerea*), cottontail (*Sylvilagus* sp.), jackrabbit (*Lepus* sp.), bobcat (*Lynx rufus*), badger (*Taxidea taxus*), and coyote (*Canis latrans*) all appear to have been used as food (Frison 1978:348). The unusual preservation of a large number of fish bones in two Paleoindian levels at the Medicine Lodge Creek site indicates that fish was a source of food as well (Frison 1978:349).

A wide variety of plants were also consumed, as attested by grinding implements, large numbers of roasting pits, and the recovery of macrobotanical remains from cooking features. The evidence reflects broadspectrum usage rather than dependence on any one type of plant such as found along the camas meadows of the Snake River in Jackson Hole, Idaho, and western Montana (see Malouf 1979; Reeve 1986).

A range of roots and tubers, including arrowroot (*Balsamorhiza sagitta*), bitterroot (*Lewisia rediviva*), sego lily (*Calochortus nuttallii*), biscuitroot (*Lomatium* sp.), and wild onion (*Allium* sp.), were gathered, supplemented by chokecherry (*Prunus virginiana*), buffalo berry (*Shepherdia argentea*), gooseberry (*Ribes flexilis*), yucca (*Yucca glauca*), goosefoot (*Chenopodium* sp.), Indian ricegrass (*Oryzopsis hymenoides*), and limber pine (*Pinus flexilis*). Because many of these plants grow at different elevations, where they mature at different times, prehistoric groups could simply move short distances to prolong the period of availability (Frison 1978:351).

Direct evidence for the use of these plants includes recent flotation analyses from the study area and southwestern Wyoming which recovered macrobotanical fossils of most of these species. Goosefoot seeds (Smith 1988) are the most common type of seed found. Charred root material has been recovered from large roasting pits in the Green River Basin (Francis 2000). In the Bighorn Basin remains of wild onion, buffalo berry, cactus (*Opuntia polyacantha*), chokecherry, juniper (*Juniperus* sp.), limber pine, thistle (*Cirsium* sp.), wild rose, wild rye, and yucca were found at a small dry rockshelter on Tensleep Creek (Frison and Huseas 1968). The remains of several hundred Mormon crickets (*Anabrus simplex*) were also found at this site.

The Paleoindian Period (11,200–8,000 B.P.)
Ample evidence of occupation during the Paleoindian period has been recovered from all portions of the Bighorn and Wind River Basins. Surface

finds of Clovis projectile points have been recorded from interior basin environments to near timberline, and Clovis points and Columbian mammoths (*Mammuthus columbi*) have been excavated from the Colby site in the interior Bighorn Basin (Frison and Todd 1986). Folsom occupation is known from numerous surface finds and the Hanson site in the foothills of the Bighorn Mountains (Frison and Bradley 1980). The Cody Complex is well known, and indeed, the Horner site in the northern Bighorn Basin (Frison and Todd 1987) provides the only evidence for communal bison procurement throughout the entire prehistoric sequence.

Stratified rockshelters and open sites in the mountains surrounding the Bighorn and Wind River Basins provide much of the extensive evidence for Paleoindian occupation of the study area. Major sites such as Medicine Lodge Creek (Frison 1978, 1991), Mummy Cave (Husted and Edgar n.d.; McCracken 1978), the Bighorn Canyon sites (Husted 1969), the Helen Lookingbill site (Frison 1983), and several others (see Frison 1991:67) confirm the region's long-term occupation. Projectile points from well-dated levels at these sites are typologically different from the "classic" Plains Paleoindian styles and reflect subsistence strategies very unlike those of the "classic" Paleoindian bison hunters. Sites such as Mummy Cave (Husted and Edgar n.d.; McCracken 1978) contain faunal assemblages dominated by bighorn sheep remains. Especially noteworthy is the recovery from the Absaroka Mountains of a net made of juniper bark: it dates to around 8,800 B.P., and its size suggests that it was used to trap deer and bighorn sheep (Frison, Andrews et al. 1986). Frison (1991:67–79, 1997; Frison, Andrews et al. 1986) believes this evidence indicates the presence of concurrent Paleoindian traditions or occupations in the Bighorn area beginning about 10,000 years ago. The foothills-mountain groups apparently practiced a more "Archaic" lifestyle, which Frison (1991:67–68) relates to differences in ecosystems and warming and drying trends leading to the Altithermal period.

The Archaic Period (8,000–1,500 B.P.)
Although differences in subsistence and settlement strategies between Paleoindian and Archaic times have become increasingly blurred, the archaeological record of the Bighorn and Wind River Basins has provided the definition of Archaic cultures for much of the Northwestern Plains. Indeed, sites around what is now Boysen Reservoir on the Wind River (Mulloy 1954) are the basis for Mulloy's characterization of Middle period groups as "culturally impoverished" cyclical nomads who exploited plants and rodent-sized game (see Mulloy 1965:24). Drawing on work in several rockshelters in the Bighorn Basin, Frison (1976, 1978) applied the term

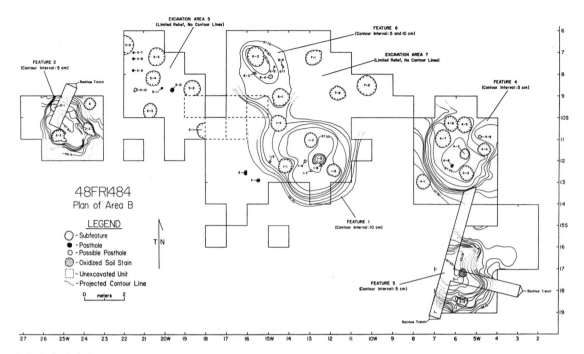

2.6. Early Archaic house pits at the Split Rock Ranch site. Courtesy of the Office of the Wyoming State Archaeologist.

Archaic to characterize the broad-spectrum hunting and gathering lifeways of prehistoric people during this time. Archaic period sites are among the most common throughout the area and include numerous rockshelters, open lithic scatters, fire hearths or roasting pits, and stone circles. Grinding implements are common, and there is a proliferation of projectile point types, ranging from stemmed to side-notched to corner-notched.

The Early Archaic period (approximately 8,000 to 4,500 B.P.) roughly corresponds to the Altithermal climatic episode (Antevs 1955). Since there were no cultural remains dating to this interval, Mulloy (1958) originally considered it to be the "gap without evidence" and suggested that prehistoric people simply abandoned the entire Plains region because of the severe climate. Frison (1976) demonstrated the presence of prehistoric occupation in the Bighorn Mountains and foothills during the Altithermal and suggested that the basins may have been abandoned in favor of the mountains (Frison 1978:41–46). When federally mandated archaeological investigations during the 1980s found evidence of numerous house pits dating to the latter part of the Early Archaic period throughout the Green River Basin (Harrell et al.1997) and immediately adjacent to the Wind River Basin (Eakin 1987; Eakin et al.1997) (Figure 2.6), Frison's hypothesis was revised. Rather than culturally impoverished and totally nomadic, it is now believed, Early Archaic groups were organized and complex to a certain degree (Larson 1990, 1997).

The archaeological record of the Bighorn and Wind River Basins includes use of semisubterranean house structures beginning about 5,200 B.P. (Martin 1999) and continuing through the Late Prehistoric period (Walker 1999). One Middle Archaic house dated to around 4,400 years B.P. has been documented at the Grass Creek site (Reiss et al. 1993). At the Dead Indian Creek site in the northern portion of the study area, what was thought to be an old stream channel is now interpreted as a house pit (Frison 1991:99–100). This site appears to be a winter camp showing extensive use of mule deer and bighorn sheep. All types of McKean projectile point variants have been recovered from Dead Indian, which has radiocarbon dates ranging from 4,400 to 3,800 B.P.

Late Archaic sites (about 2,500 to 1,500 B.P.) are extremely common throughout the Bighorn and Wind River Basins. Diagnostic artifacts reflect a change from the lanceolate and stemmed McKean varieties to large corner-notched dart points. Excavations along the North Fork of the Shoshone River indicate intensive use of bighorn sheep (Eakin 1989, 1993). Numerous perishable items, including coiled basketry, woodworking debris, bark cordage, sinew, hide, feathers, shell, and a nearly complete atlatl, have been recovered from several rockshelters (Frison 1978:59). The basketry, which is typical of eastern Great Basin baskets, was found in several rockshelters in the Bighorn Basin, including Mummy Cave, with dates ranging from around 4,400 to 1,000 B.P. (Frison, Adovasio, and Carlisle 1986:164).

The Late Prehistoric Period (ca. 1,500–500 B.P.)

The Late Prehistoric period is marked typologically by a change from large corner-notched points to small side- and corner-notched points, representing the introduction of the bow and arrow. Pottery was also introduced during this time, and populations moved and increased. Late Prehistoric period sites are extremely common in the Bighorn and Wind River Basins.

A group of early Late Prehistoric sites in these basins are related to the Avonlea complex (Fredlund 1988; Frison 1988). Avonlea points are distinctive, small, side-notched (and occasionally corner-notched) points thought to have their origins in the Northern Plains. Within the Bighorn Basin, Avonlea-like points are often found in sites on high buttes that offer excellent views of the surrounding countryside as well as defensible positions. Stone-wall features on these sites are believed to have been both residential and protective, and some have deadfall timber superstructures.

For example, Coyote House is located on the top of a free-standing remnant of sandstone overlooking the confluence of two perennial streams in southeastern Montana (Davis et al. 1994) The main feature at the site is a 6-by-6-m pentagonal deadfall structure. The timber, stacked as in a log cabin, was in a wall made of more than 100 sandstone slabs, some as large as 1.5 m across, that were laid vertically against the wood.

An Avonlea component associated with the structure contained thousands of pieces of debitage, Avonlea points, and an array of chipped-stone cutting and scraping tools (Davis et al. 1994:26). Six groundstone abraders, presumably for manufacturing arrow shafts, were also found in this level. The bone tool inventory included three awls, a punch, and a knapping tool. Cut bird bones were identified as the by-products of bead manufacturing, and several bone beads were found to support this inference. Other artifacts include shell. No ceramics were found, however.

Charcoal from a large central hearth in this level had radiocarbon ages of $1,487 \pm 64$ and $1,512 \pm 55$ years B.P. (Davis et al. 1994:84). This date is thought to represent the initial construction of the lodge. It was apparently reconstructed several times over the course of the next thousand years and was abandoned around 300 to 500 years ago (Davis et al. 1994).

The culture represented by this artifact assemblage, now called the Beehive Technocomplex (Davis et al. 1994), appears intrusive or possibly represents a cultural group that adopted the bow and arrow quite early. The defensive site locations suggest that these groups may have been in conflict with the "Archaic" groups still using the atlatl. An Athapaskan affiliation for the makers of Avonlea projectile points has been suggested (Kehoe 1966), but there is considerable disagreement (see Greiser 1994: 39–42 for an overview). Assignment of the projectile points associated with the Beehive Technocomplex to Avonlea is also debated by various investigators, who usually term them Avonlea-like. Schlesier (1994:326–35) envisions Avonlea as representing proto-Apachean groups and the Beehive Technocomplex as a predecessor to the Kiowa and Kiowa Apache.

The Protohistoric and Historic Periods
The Protohistoric period is recognized by the presence of Euro-American trade goods such as glass beads, gun flints, metal artifacts, horse bones, and related items in archaeological sites before the actual entry of Euro-Americans in the area. Several historically documented tribes are known to have occupied and/or used the Bighorn and Wind River Basins during the Protohistoric and Historic periods. These groups are quite diverse and include the Numic-speaking Shoshone, the Siouan-speaking Crow, and the Algonquian-speaking Arapaho. Traditional thought holds that these groups

are all recent arrivals in the area, and archaeologists are generally reluctant to speculate about the linguistic or ethnic affiliations of groups occupying the Bighorn and Wind River Basins before the Protohistoric period.

THE WIND RIVER SHOSHONE   Sometimes referred to as the Eastern Shoshone, the Wind River Shoshone currently occupy a reservation in the Wind River Basin and surrounding mountain region. As with other tribes in the area, their original movement to Wyoming is a matter of debate. Based on the linguistic work of Lamb (1958), several archaeologists (Bettinger and Baumhoff 1982, 1983; Young and Bettinger 1992) have suggested that the Shoshone moved across the Great Basin from a California homeland beginning about 1,000 years ago, with arrival in western Wyoming no earlier than 700 or 800 years ago and possibly as late as the Historic period (Butler 1981, 1986; Wright 1978). A variety of evidence has been used to support this hypothesis, including the spatial distributions and radiocarbon dates of Intermountain or Shoshone pottery (Madsen 1975, 1986), the occurrence of tri-notched projectile points (Holmer and Weder 1980), specific changes in basketry (Adovasio and Pedler 1994), and certain petroglyph and pictograph motifs, including the shield-bearing warrior (Keyser 1975).

Other archaeologists (Husted 1969; Swanson 1972) argue that the continuous occupation of large rockshelter sites such as Mummy Cave in Wyoming and Birch Creek Cave in Idaho, along with the occurrence over thousands of years of the same types of artifacts used by the Shoshone during the Historic period, indicates that Shoshonean groups are the indigenous occupants of the area. Recently, petroglyph and pictograph dating evidence from the Bighorn and Wind River Basins has been used to support this hypothesis (Francis et al. 1993; Francis and Larson 1995).

Based on excavations at sites in eastern Idaho, Holmer (1994) believes there has been continuous Shoshonean use of the region for 3,500 to 4,000 years, and Martin (1999) suggests the house pits in Wyoming are of Shoshonean origin. Nonetheless, the existence, timing, and directionality of a Numic expansion across the Great Basin continue to be hotly debated (see Madsen and Rhode 1994) with alternative models put forward (Aikens and Witherspoon 1986).

Ethnographically, the Wind River Shoshone have been most extensively studied by Shimkin (1947b, 1986a) and Hultkrantz (1958, 1974a). Their social units are identified as kin/cliques or small groups of families and friends who lived in overlapping territories (Malouf 1968). The Tukudika ("meat eaters" or "eaters of bighorn sheep"), the Kukundika ("buffalo eaters"), and the Agaidika ("salmon eaters") are among the Shoshonean kin/cliques that originally used northwestern Wyoming as part of their territory (Hultkrantz 1958, 1974a; Shimkin 1986a). The Wind River Shoshone are often equated with their Great Basin relatives, but they are also thought of as the most Plains-like of all the Shoshonean groups. The Mountain Sheepeaters (Tukudika) had few horses or other Euro-American artifacts and are commonly described as impoverished (Norris 1880) in comparison with their Great Plains neighbors. This characterization, based on items held in esteem by Euro-Americans, is inaccurate: the Shoshone believe the Tukudika, with their well-made horn bows and elaborate bighorn sheep drives, are relatively prosperous (see Nabokov and Loendorf 2000).

According to traditional wisdom, the Shoshone did not make petroglyphs (Trenholm and Carley 1964), reporting that the imagery abounding on their reservation was made by spirits (Hultkrantz 1986). Cole (1990: 108) and Hultkrantz (1986), among others, have assumed that the petroglyphs on the Wind River Reservation were made by cultures predating the Shoshone's arrival into Wyoming. We disagree with this assumption and directly link Dinwoody tradition petroglyphs with the Shoshone.

THE CROW INDIANS   Unlike the Shoshone, the Siouan-speaking Crow are known from both tribal tradition (Medicine Crow 1962, 1992; Nabokov and Loendorf 1994) and the archaeological record to be relatively recent entrants into the Bighorn region. The Crow Indians formed as a nation when they separated from the Hidatsa Indians and moved away from the Missouri River in North Dakota. The two tribal units of the Crow (Mountain Crow and River Crow) apparently split from the Hidatsa at different times (Bowers 1965). The Mountain Crow may have left in response to changing climatic conditions along the Missouri that limited intensive agriculture (Loendorf 1991a).

Archaeologically, Frison (1978:238) recognizes Crow ceramics in tipi ring and processing components associated with bison kill sites along the eastern slopes of the Bighorn Mountains. Radiocarbon dates on these sites range around 500 years B.P., and the prevalent explanation is that they represent the initial penetration of the Mountain Crow into the west (Frison 1979:5). The River Crow are believed to have followed their relatives to the west approximately 125 to 150 years later (Medicine Crow 1962).

At about the time the River Crow arrived in the west, Shoshonean neighbors to the south introduced horses to the Crow. A Crow narrative tells about a man who approached the first horse he had ever seen and, while inspecting it, was kicked in the belly. Thereafter this man and his followers, named the "Kicked in the Bellies," were an important division of the Mountain Crow that moved south in the Bighorn Basin during the winter. The Kicked in the Bellies were sufficiently independent of the Mountain Crow and River Crow that early Euro-American trappers and traders identified three Crow tribes (Larocque 1910).

Although the Shoshone and the Crow sometimes fought each other, the two tribes maintained fairly good relations throughout the Historic period. Friendship between them was important for their trade networks: the Shoshone supplied horses and other Spanish trade goods, and the Crow worked as middlemen, taking the horses and other items to the earthlodge villages on the Missouri River.

Ethnographically, the Crow have been extensively studied by Robert Lowie, an anthropologist who spent summers with the Crow from 1904 until 1918. Lowie published about two thousand pages on the Crow (Lowie 1956), and this information is an invaluable resource. The Crow are organized into matrilineal clans, a holdover from their Hidatsa heritage. They depended heavily on communal bison hunting (see Nabokov and Loendorf 1994 for procurement sites), and even though their environment was rich in animal and plant resources, they continued to cultivate an essential crop, ceremonial tobacco (*Nicotiana multivalvis*). Once they acquired the horse, they quickly adapted to a full-blown equestrian lifestyle. The Crow have great spiritual reverence for the Bighorn Mountains, and like the Shoshone, they claim that the spirits made the petroglyphs and pictographs that occur in and around the Bighorn and Pryor Mountains (Bradley 1961:53; Nabokov and Loendorf 1994).

THE NORTHERN ARAPAHO The Northern Arapaho live with the Eastern Shoshone on the Wind River Reservation in Wyoming. Their recent history is much better documented than their prehistory. After A.D. 1700, when horses were in use on the Plains, the Arapaho controlled a territory on the High Plains along the Rocky Mountain front range. The Northern Arapaho refused to accept a place with their southern kinsmen on a reservation in Oklahoma and were placed with the Eastern Shoshone (Clemmer and Stewart 1986:530).

The Arapaho are Algonquian in speech and related, on the Northern Plains, to the Atsina and more distantly to the Cheyenne and the Blackfoot. Their prehistoric homeland was to the west of the Great Lakes, where they were part of a group of Algonquian-speaking tribes. As Euro-Americans forced eastern North American tribes to the west, a large group of these Algonquian speakers moved west into northern Minnesota and North Dakota and the southern parts of the Canadian prairie provinces. The Arapaho, who were apparently combined with the Atsina before this move started, eventually moved south to take over their territory on the High Plains (Malouf 1967:13).

The timing of these movements is debated by historians and archaeologists. The combined tribes of the Blackfoot nation are thought to have led the Algonquian migration to the west, perhaps as early as 1,000 years ago. The Atsina and Arapaho, however, made a more recent migration, likely within the past 500 years. Although at present there is no consensus as to what archaeological complexes represent the Atsina/Arapaho (Schlesier 1994:316–323; Wood 1985:4), it is safe to assume that they were relatively late arrivals, probably not before 400 years ago, to the region north of the Missouri River along the border between the United States and Canada. The Arapaho, divided from the Atsina, were most likely not living in parts of eastern Wyoming and the High Plains until about 300 years ago, sometime around A.D. 1700. There is no evidence to suggest that the Arapaho were in the Bighorn and Wind River Basins, other than for occasional raids, until their settlement on the Wind River Reservation in 1877.

To summarize, the Bighorn and Wind River Basins have been the home of the Wind River Shoshone for centuries. Although there is debate as to how many centuries, it is apparent their religious and spiritual traditions are important for serious anthropological studies of the region's petroglyphs and pictographs. The Crow Indians were a significant force during the Protohistoric and Historic periods. Groups of Crow spent their winters in the Bighorn Basin (though their primary territory was to the north), and after the introduction of Euro-American trade goods, they were in constant contact with the Shoshone to acquire these items. The Arapaho did not arrive in the study area until the beginning of the reservation era, but they have continually maintained an interest in the petroglyphs and pictographs.

The identity of the tribes who used the region in the Late Prehistoric period is debated. Athapaskans had to travel from central Montana to their current homes in the American Southwest, and a route through portions of the Bighorn and Wind River Basins is highly probable. The traditions of the Kiowa include memories of their former homeland in the mountains, with specific references to Yellowstone Lake. Their travels within that homeland and migration across Wyoming to the Black Hills almost certainly involved portions of the study area (Mooney 1898). Petroglyphs and pictographs in the region could be related to any of these groups or their unknown predecessors.

THREE

Rock "Art"?

SINCE EUROPEAN AND AMERICAN COLONISTS, EXPLORERS,
and military personnel first noticed the complex images rendered
on stone throughout the North American continent, two major paradigms
have been used to interpret petroglyphs and pictographs. The first is a
predilection to see these designs as a written language with universal meaning; the second is the interpretation of these images as "art," in the same
context as "art" in Euro-American culture.

Colonel Garrick Mallery (1886, 1893) was one of the first to interpret
the paintings and engravings of the Wind River and Bighorn areas from a
pictographic perspective. The well-known winter counts made by the
Lakota, Yankton, Blackfeet, and Kiowa employ true pictographs. These
hide paintings used symbolic notation to record a year's name and its
memorable events. The hide was cared for by a keeper who passed it on
to others at his death so that they might continue the notations.

Mallery recognized the importance of this information, and during his
stay at Fort Rice in Dakota Territory, he recorded various symbols and
their meanings, which he attributed to the Lakota. After joining the
Bureau of American Ethnology in 1880, Mallery expanded his study to
other types of imagery, including rock paintings and engravings. He published two volumes of the results of the project (Mallery 1886, 1893), and
although he was able to offer explanations for the pictograph motifs on
winter count calendars, he found that it was not possible to translate symbols on stone into messages that were understandable as a form of written
communication.

Many researchers still maintain that certain symbols must be translat-
able as representations of natural features or occurrences. For example, a

spiral must designate the nearby location of a freshwater spring; a rayed circle next to a crescent is an obvious symbol for a supernova, and a depiction of a bighorn sheep with an arrow in it must mean the artists were hungry and made a great kill. Martineau (1973), a leading proponent of these ideas, believed it is possible to read all petroglyphs in much the same way that one can interpret Indian sign language. Unfortunately, when others try to follow the Martineau system, they learn that few examples can be replicated. The petroglyph spiral may be near a freshwater spring in one canyon but not in the next canyon, or there is a freshwater spring near other petroglyphs but no spirals among them.

In addition, petroglyphs and pictographs have often been interpreted as "art," rendered for art's sake or simply to depict a scene or person, as an artist would create a painting in Euro-American culture. This perspective imposes art historians' models of the development of art in Western society (see Schapiro 1953) on hunting and gathering groups. It ignores the non-Western culture of the Native American people who made the images and often leads to judgment of the images based on their realism and the artistic talents of the maker. Thus, style is often described in terms of realistic and abstract elements, with more realistic or representational images considered advanced and often younger in age (Gebhard 1969; Heizer and Baumhoff 1962). Even more detrimental, this perspective leads to ethnocentric and racist interpretations of Native American cultures, as in an example published as recently as 1982: "There is an immense and very important difference between such a knowledgeable abstraction process and what actually happened when a nomadic, half starved Archaic level Indian stood scratching straight or curved lines into a cliff, or a simple stick-man onto a boulder or hand-held rock. That native's knowledge of graphics was far less sophisticated than that of a modern child just a few months old, a child that has been surrounded by diverse and complex graphic images from its birth on" (Barnes 1982:33). It is extremely unfortunate that literature offering these types of interpretations is still sold at many parks and recreation areas and in the Native American sections of bookstores.

These frameworks for interpreting Native American petroglyphs and pictographs are etic, derived from Euro-American concepts that are external to the people and cultures who made the images. Notions from cultures in which written language is a primary form of communication have been imposed on images and material objects that are the product of nonliterate societies. Such interpretations are implicitly founded on what would now be considered naive acceptance of statements by Native American informants that spirits made the images (e.g., Bradley 1961) and on widely held beliefs that most of the petroglyphs and pictographs predate a presumed recent arrival of the Shoshone into western Wyoming (e.g., Cole 1990:108; Hultkrantz 1986; Trenholm and Carley 1964). Therefore, modern Indian people would know nothing of the images.

Since about 1980 something of a revolution has taken place in the study of Native American rock drawings (Whitley and Loendorf 1994). One important aspect of this revolution is the recognition that the North American ethnographic record can help us understand and interpret Native American paintings and engravings. Furthermore, the ethnographic record from much of the Great Basin and California (Whitley 1982, 1992, 1994a, 1994b), the Columbia Plateau (Keyser 1997), and the Black Hills (Sundstrom 1997) clearly demonstrates relationships between spiritual and religious practices and the manufacture and use of pictographs and petroglyphs.

In addition, consultation with Native American elders (as is now required by the regulations of the National Historic Preservation Act and the Native American Graves Protection and Repatriation Act) has revealed that knowledge of petroglyphs and pictographs is still extant, that sites in many areas are still being used, and that these areas are considered by Native Americans to be of critical spiritual and sacred value. In short, it has become apparent that the traditional interpretive models that view the imagery as written communication or as "art" are completely inappropriate to its original cultural context and use. Many Native Americans consider the term *rock art* to be offensive, in that it imposes Euro-American values and belief systems on their religious and spiritual beliefs. For this reason, we attempt to use the terms *petroglyphs* or *engravings, pictographs* or *paintings, figures,* and *images* to label these manifestations as much as possible. Nevertheless, we recognize that the term *rock art* is so ingrained in the literature and in the consciousness of archaeologists and other researchers that it will take time to change its use.

The Shamanistic Hypothesis

For scholars of petroglyphs and pictographs around the world, the most controversial single event since 1980 was the publication of Lewis-Williams and Dowson's neuropsychological model in 1988. The most widely known formulation of the neuropsychological model owes it origins to the ethnography of the southern San (Bushmen), which indicates that shamans executed paintings and engravings to depict the images and physical reactions experienced during the altered state of consciousness central to the trance dance (see Lewis-Williams 1981, 1983, 1984). Lewis-Williams sought to use independent data to build a model that would explain many characteristics of southern San painting and then to apply such a model to a geographic area and time period for which there was no direct ethnographic record: the Upper Paleolithic paintings of Europe. To this end, he turned to the neuropsychological literature related to altered states of consciousness and mental imagery.

In their landmark article Lewis-Williams and Dowson (1988:202) note that the human neuropsychological system generates a range of luminous percepts that are independent of light from an external source. These visual phenomena generally take geometric forms such as grids, zigzags, dots, and spirals and are experienced as incandescent, shimmering, moving, rotating, and sometimes enlarging patterns that grade into one another and combine in bewildering arrays. This imagery is induced by many means, including psychoactive drugs, fatigue, sensory deprivation, intense concentration, repetitive auditory stimuli, migraine, schizophrenia, hyperventilation, and rhythmic movement (Horowitz 1964; Klüver 1942; Sacks 1970; Siegel and Jarvik 1975 cited in Lewis-Williams and Dowson 1988:202).

Other researchers (Hedges 1982a) had previously linked these images to petroglyphs and pictographs, but Lewis-Williams and Dowson expanded the model to three stages that appear to be common in the progression of mental imagery during altered states of consciousness (1988:203–204). The first stage is the perception of simple geometric shapes, termed *entoptics* by Lewis-Williams and Dowson. In the second stage subjects try to make sense of these images by elaborating them into iconic forms. In other words, the brain attempts to recognize or construe the perceived images as culturally meaningful items. For example, in southern Africa, patterns of grids may be arranged to form a giraffe (Dowson 1992:54). The final stage marks the transition to fully iconic hallucinations, in which the images are often associated with culturally influenced items, memories, or powerful emotional experiences. Iconic imagery is often projected onto a background of entoptic phenomena, and the imagery increases in vividness. Subjects report that images are "what they appear to be" and lose the difference between real and analogous meanings (Siegel and Jarvik 1975 cited in Lewis-Williams and Dowson 1988:204). Subjects also may experience a variety of powerful physical sensations, including pain, tingling, and trembling throughout the body, and often confuse somatic experiences with optic experiences, a phenomenon referred to as synesthesia. Legs may feel like spirals or a touch may feel like a color (Lewis-Williams and Dowson 1988:211).

Of critical importance is the fact that because the geometric visual percepts derive from the human nervous system, all people who enter altered states of consciousness, no matter what their cultural background, are likely to perceive similar images (Eichmeier and Höfer 1974; Reichel-Dolmatoff 1978 cited in Lewis-Williams and Dowson 1988:202). Subsequent research (Hobson 1994 cited in Whitley 1998b) has shown that varying brain-mind states, including waking, sleeping, dreaming, and trance, are controlled by interactions of the aminergic-cholinergic chemical systems in the neural structure of the brain. Thus, much of the mental imagery experienced during altered states of consciousness and the somatic reactions during these states are cross-cultural in nature.

The neuropsychological model lays a foundation for a "shamanic" explanation for hunter-gatherer artistic traditions worldwide. Many of the universal symbols found in shamanic religions have their origin in cross-cultural neuropsychological and somatic reactions to altered states of consciousness (Whitley 1994b:1). The model develops an explanatory mechanism for the occurrence of numerous design elements found in paintings and engravings in southern Africa and indeed throughout much of the world. These images are the product of the hallucinations experienced during shamanistic trances; that is, they are metaphorical depictions of the images, visions, and somatic reactions experienced during the trance state.

The neuropsychological model is now being used to interpret Upper Paleolithic paintings (e.g., Clottes and Courtin 1996; Clottes and Lewis-Williams 1998). In North America, Whitley (1998b,1998c) has been the most vocal proponent of the neuropsychological model, and his reanalysis of Great Basin and California ethnographic data demonstrates clear relationships between the activities of shamans and the manufacture of paintings and engravings, especially for Numic-speaking groups. This approach is growing in popularity, and other North American researchers (Boyd and Dering 1996; Schaafsma 1994; Turpin 1994) are exploring such associations in different regions.

Despite the fact that most hunter-gatherer religions include a strong shamanic basis (Malefijt 1968:229), the neuropsychological model has come under a great deal of criticism, principally because it is seen as too monolithic. Many of these criticisms are quite obvious. For example, geometric figures are so widespread that they could not possibly have the same origins. Or geometric designs are so simple that anyone, including children, could have made them. Going into trance may not always result in the manufacture of paintings or engravings, and not all individuals who enter trance are shamans. Furthermore, some critics have argued that not all hunter-gatherer religions are shamanic.

Visionary Perspectives

Anthropological definitions of shamans and shamanism vary widely, and many criticisms of the neuropsychological model take a very narrow view of shamanism. Kehoe (2000), for example, notes that the terms *shaman* and *shamanism* are now being uncritically applied to anyone who enters trance for any purpose. She outlines several key characteristics of shamans, including performance of community-oriented rituals for healing and divining, using drum, song, and dance; intense mental concentration to the point of apparent dissociation from sense perception; stated belief that the adept's soul leaves the body to travel in company with spirits; and receipt of specific knowledge from the spirits (2000:57). She feels the term should be applied only to religious adepts in Siberia and perhaps in the Circumboreal region of North America.

Hultkrantz (1974b:34) defines a shaman as "a social functionary who, with the help of guardian spirits, attains ecstacy in order to create a rapport with the supernatural world on behalf of his group members." Whitley (1998b) suggests that not all trances should be considered "ecstatic." Nonetheless, the key elements in Hultkrantz's view are that the shaman is recognized by other members of the social group as the mediator between the group and the supernatural, that the shaman acts for benefit of the community, and that not all visionaries are shamans. Walsh (1990:9–10) identifies these same key features of shamanism: voluntary entry into an altered state of consciousness, supernatural travel to spiritual realms, and use of knowledge or power acquired on this journey for the good of the community.

It is this definition of shaman, as a recognized specialist who employs certain techniques to acquire supernatural knowledge and power for the benefit of the community, that we employ throughout this book. We argue that not all Native American paintings and engravings in the Bighorn and Wind River Basins were made by shamans. But if we look beyond the specific connotations of shamanism, it is clear that a great deal of hunter-gatherer religious belief and practice and artistic expression is rooted in visionary experiences, whether or not these practices would be considered shamanistic. For example, southern San paintings can be interpreted with respect to emic concepts of supernatural power and potency, what creatures hold what types of power, and how humans may acquire this power

(Lewis-Williams 1981, 1983; Lewis-Williams and Dowson 1989). Many aspects of mundane activities, such as hunting eland, are imbued with religious meaning, and aspects of personal dress, decoration, and ritual are grounded in beliefs about the invocation of supernatural power that have visionary origins. In Australia, where aboriginal religions are not considered shamanistic, many painted and engraved locations can be directly related to important ancestral sites and the "Dreamtime" (Flood 1997), often considered the epitome of the visionary experience.

In North America the Plains vision quest has been widely studied and documented, and there is considerable evidence to suggest a visionary origin for the imagery seen in all media throughout Great Plains material culture. Irwin (1996) argues that the individual visionary experience is the basis for the Great Plains religious worldview. Whether spontaneous or formalized as a quest, the visionary experience is a source of personal empowerment that guides individual behavior and action, structures social and religious behavior within the community, and reinforces communally held values and beliefs. At the same time, because each experience is intensely personal and unique, it serves as a source of innovation in religious belief and practice.

Visionary experiences are part of the "lived" world for nearly all individuals in Plains societies, but it is only those individuals with heightened abilities to enter altered states of consciousness who go on to become religious specialists or shamans. Through the synthesis of a substantial body of ethnographic data, Irwin (1996) identifies key elements of cosmology and the visionary experience shared by the entire range of Great Plains groups. The world is organized into at least three realms—the above, middle, and below—which are inhabited by a variety of beings, including humans. Travel between the realms is an integral part of ordinary visionary experience. This aspect of Great Plains religious practice has been downplayed, in part because our culture perceives it as irrational.

For Plains people, the visionary experience presents a dialectic between the need to keep the dream or vision private and the need to communicate some aspect of the experience (Irwin 1996:172–184). Many groups had strict prohibitions against recounting the details of the visionary experience (Cooper 1957; Hallowell 1975; Mandelbaum 1940; Skinner 1914), for fear of losing the knowledge and power conferred during the vision and endangering one's relationship with the dream spirits. Among other groups, speaking of the visionary experience could occur only under certain ritually prescribed circumstances (Dorsey 1890; Fletcher and La Flesche 1911; Wallace and Hoebel 1952), such as to the directing shaman or elders or to fellow members of a ceremonial society.

Beyond these restricted circumstances, the dream experience was communicated through personal action and through imagery, as Irwin describes:

> The most expressive means for communicating the dream experience, according to the ethnography, involves the use of visionary images and the making of an extremely wide range of objects. Although certain of these forms are part of a shared symbolic repertoire of symbolic items normally associated with visionary experience, any item of either nature or culture can be incorporated into a visionary assemblage that expresses the unique experience of the individual. Such an item is treated with care and attention as a means for evoking and manifesting power. The nature of the assemblage varies in relationship to the contents of the vision and the instructions received. The visionary usually experiences visual imagery of a very explicit and vivid kind. This imagery is then transformed into objects or recreated in visual form symbolizing the presence of the power of the vision. Because the contents of the vision are highly variable, so are the explicit images adopted by the visionary. (1996:211)

Visionary imagery includes objects and symbols illustrated in individual dress, paint, tattooing, and sacred objects such as feathers, stones, rattles, pipes, medicine bundles, and robes (Irwin 1996:212). The imagery seen on the painted lodges of well-known shamans was derived from their visionary experiences (Ewers 1958; Grinnell 1923; Lowie 1909a), and that depicted on warrior shields was derived from the vision experience of the shield's owner (Dorsey 1890; Grinnell 1923; Horse Capture 1980; Wallace and Hoebel 1952), with occasional transference of designs to other individuals. Among the Ponca the images seen in women's crafts, clay figurines, and petroglyphs were also derived from visionary experiences (Howard 1965).

All human beings have the ability to dream and entered altered states, and dreaming and visions are important in innumerable hunter-gatherer societies and religious worldviews. Clearly, how dreaming and visionary experiences are expressed varies among cultures and over time and space. For example, Whitley (1998b) notes that in the Great Basin, manufacture of petroglyphs and pictographs appears to have been the exclusive work of shamans whereas in portions of California, images were made by shamans, puberty initiates, and adults as part of life-crisis rituals. Similarly, Salish-speaking people on the Columbia Plateau report that some rock paintings are the products of interaction with guardian spirits in visions or dreams and others are part of puberty ceremonies (see Boreson 1998). Ultimately, it is variability in the expression of religious worldview and visionary experience that is reflected by the prehistoric imagery of the Bighorn and Wind River Basins.

Metaphors of the Imagery

Both Irwin (1996) and Whitley (1994b) argue that the mental imagery of altered states of consciousness is metaphorically reflected in the iconography and symbolism of Native American cultures. Whitley (1994b) further suggests that the imagery and symbolism are metaphorical expressions for the aural and somatic experiences of the trance state. Many petroglyphs in the Bighorn and Wind River Basins, especially Dinwoody anthropomorphic figures, unquestionably depict aspects of the trance state (see frontispiece).

North American ethnographic accounts indicate that trances often began with aural hallucinations, described as roaring, whirring, ringing, whistling, or buzzing and likened to the sound of the bullroarer or flute (Whitley 1994b:12). Among Numic speakers the bullroarer was the special ritual instrument of the weather-control shaman (Kelly 1932:177), and as seen throughout western North America, anthropomorphic images occasionally hold stick-like objects or other ritual paraphernalia.

Native tobacco was associated with "a noise something like the buzzing of a bee" (Zigmond 1980, 1981:45), also a common metaphor among southern African Bushmen, or San (Lewis-Williams 1984:46), who believed bees had great supernatural power. Bees were commonly illustrated as dots and flecks in paintings throughout southern Africa (Dowson 1989). Dots and flecks occur as design elements in many paintings in the Bighorn and Wind River Basins.

Throughout much of the Great Basin and California, entry into the supernatural world was dangerous and cannot be viewed as an ecstatic trance (Whitley 1998b). Visionary experiences often began with perilous tests, and supplicants had to overcome highly negative emotions such as fear and anxiety, often reflected by violent scenes. Such scenes are certainly found in the Bighorn and Wind River Basins, as in a painting near the Medicine Lodge Creek site (Figure 3.1) which features disembodied heads, hovering axes, and pierced bodies surrounded by red finger dots.

Whitley (1994b) outlines four principal metaphors for trance states common in the ethnography and illustrated in the imagery of western North America. Death is one of the primary metaphors because of the physical similarities between "real" dying and collapsing in a trance (loss of consciousness and motor control, loss or diminution of vital signs,

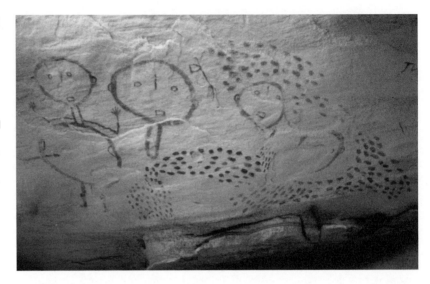

3.1. Red-painted panel from the Medicine Lodge Creek area in the Bighorn Mountain foothills. Finger dots surround disembodied heads. One human figure has been pierced by an arrow; an ax hovers next to another head. Death is often used as a metaphor for entering the trance state, whose physical symptoms frequently mimic dying.

rolling back of the eyes, convulsions, etc.). This connection was expressed linguistically by the Northern Paiute word *tutaigep*. The root of this word is *tai*, "to die" (Fowler 1989:158 cited in Whitley 1994b:14), but it is translated as both "paint" and "poison." Thus, dying, painting, and holding supernatural or medicinal powers are clearly associated (Whitley 1994b:14).

The death metaphor was commonly represented by hunting scenes. Whitley (1994c) offers compelling information that the hunting scenes and killed mountain sheep common in the Coso Range of eastern California are metaphorical expressions for the visions that must be acquired by weather-control shamans to make rain. Hunting scenes and killed animals occur throughout the Bighorn and Wind River Basins. They are most explicitly represented by bow-and-arrow hunters and associated animal figures or by animals that have been pierced by arrows or spears. Significantly, many of the animals depicted in such scenes were not commonly hunted for food; elk, for example, often appears in these images, but elk bone is extremely rare in archaeological faunal assemblages. Furthermore, many groups explicitly prohibited individuals from hunting animals they encountered during visions (Lowie 1909a:47).

Bleeding from the mouth, nose, or eyes is also a common cross-cultural metaphor for the ritual death experienced during trance and is of great importance in southern African painting (see Lewis-Williams 1981, 1982). Facial hemorrhages in humans may be caused by rupturing of the sinus membranes due to hyperventilation; by hypertension, which may be a result of tobacco ingestion; or by ingestion of anticoagulant poisons such

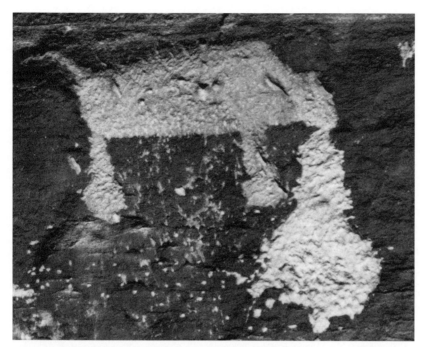

3.2. At the Petroglyph Canyon site in the Pryor Mountains, this en toto pecked bison appears to be in the throes of a nasal hemorrhage, a typical metaphor for death. The darker body of the bison shows some varnish development whereas the "blood" appears to be fresher, and therefore younger, than the animal. The AMS age for the bison is about 1,470 years ago; the blood was CR-dated to less than 1,000 years (Francis et al. 1993). Both figures can fairly certainly be ascribed to the Late Prehistoric period and demonstrate continued use and modification of images over time.

as rattlesnake venom (Whitley 1994b:14). In animals, bleeding can be caused by lung trauma, poisoning, or diseases such as anthrax. Facial bleeding is commonly reported during trance experiences in western North America, and nosebleeds were ascribed supernatural causes (see Whitley 1994b:16). Such hemorrhages by humans are not commonly illustrated, but images of animals in the throes of a facial hemorrhage and presumably dying are occasionally found in the Bighorn and Wind River Basins (Figure 3.2). Furthermore, such images are not necessarily associated with explicit hunting scenes or an obvious wound or trauma. Although this type of image has a clear basis in nature and potential real events, a metaphorical meaning and a basis in trance must also be considered.

Mystical flight is one of the most common metaphors for altered states of consciousness among hunter-gatherers around the world and is widely illustrated in the American West (see Schaafsma 1994, Turpin 1994, and

Whitley 1994b for examples). The ingestion of certain alkaloids, some-times taken to induce trance, results in feelings of weightlessness and of having the ability to fly (Mariategui and Zambrano 1959:22). Hand in hand with the ability to fly is the transformation of humans into bird-like forms or the conflation of the two. This is the most common metaphorical expression of the trance state in the Bighorn and Wind River Basins, par-ticularly in the Dinwoody tradition figures. Scattered along the major tributaries draining into the Wind River upstream from what is now Boysen Reservoir are countless examples of bird-like images or anthropomorphic figures with wings for arms and bird-like feet (Figure 3.3). Indeed, this is one of the dominant figure types at the Dinwoody type site. And though winged figures are not as common downstream from Boysen Reservoir, many Dinwoody tradition sites in the Bighorn Basin contain images of humans with bird-like feet.

Drowning and the experience of being underwater induce many of the same physiological reactions as dying and the trance state, including re-stricted body movements, difficulty breathing, weightlessness, changes in hearing, and altered or blurred vision (Lewis-Williams and Loubser 1986:271; Lewis-Williams and Dowson 1989). Graphic metaphors of being underwater are not illustrated in a straightforward manner in the Bighorn and Wind River Basins. Nevertheless, the role of lakes and springs as portals to the supernatural and home to a variety of malevolent spirits is well documented ethnographically (Liljeblad 1986:653), and shamans often ritually bathed at such places before the vision quest. Within the Dinwoody tradition some anthropomorphic images are occasionally completely surrounded by wavy lines or circles (Figure 3.4), giving the impression of being surrounded by or underneath something. Such images could represent the experience of the shaman during the vision quest or depict the supernatural creatures that lived in the lakes and springs.

Sexual arousal is also a common response to altered states of conscious-ness, and the ethnographic literature is replete with references to the unusual virility and extreme sexual appetites of shamans, along with the sexual symbolism of many rituals, which also involved trance states and shamanistic performances (see Stone 1932:55; Whitley 1994b:21–22). Whitley (1994b:23, 1998) argues that sexual symbolism is expressed at the level of the site and at the level of specific iconographic motifs. In the Bighorn and Wind River Basins this symbolism is most apparent in numer-ous phallic figures, often with exaggerated or multiple male genitalia (Figure 3.5).

Whitley (1994b:24–28) argues that natural models were often used as visionary symbols, in particular certain kinds of animals. Because of the

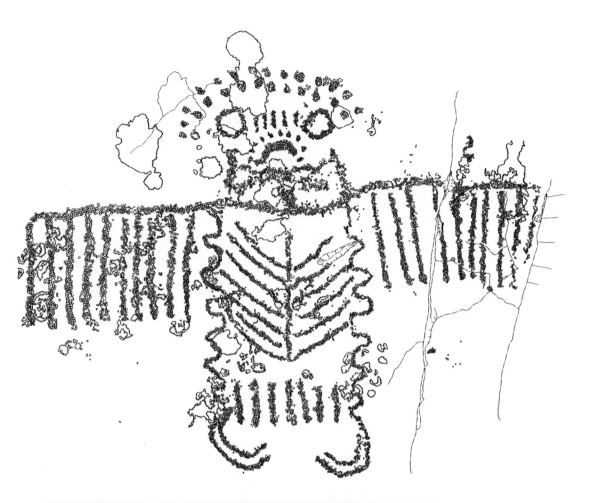

3.3. Winged figure from the upper Wind River area. Drawing by Linda Olson and Courtney Yilk.

3.4. Interior-lined Dinwoody figure from the Bighorn Basin. This claw-footed figure is completely encircled by a wavy line, perhaps conveying the impression of being surrounded by or underneath water. The height of this image is well over 1 m. This site is quite close to one of several hot springs in the Thermopolis area.

3.5. En toto pecked figures with exaggerated male genitalia from Petroglyph Canyon, Montana. Photo by Dennett, Muessig, Ryan, and Associates. Courtesy Bureau of Land Management, Montana.

ambivalent and often dangerous nature of the supernatural, deadly animal species were strongly associated with shamans and supernatural power in southern California. These animals were most often the grizzly bear and rattlesnake, which also served as guardians of the supernatural world. Shamans could transmogrify into these species, and linguistic evidence suggests that some groups considered the animals to be the shamans. Bear power was also of central importance among many Plains groups (Irwin 1996:158). Thus, it should come as no surprise that we see numerous images and tracks of these animals at sites not only in southern California as observed by Whitley (1994b) but also throughout the West, including the Bighorn and Wind River Basins. Indeed, bears and bear tracks are some of the most common zoomorphic images in the study area.

Other species frequently illustrated in the Bighorn and Wind River Basins and many other areas are liminal; that is, they move between the earth and air or underground and serve as metaphors for the shamans' travel between the natural and supernatural worlds (Whitley 1994b:26). Among these species are frogs, turtles, salamanders, and lizards. These animal images appear in all the major classes of petroglyphs and pictographs in the Bighorn and Wind River Basins. For example, turtles occur in the Dinwoody tradition, in the Castle Gardens shield style, and as painted images and are at least as old as the Late Archaic, indicating their importance in the visionary and spiritual world for many different people over thousands of years.

1. Two en toto pecked anthropomorphs from Petroglyph Canyon with fan-shaped, incised headdresses. (Lawrence Loendorf)

2. Profile view of en toto pecked anthropomorph pointing a bow toward an antlered animal, Petroglyph Canyon. (Lawrence Loendorf)

3. En toto pecked figure from the Legend Rock site, Wyoming. (Mike Bies)

4. Dinwoody tradition ghost figure on a glacial boulder from the upper Wind River area. The figure is well over 1 m tall. Note the elongated fingers and claw-like feet with wavy lines running out to the boulder's edge. (Julie Francis)

5. Dinwoody tradition owl-like figure from the upper Wind River area. (Julie Francis)

6. Dinwoody tradition winged figures from the upper Wind River area. The highest figure has pendant feathers; the propeller-winged figure on the lower right may represent a hummingbird. (Julie Francis)

7. Complex Dinwoody tradition panel from the Legend Rock site showing anthropomorphic figures intermixed with animals. The horizontal line in the center appears to represent an arrow and goes around three sides of the boulder. (Julie Francis)

8. Dinwoody tradition anthropomorphic figures at the Legend Rock site. Note the small attenuated figure with one foot on the right side of the large anthropomorph. (Mike Bies)

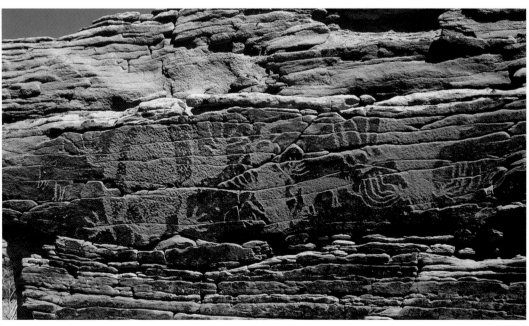

9. Fully pecked Dinwoody tradition figures from the Thermopolis area. (Julie Francis)

10. Fully pecked Dinwoody anthropomorphic figures completely encircled by wavy lines. Exaggerated hands protrude from the circles and are typical of water ghosts. The small canine figures at the base of the panel are characteristic of these sites. (Julie Francis)

11. Composite Dinwoody anthropomorph from the Thermopolis area. The figure's right foot disappears into a crack in the rock. (Julie Francis)

12. Red-and-yellow-painted shield-bearing warrior, southern Montana.
(Lawrence Loendorf)

13. V-shouldered figure with herringbone chest decoration from the Trapper Canyon site in the Bighorn Mountains. On the same panel are intricate incised animal and human forms. (Julie Francis)

14. Red-painted anthropomorphic and zoomorphic forms at Little Canyon Creek Cave superimposed by a V-shouldered figure. At least one bison is discernible. (Lawrence Loendorf)

15. Red-painted, rectangular-bodied bighorn sheep and anthropomorph from the Cook's Canyon area of the southern Bighorn Mountains. (Lawrence Loendorf)

16. Unidentified animal figure with cloven hooves from the Beaver Creek area. (Julie Francis)

17. Large outline-pecked bison superimposed by numerous pecked figures near Greybull, Wyoming. Note the damage caused by bullets, shotgun pellets, and paint. Photographs of this panel from the 1950s show no vandalism. (Lawrence Loendorf)

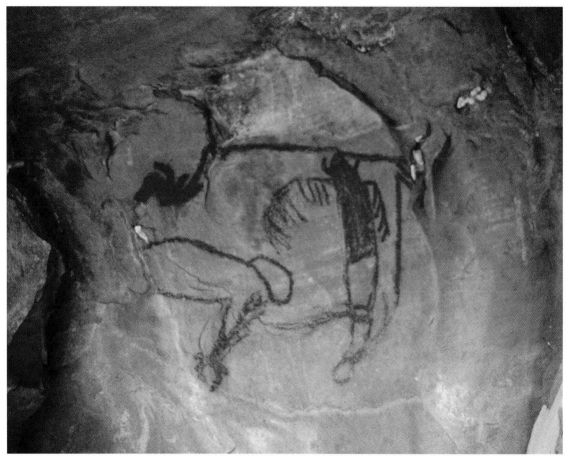

18. Red-painted bison superimposed by a winged anthropomorph, southern Montana. The bison is missing a portion of its head and has the remnants of a heart line and a clawed front leg. (Lawrence Loendorf)

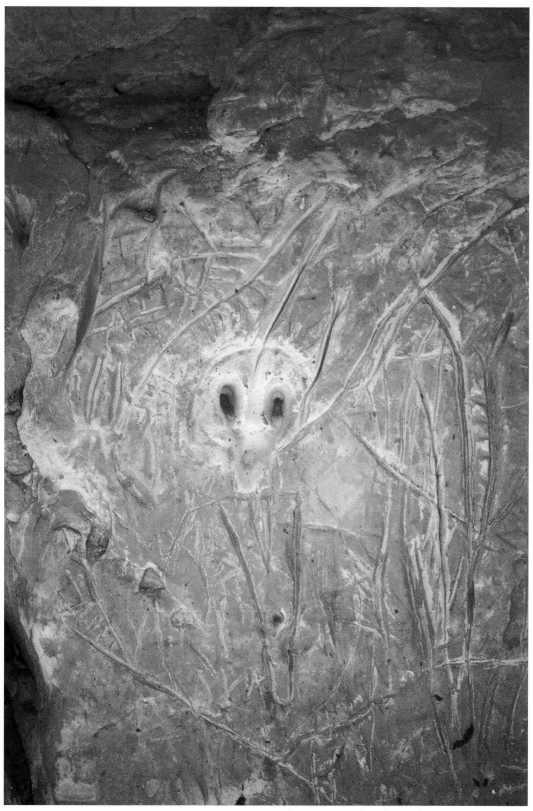

19. Deeply incised and abraded avian form, Trapper Canyon area.
(Lawrence Loendorf)

20. Flat-headdress anthropomorph and tobacco plant images, Frozen Leg Cave, Montana. (Lawrence Loendorf)

FOUR

Style and Classification

NATIVE AMERICAN PETROGLYPH AND PICTOGRAPH SITES
were among the first archaeological localities mentioned and documented by Euro-American explorers in the Bighorn and Wind River Basins. Extensive United States military exploration of northwestern Wyoming began in the 1870s after the Civil War and completion of the transcontinental railroad in 1867. The reports of these expeditions provide the earliest drawings and interpretations, and some of these accounts have proved to be most influential for archaeological interpretations of the area's prehistory and history. For example, Clark (1885:320) reported that supernatural power was sought at sites. Other early accounts hinted at the spiritual use of these sites and also made observations regarding cultural origins and suspected antiquity.

Captain William A. Jones (1875:267–270) published the first drawings and reports of petroglyph and pictograph sites in the Wind River Basin after his 1873 reconnaissance of the northwestern part of Wyoming, including Yellowstone Park. Jones marched north from the Union Pacific Railroad through the Green River Basin to the vicinity of present-day Lander. His report mentioned four localities. The first was a small, walled rockshelter on the left bank of the Little Popo Agie River. The shelter contained a few twigs and leaves, leading Jones to speculate that "the retreat may have been used as a place of incantation by some Indian medicine-man" (1875:267). He also noted three black-painted figures—two horses and a possible mule—on the cliff above the entrance to the shelter. The second site, also in the Little Popo Agie valley, was located on a nearly vertical sandstone cliff face. It had several pecked or incised human, animal, and abstract figures, including at least one shield figure. Jones's Shoshone guide interpreted the scene as representing some unknown battle. This site was also reported by Putnam (1876) and relocated by Hendry (1983).

Jones also provided documentation for two other sites in the Wind River valley, about 30 km north of the Little Popo Agie sites. One site was found where the woodcutters' road from Camp Brown (near present-day Lander) crossed Trout Creek (a tributary of the Wind River). The site consisted of a complex panel of deeply "cut" figures on a buff-colored sandstone cliff overlying the Triassic red beds (Jones 1875:269). Jones's description of the broad, coarse lines used to manufacture the petroglyphs and his inference that they were made by a blunt instrument suggest that they would be classed as deeply incised in modern terminology. Jones also felt that because of the greater number of figures, this panel represented a more complete story than the Little Popo Agie sites. The final site Jones described occurred along the Wind River near the mouth of a tributary. It consisted of multiple figures: at least two human, one animal, one round, and several unknown. It was also located on a buff-colored sandstone cliff and was interpreted as a battle scene between Shoshones and Cheyennes by the Shoshone guide.

Several of Jones's observations and generalizations have relevance for modern interpretations. First, Jones noted a concentration of sites in the Wind River area. Second, he observed that figures were located on soft buff-colored sandstones that were extremely subject to weathering. This, along with the depiction of some horses and guns, led him to speculate that most of the glyphs were "modern relics" (1875:270). Finally, although he suspected that all the figures had a common cultural origin, he was strongly of the opinion that they were not made by the Shoshone.

Another site on the Wind River Indian Reservation was sketched by Dr. William H. Corbusier of the U.S. Army in 1882. He forwarded his drawings to Garrick Mallery (1886, 1893). This site consisted of a panel of pecked figures that was later photographed by Sowers in 1939 and Hendry in 1979 (Hendry 1983:12). In present terminology it would be classified as Dinwoody tradition. Comparing the 1882 drawing with the 1939 photographs, Hendry (1983:12–14) noted some additions to the headdress of one figure. This finding is significant because it documents continued Native American use of sites on the reservation during the late nineteenth and early twentieth centuries. Hendry (1983:12) also mentioned that the "patina" on the drawings had nearly returned to its original color and that the additions had a much lighter patina than the surrounding figures. She observed that this panel would be an excellent place to study weathering and the formation of patina, presaging the rock varnish and dating studies of the 1990s.

Early Investigations

Systematic investigation of Native American paintings and engravings in the Bighorn and Wind River Basins began in the early part of the twentieth century with the work of E. B. Renaud and the Archeological Survey of the Western High Plains. In the eighth field season, 1931, Renaud visited sites in Wyoming, South Dakota, Colorado, and New Mexico, and he prepared numerous plates for the report (1936) from photographs and sketches. Renaud was most taken by the Castle Gardens site, which he visited on a side trip to the Moneta area. The only other site that he apparently visited in the study area was a panel of pecked animal figures on Twin Creek some 32 km southeast of Lander (Renaud 1936:9).

Guided by J. D. Love, Renaud provided detailed descriptions of the Castle Gardens site in the central Wind River Basin before much of the vandalism that occurred after about 1940. This work included in situ observations and measurements of the "Great Turtle" glyph, which has since been removed from the site and is now located at the Wyoming State Museum. Through Renaud's eyes, the modern reader gains a far different view of the now faded and extensively vandalized figures at this site. In addition to noting that several burin-like implements used to manufacture the figures were found at the base of panels, Renaud (1936:11) described vivid polychrome paints—red, black, brown, yellow, white, strong greens, pale oranges, purplish red, and white—applied to many of the figures. Today most of these paints are barely detectable, even with careful observation, and it quickly becomes apparent that the truly spectacular nature of the Castle Gardens site has been lost.

Other early investigators also visited and described Castle Gardens, along with a few additional localities in the study area, during the late 1930s. As part of the Works Progress Administration, the Archaeological Survey of Wyoming, under the direction of Ted C. Sowers, visited Castle Gardens in 1939. In his report Sowers (1941a:16–20) relied heavily on Renaud's (1936:12–13) description and a photograph of the Great Turtle petroglyph given to him by the Love family, as this figure had already been removed from the site.

Because they are so unusual and spectacular, what are now called Dinwoody tradition petroglyphs have long been studied and photographed. In the early 1930s Rennick (n.d.) and Epperson (1936) completed extensive photographic documentation of Dinwoody sites and attributed the petroglyphs to the Sheep Eater Indians. In addition to visiting Castle Gardens, Sowers (1940, 1941b:12–16) described eight other sites, most of which would now be classified as Dinwoody tradition. Several of them are located on the Wind River Indian Reservation, and he provided brief descriptions of sites on Twin Creek, at Crowheart Butte, and along Big and Little Dry Creeks. Sowers (1941b:12) stated that the outlines of all the petroglyphs he observed had been pecked. On some of the figures he also noted traces of paint, but they were so faint that he could not describe the figures as pictographs (Sowers 1941b:12). This description is significant because it provides one of the few indications that Dinwoody petroglyphs were sometimes painted.

One of the major projects undertaken by the Archaeological Survey of Wyoming was excavation at the Dinwoody Cave and Camp sites and documentation of the Dinwoody site on the Wind River Indian Reservation in 1938 and 1939 (Sowers 1939, 1941b:4–10). Sowers estimated that less than half the Dinwoody Camp site was excavated before the conclusion of fieldwork. These excavations yielded more than 4,000 artifacts including paint, which led Sowers (1941b:7) to infer that the Dinwoody Camp site was also used as a Sun Dance ceremonial ground.

Sowers visited 84 petroglyphs within a 3.2-km radius of the Dinwoody Camp site. He noted the presence of only two pictographs in the entire area, both of which were found on the walls of Dinwoody Cave (Sowers 1941b:7). Although Sowers recognized that Native American paintings and engravings could not be considered true "writing" and that some of the figures in the Dinwoody area could be symbolic, his interpretations reflect the Euro-American tendency to ascribe specific meanings to specific figures that can be directly interpreted or "read" and have the same meaning to all individuals who visit a site. Thus, he interpreted the "famous Dinwoody panel" as documenting the death and mourning of a great medicine man, complete with his departed spirit, crying wife, chief, medicine man, and the giving of blankets and bags to the loudest mourners (Sowers 1941b:7–10). Another panel was said to represent the birth of a twin boy and girl and the superstitions surrounding such a birth, along with representations of the midwife, the birthing hut in which new mothers were confined, hermaphrodites, and a shamed father (Sowers 1941b:7). Sowers clearly did not consult with the Wind River Shoshone about the meaning of the petroglyphs, and it is apparent from other anthropological studies of the Wind River Shoshone (e.g., Hultkrantz 1986) that most of his observations are conjectural.

World War II interrupted archaeological research throughout the United States, and the Wind River and Bighorn Basins were no exception. Investigations resumed soon afterward, and the archaeological survey of Boysen Reservoir area began in 1946. This survey, conducted by the Smithsonian

Institution River Basin Surveys, documented 12 sites containing engravings and paintings in the Boysen Reservoir area (Bliss 1948; Bliss and Hughes 1947). As part of the documentation, small test units were excavated below panels at several sites. Excavations at three sites proved unproductive, but hearths and some bison bone were discovered at 48FR13. A Late Prehistoric or early Historic period age was inferred for most of the figures by the original investigators (Walker 1994a:122). Several of these sites were reinvestigated during the 1980s and 1990s (Tipps and Schroedl 1985; Walker 1994b), with Walker (1994b) publishing the most detailed descriptions, including original field notes from the River Basin Survey projects.

The River Basin Survey projects made some important observations regarding petroglyphs and pictographs in the Boysen Reservoir area. First, Wheeler (1957:337) suggested that the Boysen glyphs and those found in the Dinwoody area had a direct relationship and a common tradition. In addition, he felt that most of the pecked images represented supernatural beings or shamans impersonating such beings, along with totemic animals and birds (Wheeler 1957:334). Finally, he noted that the rare, finely incised and scratched figures dated to the Historic period and were no more than 100 years old (Wheeler 1957:336).

The research of art historian David Gebhard on Dinwoody tradition imagery has probably been most influential on subsequent scholars. Gebhard began his work in the post–World War II era (Gebhard 1951, 1954; Gebhard and Cahn 1950) and continued to refine a widely used stylistic sequence (Gebhard 1969, 1972). He suggested a recent Shoshonean authorship for Dinwoody sites but noted, "If one knew or even had an inkling as to the specific purposes of these drawings, an analysis of style could be carried a step further into a study of their iconography" (Gebhard 1969:22).

Research has continued in the Dinwoody area. Extensive photographic documentation of Dinwoody tradition sites in the upper Wind River area was undertaken by Adams (1974) and Swaim (1975). In 1984 Childers (1984, 1991) began an intensive study in this same area, identifying two classes of winged anthropomorphic figures. She is also one of the few to suggest a great antiquity for the area's petroglyphs, hypothesizing that some of the imagery could date to Altithermal times (Childers 1994). A National Register nomination for this area was prepared by Swenson and Chapman (1992). Other important documentation of numerous Dinwoody sites was completed by Hendry (1983) and Stewart (1989).

In the northern portion of the study area William T. Mulloy was the first professional archaeologist to extensively describe the major complex of paintings at Pictograph Cave near Billings, Montana. In the excavation report Mulloy (1958:121–122) described all 141 paintings on the walls of the cave, providing the first descriptions for the shield-bearing warrior and V-necked human figure types, descriptions that are still in use today. Mulloy (1958:118) noted that the paintings were completed in three colors: black, red, and white. He also recognized a difference in the shades of red, suggesting that the brighter red was derived from Euro-American trade paint, referred to as vermilion.

One of the problems with Mulloy's analysis of the pictographs is the absence of information on the juxtaposition (relationship of one figure to another) of the figures. It should be noted that this lack is not Mulloy's fault: the pictographs were recorded by the Works Project Administration field crews before his involvement with the project. Mulloy completed his research by using a set of drawings made of each individual pictograph on butcher paper, and these drawings, now curated in the University of Montana library archives, did not present the pictographs' relative positions.

Mulloy discussed superimposition, using it to help divide the pictographs into two groups. One group was believed to have been made by the occupants of the cave during the period known as Pictograph Cave III, and the second group was thought to represent Pictograph Cave IV occupants. The latter figures include a row of muskets. These guns as well as other paintings in the cave are executed in the bright red trade paint obtained sometime ca. A.D. 1700. According to Mulloy, the historic figures are always superimposed on older Pictograph Cave III pictographs, which are primarily in black, do not portray objects of the Historic period, and are more faded than the Pictograph Cave IV figures.

Although Mulloy resolved some of the chronological questions regarding the paintings at Pictograph Cave, he held an extremely pessimistic view of our ability to understand and interpret these and other figures found throughout Wyoming and Montana: "Their pictographic significance must remain obscure, however, for such symbolism is a highly individualized thing, capable of decipherment only by the original artists and his community.... archaeologically we cannot cope with petroglyphic meanings" (Mulloy 1958:119).

Throughout the 1960s members of the Montana Archaeological Society, led by Stuart W. Conner and Kenneth Feyhl, documented many localities in Montana. These investigations resulted in the refinement of type descriptions for both the shield-bearing warrior and the V-necked human figure (Conner 1962; Conner and Conner 1971). More recently, Conner (1984) noted the contemporaneity of these figure types and discussed their relationship to the introduction of the horse in the Lower Yellowstone valley.

Previous Treatments of Style

Numerous chronological sequences and stylistic definitions have been developed for pictographs and petroglyphs throughout Wyoming and Montana (see Francis 1991 for a summary). In addition to Mulloy's (1958) treatment of Pictograph Cave, Malouf (1961) proposed a chronological sequence of pictographs throughout Montana. Based on work at Writing-on-Stone in southern Alberta, Keyser (1977) defined the Ceremonial style to describe the shield-bearing warriors and other motifs of the Late Prehistoric period. Most significantly, he noted a major change to the Biographical style, which depicts action and specific events during the Historic period, and subsequently, through an examination of ledger art and hide paintings, offered detailed techniques for the interpretation of Historic period imagery (Keyser 1987, 1996). Other sequences have been developed for the Black Hills, beginning with Buckles's (1964) work at Medicine Creek Cave. Sundstrom (1984,1990) and Keyser (1984) have outlined chronological sequences of petroglyphs and pictographs for the Black Hills and North Cave Hills, respectively. Sundstrom (1984, 1989, 1990) was the first to postulate an Archaic age for some of the figures in the Black Hills. More recently, Tratebas (1993) has established a chronology for petroglyphs at the Whoopup Canyon site in the southwestern Black Hills. Ranging from Paleoindian to Historic times, the sequence uses chronometric dates and a principal components analysis based on style.

Within the Wind River and Bighorn Basins, only three investigators have developed chronological sequences or have attempted a synchronic analysis of style. Renaud (1936:7) was the first to recognize that "stylistic" differences could be ascribed to chronological variation, and he constructed a relative chronology based primarily on manufacturing technique. Thus, pecked figures were thought to be the most ancient, dating to some unknown prehistoric period, followed by "deeper" incising and "finer" incising during the Historic period. The chronological differences between deeply incised and finely incised figures are still recognized today (Loendorf and Porsche 1985), with similar sequences recognized throughout the Plains (Keyser 1977; Sundstrom 1984).

At the Castle Gardens site Renaud (1936:16) suggested that some of the figures had to be at least 200 years old, based on a count of tree rings from a pine tree that had grown over and damaged some shield figures. He also noted a lack of depictions of horses throughout the site and the fact that the height of many figures above the present ground surface indicated considerable erosion of the cliff faces since the glyphs' manufacture. Thus,

Renaud (1936:16) ascribed the images at Castle Gardens to a true "prehistoric period."

Relying heavily on a report prepared by J. D. Love (1932), Renaud defined four types of petroglyphs at Castle Gardens, based on methods of manufacture as well as subject matter. The first type proposed by Love (1932) and Renaud (1936:10) included deeply incised, parallel lines thought to represent tool grooves, as well as drawings of single arrows, bear tracks, and tipis and one representation of what Love (1932) inferred to be a corn plant. Geometric designs, including circles, squares, triangles, "ladders," and zigzag lines, made up the second, and somewhat uncommon, type. Renaud (1936:10) stated that this type contrasted with the naturalistic style of other figures at the site. Both Renaud (1936:11) and Love (1932) recognized shields and shield-bearing warriors as the third and most striking type at Castle Gardens. These figures were made by first smoothing the surface of the cliff with a flat, mano-like implement and then deeply incising a large circle, inferred to be the shield, around the smoothed area. Figures such as warriors, turtles, birds, and quadrupeds were then incised and painted in a variety of colors on the inside of the shield. Naturalistic human figures with pointed shoulders (now termed V-necked figures), rectangular bodies often covered with garments, and frequent depictions of sexual organs comprised the fourth type defined by Renaud (1936:13). This group also included human figures without pointed shoulders and was always incised, with no painting.

Building on his work in the Dinwoody area, Gebhard (1969) formulated a chronological sequence of styles that has been applied throughout Wyoming (Gebhard et al. 1987a, b, c). The style definitions and chronology he proposed have also been the most frequently used by subsequent investigators (Stewart 1989; Tipps and Schroedl 1985).

Gebhard (1969) adopted a concept of style similar to that used by Schapiro (1953:287), which views style as the constant of form, elements, quality, and expression of an individual or a group. Style is assumed to be unique to a given time period and culture, and there is only one style or a limited range of styles within a given culture or epoch of culture. Thus, style can be used as a temporally and culturally diagnostic tool. Style ultimately is defined on the basis of overall aesthetic qualities of panels (Schaafsma 1985), which are assumed to reflect the cultural preferences of the makers.

Gebhard (1969:11) defined styles at Dinwoody and other sites in the southern Bighorn Basin using artistic characteristics of panels and individual figures, including modes of conventionalization, scale, composition and arrangement, techniques of rendering, and subject matter. He observed several instances of superimposition and some obvious differences in the degree of weathering of figures on the same panel or rock exposure, which he used to infer chronological differences between the styles. He defined the Early Hunting style as including small (about 5 to 10 cm) fully pecked animals with some humans (also fully pecked) (Gebhard 1969:15–16). These figures are typically arranged in herd or hunting scenes, with bighorn sheep, mountain goats, pronghorn, rabbits, bears, and canids most often depicted. No dates, other than earlier than the Interior Line style, were suggested for the Early Hunting style.

Gebhard (1969:16–17) considered the Interior Line style the predominant style at the Dinwoody site. It was defined as including large (ranging to over 1 m in height) human figures pecked in outline form with elaborate patterns of interior lines in the torso. These figures exhibit horns or some type of headdress and often are connected to intricate geometric patterns. Gebhard also noted that some fully pecked (human?) figures occur. Animal figures are not as common, and when they occur, they are less detailed than the human figures and are generally solidly pecked, with a few instances of simple interior lines.

Gebhard (1969:18–19) was the first to note that the Interior Line style was restricted to the Wind River Basin and southwestern portion of the Bighorn Basin. He also observed stylistic similarities between the interior-lined human figures of these basins and interior-lined human figures found throughout the Great Basin and in the Coso Range (Gebhard 1969:20–21; see Grant et al. 1968; Heizer and Baumhoff 1962; Steward 1929; and Younkin 1998). Although some elements of the human figures occur in both Great Basin and Plains Indian imagery, Gebhard (1969:22) suggested that the Wyoming interior-lined figures "grew out" of Fremont and provided some stylistic elements for late Plains Indian art, with the Shoshone as the most likely candidates for authorship. In view of the freshness of many of the drawings, the lack of specific ties to the historic Plains Indian buffalo hunting culture, and the lack of historic items in the drawings, Gebhard suggested dates between A.D. 1650 and 1800 for the Interior Line style.

The final style defined by Gebhard (1969:17–18) was the Late Plains Hunting style, which was not particularly common at Dinwoody. It includes lightly pecked or incised human figures that are smaller and simpler than the Interior Line style figures. The human figures can apparently exhibit some interior lines, and animals include deer, elk, birds, and large insects. Gebhard (1969:18) relates this style to Historic-period Plains Indian cultures.

Gebhard attempted to extend the stylistic sequence for Dinwoody to other portions of Wyoming. The vast majority of the pecked animal figures at Whoopup Canyon in the southern Black Hills were considered to be examples of the Early Hunting style (Gebhard et al. 1987c:39), and Gebhard et al. (1987c:58) follow Sundstrom (1984:100) in suggesting that these figures date to the Archaic period. At Cedar Canyon in the Green River Basin, Gebhard et al. (1987b:3, 23) considered most of the petroglyphs to be classic examples of the Late Plains Hunting style.

At Castle Gardens, Gebhard et al. (1987a:81) defined the Late Prehistoric Northern Plains style, with a postulated age between the early seventeenth century to the late eighteenth century, approximately A.D. 1600 to 1800. More specifically, Gebhard et al. (1987a:13) suggested that most of the drawings were produced either just before or just after A.D. 1700. This style includes shield figures and V-necked anthropomorphs, and according to Gebhard et al. (1987a:56–57), the shield figures most likely predated the V-necks. Although the dates for the Late Prehistoric Northern Plains style are basically coeval with the suggested age range for the Interior Line style (Gebhard 1969:18–19), Gebhard et al. (1987a:83) believed the Interior Line style to be earlier. A Shoshonean origin was suggested for Castle Gardens, as well as for many other sites containing shields and shield-bearing warriors throughout northwestern Wyoming and into Montana (Gebhard et al. 1987a:102).

Wyoming artist Mary Helen Hendry, who completed extensive documentation of sites throughout the state, had a much different perspective on style. She recognized a concentration of sites with many distinct qualities surrounding the Wind River Indian Reservation and inferred that most of the images in the Wind River and Bighorn Basins had been manufactured after the reservation was established in 1872 (Hendry 1983:7). She related many of the symbols on the rocks of Wyoming to the Ghost Dance religion, which spread to the area in 1890. These symbols include a circle representing the sun, a horizontal crescent representing the new moon, the morning star, sacred birds, handprints, dots, slashes, fish, pipes, buffalo, turtles, and the cedar or pine bough (Hendry 1983:56).

Because of her assumed recent age for Wyoming pictographs and petroglyphs, Hendry's (1983) analysis of style is basically synchronic. Style is used to refer to characteristic features or elements of individual figures, such as body shape and head shape, as well as to overall composition of figures in relation to one another. The most common body or figural styles represented are circular, rectangular, or a "D" turned on its side. Compositional styles, as seen in historic Plains Indian hide paintings, are related to the ultimate purpose of the painting or drawing (Hendry 1983:21–23). Thus, Winter Count paintings often exhibit a different compositional style (spiral) than biographical paintings or the geometric composition found on clothing. Biographical composition is seen as the most common style. Hendry (1983:28–47) also identified several types of a composite style in which one figure can have secondary figures or additional limbs integrated into the overall design.

Hendry (1983:7) found spatial variation in the occurrence of both body styles and compositional styles. Outside the Wind River and Bighorn regions a modified biographical style is most prevalent; within the Wind River and Bighorn areas composite style predominates. Hendry noted that circular and rectangular body styles were more common in the eastern half of Wyoming whereas the sideways "D" was most common in the Bighorn and Wind River Basins (Hendry 1983:7).

Classification, Style, and Tradition

It is apparent that styles have been defined in vastly different ways by researchers in the Bighorn and Wind River Basins. These differences illustrate one of the problems of stylistic analysis: the proposed styles cannot be used as classificatory devices to compare sites or regions. The designated styles do not necessarily represent mutually exclusive categories, and the characteristics that differentiate one style from another are unclear. For example, Gebhard (1969) stated that fully pecked human and animal figures occur in both the Early Hunting style and the Interior Line style. Unless instances of superimposition of different figures occur on a panel or within a site, it is impossible to classify these figures as one style or the other. Hendry's (1983) scheme presents similar problems. One figure could be classified as three different styles, based on its body shape, type of headdress, and composition. In essence, "style" has been used to describe attributes of the same figure.

With no chronological data derived from archaeological investigation of pictograph and petroglyph sites available, past researchers presumed that severe environmental conditions and soft rock surfaces would not be conducive to long-term preservation. Thus, a "compressed" time frame and a fairly recent age (no greater than the latest portions of the Late Prehistoric period) for styles were taken for granted. Gebhard (1969) and Gebhard et al. (1987 a, b, c) assumed that only one style of rock art should be present during any one time period. These assumptions mask potential important variation in form and function across the study area and throughout most of Wyoming. Hendry (1983) discounted time as a variable, even in cases of superimposition, and considered all images across Wyoming to be contemporaneous.

In this book we use a much different approach, one based on traditional archaeological method and theory and principles of classification that have been debated, developed, and refined over the past century (Hill and Evans 1972; Willey and Sabloff 1974:104–115). We follow the traditional North American paradigm, which emphasizes temporal and spatial variation in different classes of material culture and classification as the central prerequisite to problem-oriented research, analysis, and interpretation (Hill and Evans 1972:234) from either processual or postprocessualist perspectives. Not only should classification systems bring order to a particular data set; they must also seek to maximize variation between groups in order to explain variability and change between them (Plog 1974).

In order to document temporal and spatial variation in pictographs and petroglyphs, with the ultimate goal of understanding that variation, it is necessary to devise a replicable classification system that can be used to compare figures across time and space. We do not assume the classification system used here represents the only means of classifying petroglyphs and pictographs in the Wind River or Bighorn Basins. This system is based on the one developed for Carbon County, Montana, in the northern portion of the study area (Loendorf and Porsche 1985) and elaborated on at Pinon Canyon in southeastern Colorado (Loendorf 1989).

The first step is devising a method by which figures can be consistently described by different investigators. Primary to this system is the identification of attributes or characteristics of images and sites that vary: such things as age, location (in a rockshelter, along a cliff face, on boulders), site location (along drainages or in upland settings), and geographic region. Other attributes are orientation of figures on the rock face, height above the ground surface, the amount of rock varnish, and the degree of weathering. Many other attributes are intrinsic to the image itself: technique of manufacture (pecked, incised, painted), color of paint, type of figure (anthropomorphic, zoomorphic, abstract, etc.), animal species, body shape, type of headdress, view (frontal or profile), and posture (sitting, standing).

Many intrinsic attributes can be considered *design elements,* which are central to the accurate and replicable description of individual figures. As used in this book, a design element is a formal unit used to divide and describe an individual design or figure. It is designated by the researcher and recognized as being arbitrary. Examples include zigzag lines; patterns of dots; conventions for rendering eyes, hands, feet, or limbs; details of antlers or hooves; body or torso shape; and other characteristics that describe formal or morphological variation in the figure. An individual figure can be composed of one design element or many.

Designation of *descriptive types* is the next step in the classification process. A descriptive type refers to a grouping of figures based on conscious recognition of dimensions of formal variation and consistent patterning of attributes (Hill and Evans 1972:233; Krieger 1944, 1960: 143; Sackett 1966; Spaulding 1953). A simple fact in all systems of typology is that one cannot describe all the variability in every arrowhead, pot, or figure and hope to communicate such lengthy descriptions to others. One has to search for similarities between artifacts or figures so that those with common attributes can be described together. Types created at this early stage of analysis are not necessarily intended to fit into a given time period or chronological scheme. In fact, it is often impossible to determine the age of individual figures that form a descriptive type, and one descriptive type could have been manufactured for thousands of years. Nor is there a presumption that descriptive types must occur in a spatially restricted area—some occur throughout the Great Plains or Great Basin. Given the broad occurrence of some descriptive types, there is not necessarily a presumption of taxonomic relationship or common cultural origin among all members of a given type.

Another important feature of descriptive types, as used here, is that the rules of classification for any given type can be both monothetic and polythetic. That is, some of the attributes that form the type are absolute; other rules of classification allow for some variability. Often these rules are hierarchical. For example, painted figures on the interior of caves could be defined as a descriptive type. The occurrence of these images in caves is an absolute rule of classification. That they must be painted is also an absolute criterion. However, that they are usually executed in either yellow or red paint allows for some variability in that criterion and allows for a few designs in the type to be of a different color paint.

Several descriptive types from the Wind River and Bighorn Basins are well known. For example, large pecked human figures with interior lines or patterns in the torso and some type of headdress form the descriptive type that was designated the Interior Line style by Gebhard (1969). Shield figures or shield-bearing warriors and V-necked human figures comprise two other descriptive types that occur throughout the Plains. Other descriptive types employed in this book are discussed in subsequent chapters.

The second analytical grouping used here is *class,* which refers to any division of figures based on readily observable similarities and differences in a few attributes (Hill and Evans 1972:233). Thus, class is a more generic term than type and can often be defined by a single attribute. Classes are not simply a higher-order, hierarchical grouping of descriptive types; a taxonomic relationship between descriptive types and class is not assumed.

In the case of the Wind River and Bighorn Basins, general geographic location with reference to the Bighorn River and method of manufacture appear to be extremely important variables, accounting for a great deal of variation in descriptive figure types. We define two basic classes: imagery west of the Bighorn River is almost entirely pecked whereas imagery east of the river is incised, painted, and occasionally outline-pecked. These two classes are fundamentally different and are dominated by different descriptive figure types. The classes do not represent a chronological sequence. In fact, as seen in subsequent chapters, current data indicate that for at least the last millennium, the two classes were manufactured concurrently throughout the Bighorn and Wind River Basins. There appear to be important differences in terms of how images in each class relate to other archaeological sites. In short, within the Wind River and Bighorn Basins this simple division appears to measure some differences in the manufacture and use of visionary imagery.

We also use other analytical constructs: *style* and *tradition*. Because of the problems associated with stylistic constructs (see Hedges 1982b; Schaafsma 1985; and Whitley 1982), we use *style* sparingly and in a far more restrictive sense than other researchers. A style is a repetitious form or series of forms that shows internal continuity with respect to specific techniques of manufacture and combinations of design elements, has a limited temporal distribution, and has a widespread spatial distribution. Style in this sense is much more akin to the concept of horizon style, as defined by Willey and Phillips (1958:32), who used the term to infer a specialized cultural continuum represented by the wide distribution of a recognizable art style. As an example, we define the Castle Gardens shield style (Loendorf 1995) to refer to abraded, incised, and painted shields and shield-bearing warriors that occur at several sites throughout the study area and consistently date to around 1,000 years ago.

We also follow Willey and Phillips (1958) in our use of the term *tradition*. Willey and Phillips defined tradition as a temporal continuity represented by persistent configurations in single technologies or other systems of related forms (1958:37). In its broadest sense, tradition could be equated to the classes defined above, but we primarily use the term to refer to the complex of pecked anthropomorphs and associated figures that occur in the southwestern portion of the study area. The distinctiveness of this complex, called the Dinwoody tradition (Francis 1994), has been recognized by many other researchers (Gebhard 1969; Hendry 1983). The

Dinwoody tradition shows a great deal of internal cohesion. Yet its time depth is far greater than suspected by earlier investigators, spanning at least the Archaic, Late Prehistoric, and Protohistoric periods. Although the tradition shows a great deal of internal cohesion with respect to overall form and function, the Dinwoody tradition also exhibits evolutionary change.

The variability seen in the distribution of figure types within and between classes argues strongly for a great deal of variability in ideological expression on the part of the prehistoric people of the Wind River and Bighorn Basins. In addition, although only a small portion of this imagery can be subsumed under the analytical constructs of style and tradition as used in this book, these constructs have important implications for patterns of culture process and change generally not found in other aspects of material culture.

FIVE

So How Old Is It?

ONLY SINCE ABOUT 1980 HAVE SPECIALIZED TECHNIQUES been developed to obtain chronometric age estimates for rock paintings and engravings. In the absence of direct dating techniques, archaeologists and other researchers used various criteria to infer relative ages of glyphs (see Gebhard et al. 1987a, b, c; Grant 1967; Sundstrom 1984:67; and Wellmann 1979:20–24). These criteria provide evidence only that one figure or panel is older than another, and rarely can they be anchored to a specific calendrical date. Because many petroglyphs and pictographs are not suitable for numerical dating, however, these criteria remain important and are often used in conjunction with other, direct techniques to develop regional chronologies.

Subject matter is one way to tie figures to calendrical dates in a relative sense. This is most apparent with Historic period items. For example, since the earliest reported occurrence of guns and horses in southern Montana is around A.D. 1725 or 1730 (Ewers 1955), images of guns and horses must postdate this time. For older figures, temporally diagnostic items that have been dated in other archaeological contexts can be used to infer age. Use of the bow and arrow began about 1,500 years ago (see Chapter 2) in the Bighorn and Wind River Basins, and therefore panels containing images of bows and arrows must be younger than 1,500 years.

Superimposition provides an intuitively obvious way to infer relative age. At many sites one figure has been pecked, incised, or painted on top of another figure. The figure on the bottom clearly must be older than the figure on the top. Nevertheless, there is rarely any way to infer the difference in ages between the two images. Reported consistencies in superimposition have been used to suggest chronological and cultural differences on a regional scale. For example, Bettinger and Baumhoff (1982: 494) use the superimposition of scratched over pecked figures as evidence of the Numic expansion across the Great Basin beginning about 1,000 years ago. Ritter (1994:57, 61) has challenged this interpretation, however, noting that pecking is just as likely to overlay scratching and that some scratched images may be Archaic.

Visual differences in weathering and the development of rock coatings can sometimes be used to suggest age differences. Within the same panel or rock surface exposure, and assuming similarity in the method of manufacture, figures that are more weathered and therefore more faint than others generally are assumed to be older. Again, there is no way to assess the extent of age differences, and one cannot reliably extrapolate age differences between paintings and engravings on different rock surfaces or between sites owing to variation in exposure to wind and water.

Like weathering, the visual development of rock varnish, often referred to as patination (Gebhard et al. 1987a, b, c; Sundstrom 1984:67), has been used to make inferences about age. But as Liu and Dorn (1996) note, varnish does not form evenly: variation in the microtopography of a rock surface or petroglyph or between a crack and a surface continuously exposed to air causes considerable variation in varnish development. The visual development and color of rock varnish can be greatly influenced by a host of other factors as well: the differential growth rates of different types of rock coatings, varying chemistry of the same type of rock coating, the underlying lithology, the underlying weathering rind, water flow and water ponding, interdigitation of different rock coatings, epilithic organisms, corrosion, surface roughness, and soil proximity. Thus, visual development of varnish, even on the same panel, is not necessarily a reliable indicator of age.

The relative age of different rock surfaces has also been used, in conjunction with the degree of weathering or varnish development, to suggest age differences. For example, figures made on a surface that has been created by recent spalling are presumed to be younger than those on an adjacent varnished surface, if and only if the figures on the varnished surface exhibit a similar degree of varnish development as the surrounding surface (see Sundstrom 1984:67).

Surfaces at the base of panels on cliffs are not stable and are often subject to complex erosional and depositional conditions. In some cases, lines marking the level of previous ground surfaces are visible on cliff faces. Thus, relative height above the present ground surface can sometimes be used as an indicator of age: higher figures may be older than lower figures on surfaces exposed by recent erosion. Again, this technique can be used

only in limited circumstances. It assumes that erosion of the ground surface has been continual and that the highest figures have never been
covered by more recent deposition. It also assumes that the manufacturers
did not use any kind of a device such as a ladder or scaffolding to reach
high, inaccessible surfaces on cliffs.

Sediments at the base of panels sometimes contain artifacts associated
with the figures and other datable materials. We have been excavating
directly beneath petroglyph and pictograph panels since 1983 at several
sites in Petroglyph Canyon (Loendorf 1984:107–123). Excavations were
subsequently undertaken at a half-dozen other sites in Carbon County,
Montana (Loendorf and Porsche 1985). At the Valley of the Shields site we
recovered a sandstone abrader used in the manufacture of the petroglyph
in direct association with a charcoal-filled hearth that provided a radiocarbon age (Loendorf 1988, 1990). We have also excavated deposits
partially covering petroglyphs and pictographs. In these cases, the figures
must predate the deposition of the sediments and any associated archaeological materials. Radiocarbon dating of charcoal recovered from sediments
partially burying a Dinwoody anthropomorphic figure at the Legend Rock
site was used to suggest that the figure was made sometime before 2,000
years ago (Walker and Francis 1989:42).

Advances in Dating Techniques

The terminology of dating, as well as the techniques, has changed
in the last decade (Colman et al. 1987; Dorn 1998a). We have already
introduced the concept of relative dating, which provides only an ordering
of events, and most readers are familiar with the term *absolute* in conjunction with dating techniques. This term is no longer used because measured
ages are never so certain as to be absolute. Instead, we use *numerical* for
methods such as radiocarbon which yield specific ages with uncertainties.
Calibrated methods are those tied to numerical measurements, and *correlative* methods use particular events (such as volcanic eruptions) to establish
equivalency. Finally, the term *age* is preferable to *date* because of the false
connotation of precision implied by the latter.

AMS *Dating of Pictographs*
Researchers have long recognized the theoretical possibilities of radiocarbon (^{14}C) dating the organic constituents of paint. In the past, however, use
of ^{14}C dating was prevented by the inability to date minute quantities of
organic material, technological problems associated with the extraction of
organics from the paint, and contamination from other sources. Improve-

ments in accelerator mass spectrometry (AMS) now permit ^{14}C dating of extremely small samples of organic materials, and advances in chemistry have improved extractive techniques. As a result, AMS is being used to date rock paintings throughout the world. Moreover, scientists have refined the ability to identify the chemical constituents of paints, thus providing valuable clues about the types of pigments and binders used by prehistoric peoples.

Only organic pigments or those incorporating organic material are datable with AMS techniques. Not all paints are organic. For example, Tipps (1995:157) found that some paintings in Barrier Canyon, Utah, had been executed by coloring the rock surface with a lump of inorganic pigment such as hematite or manganese oxide. A variety of organic materials were used in prehistoric pigments. Charcoaled figures from several Paleolithic caves in Spain and France (Clottes 1994) and beeswax figures in Australia (Watchman 1992) have now been successfully dated by AMS.

Ancient painters often used ground pigment suspended in a liquid medium and applied to the rock surface with fingers or brushes or by spraying. Liquid binders include such materials as animal fat, blood, and vegetable oils. If the type of organic component is known, specific techniques can be used to selectively extract that material. In Australia paints made with blood (Loy et al. 1990) or containing plant fibers (Watchman 1992) have been dated.

More often, however, minuscule quantities of organic material are dispersed throughout largely inorganic pigments, and it is impossible to know their exact nature. The primary problem is to extract organic components from the paint only, without also gathering older or younger carbon from other sources (Chaffee, Hyman, and Rowe 1994). Carbon occurring in the rock on which the painting was made is one potential source of older material. Carbon is a principal component not only of limestones and sandstones but also of mineral coatings that overlie paintings such as silica glaze, calcite ($CaCO_3$), and calcium oxalate ($CaC_2O_4.H_2O$).

Modern human activities can also seriously contaminate the organic components of rock paintings. Spraying figures with antifreeze (which contains ethylene glycol) or other water-repellent compounds to attempt erosion control, or with biocides to remove lichens, algae, or fungus (see Ford and Watchman 1990), can render pictographs undatable. Application of kerosene to improve the photographic quality of paintings (Grant 1967; Kirkland and Newcomb 1967) can have the same result (see Chaffee, Hyman, and Rowe 1993, 1994:9).

Chemists at Texas A & M University have refined new techniques for the extraction of organic materials from paints that are mostly inorganic.

Low-temperature, low-pressure oxygen plasma extraction (see Chaffee, Hyman, and Rowe 1994) can selectively remove organic carbon. Prior knowledge of the nature of the organic matter in the paint is useful but not necessary. In a high vacuum the oxygen plasma oxidizes the organic component of the paint, which is collected as gaseous carbon dioxide.

One of the difficulties in dating pigment is the interdigitation of organic and inorganic compounds. A great advantage of the oxygen plasma approach is that it is unaffected by inorganic carbon found in the host rock or subsequent mineral overcoatings. Further research has attempted to reduce the possibility of contamination by organic carbon and to date materials with a known and restricted age range (Chaffee, Hyman, and Rowe 1994:10).

The oxygen plasma technique was first used to date pictographs from the Lower Pecos valley of southern Texas (Russ et al. 1990). Additional pictographs in the Lower Pecos valley (Chaffee, Hyman, and Rowe 1994), the All American Man figure in Utah (Chaffee, Hyman, Rowe, Coulam et al. 1994), and several other sites in Canyonlands National Park (Tipps 1995:156) have now been successfully dated, although contamination from organic carbon in the underlying sandstone resulted in unreliable ages for some figures (Tipps 1995:160). In the Bighorn region, pictographs at three different sites have been dated. Three separate AMS ages from a black, outline-painted turtle at Pictograph Cave fall into the Late Archaic period (slightly older than 2,000 years) and constitute the oldest age estimate for any painting in the region. A solid, red-painted anthropomorphic figure at Elk Creek Cave in the Pryor Mountains yielded a Late Prehistoric AMS age of about 800 years ago (Chaffee, Loendorf et al. 1994). Collection and processing of paint samples is an ongoing process, depending on time and funding constraints. During the summer of 1998, with the assistance of Mike Bies of the Bureau of Land Management, we accompanied Marvin Rowe of Texas A & M to collect samples from several figures in Little Canyon Creek Cave and from several other sites on Nature Conservancy holdings in the southern Bighorn Mountains. One age is thus far available: a series of charcoal painted lines adjacent to a similarly painted shield-bearing warrior in Little Canyon Creek Cave yielded an AMS age of 550 ± 40 years B.P.

Estimating the Age of Petroglyphs
Nearly all who visit sites containing pecked images have observed that some figures appear quite fresh with peck marks showing the bright colors of recently exposed rock, in stark contrast to the surrounding unmodified surface. Other figures appear more faint with the colors of the peck marks

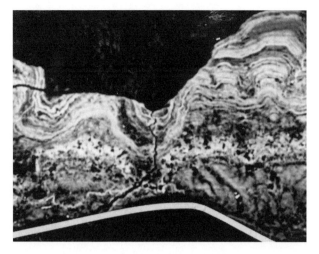

5.1. Cross section of a varnish sample collected from a figure in Petroglyph Canyon, Montana. The clearly visible layers demonstrate the accretionary nature of rock varnish. This sample also shows truncation of the varnish due to erosion or abrasion. Photograph courtesy of Ron Dorn.

gradually returning to those of the surrounding rock. Although researchers have generally assumed that the gradual color change is due to weathering, the patina, or more properly, rock varnish, is actually an accretionary coating of clay minerals cemented to the underlying rock by oxides of manganese or iron and is chemically and morphologically distinct from the underlying substrate (Dorn and Oberlander 1982; Perry and Adams 1978; Potter and Rossman 1977) (Figure 5.1). It has usually been assumed that heavily varnished figures are older than ones that appear fresh, and it has long been hoped that a dating method would be developed for the varnish (Basedow 1914; Heizer and Baumhoff 1962), as dating the onset of rock varnish formation would provide a minimum limiting age for the petroglyph.

AMS DATING   Geographers and geomorphologists have used a variety of techniques to obtain numerical age estimates for Pleistocene and Holocene landforms. These techniques include uranium-series measurements; cosmogenic helium (^{3}He), chlorine (^{36}Cl), and aluminum (^{26}Al); and AMS radiocarbon dating of organic matter entombed in rock varnish. Ronald Dorn, of Arizona State University, has been one of the pioneers in the application of AMS dating to petroglyphs.

The manufacture of a petroglyph, assuming that the engraving completely truncates the rock coatings on the older surface, exposes fresh rock to the elements. This is an open system with respect to the accumulation of organic carbon (Dorn 1994). New carbon is continually being added through the growth of organisms such as lichens, fungi, bacteria, mosses, cyanobacteria, and algae (Danin 1983; Jones and Goodbody 1982), and as organisms die, some material remains in pockets and fractures. The net effect is an organic accumulation that is a mixture of old and new carbon and that should postdate the exposure of the rock surface in the petroglyph. As long as this weathering rind remains exposed, the system is open to the accumulation of new carbon. When the weathering rind is sealed by the formation of rock varnish, the system has been assumed to be closed to the introduction of new carbon (see Dorn 1994:22–23). Once the weathering rind organics (WROS) are encapsulated by accreting rock varnish, AMS dating of the WROS should provide a minimum limiting age for the manufacture of the petroglyph. It has also been assumed that the system is closed to the introduction of older organics from the host rock. Recent research by Dorn, however, discussed in detail later, questions these assumptions.

Not all petroglyphs are suitable for dating by AMS, and there are uncertainties associated with the technique. First, there may not be enough organic matter in some WROS, even for AMS. Second, petroglyph manufacture must have completely removed any older varnish and the previous weathering rind; otherwise, AMS dates of WROS would include much older carbon and yield an unreliable age estimate. Whether the older weathering rind was completely removed can be determined through depth profiles of organic matter in panel material and careful analysis of sample thin-sections before any chemical processing.

One must also evaluate the preservation and condition of the overlying rock coating. Younger organic material from organisms growing on the varnished surface can truncate the varnish and become incorporated into the weathering rind. It is important to sample weathering rinds that are overlain by stratified layers of varnish. Just as in an archaeological site, distinctly stratified layers imply comparatively little disturbance. The degree of disturbance and potential for introduction of younger organics can be evaluated through analysis of sample thin-sections. Samples that do not exhibit the proper stratification of varnish are not deemed suitable for dating.

In addition, there is evidence that water continues to move through the overlying varnish and weathering rind (Dorn and Krinsley 1991; Krinsley et al. 1990; O'Hara et al. 1989, 1990), thus introducing younger organic material. This issue can be resolved by appropriate pretreatment with hydrofluoric, sodium hydroxide, and hydrochloric acids to remove invading younger organics (Dorn et al. 1989), in the same fashion as these acids are used to remove rootlets and humic material from conventional charcoal samples (Gillespie 1991).

Recent research by Dorn has called into question some of the assumptions on which the accuracy of AMS dates of WROS are based. At Côa,

Portugal, Dorn (1997) has shown that rock coatings may not always act as a good seal to prohibit the introduction of younger organics into the weathering rind. Briefly, Dorn (1997) noted major differences between ^{36}Cl ages on panel surfaces and ^{14}C ages on engravings on these same surfaces. The ^{36}Cl ages, which date the exposure of the surface, ranged from 16,000 to 136,000 years B.P. whereas ages based on ^{14}C measurements of WROS were thousands of years younger.

In order to test the assumption that no younger organics had been introduced into the weathering rinds, Welsh and Dorn (1997) used ^{14}C to date organics in the weathering rinds of unengraved control samples adjacent to the petroglyphs. These ages should have been directly comparable to the ^{36}Cl ages, but they ranged from 11,000 to 9,000 B.P. In this case, younger organic materials have been continually introduced into the weathering rinds, despite their appearance under electron microscopy of being well stratified and sealed. Dorn has concluded that the Côa petroglyphs are undatable by AMS techniques.

The possibility of contamination from older carbon has also been examined. Dorn et al. (1989) and Reneau et al. (1991) have both suggested that it is theoretically possible for older material to become incorporated into the sample. In Portugal, Watchman (1995) argues that older detrital carbon has contaminated samples on petroglyph faces. To test for contamination from older carbon in the host rock, Welsh and Dorn (1997) analyzed organic materials collected from control samples adjacent to engravings at the Hedgepeth Hills site in Deer Valley, Arizona. Two types of organic materials (dense particles and granular particles), with a combined ^{14}C age of 20,450 B.P., were found in the control sample. Minute quantities of these same organic materials were found in the petroglyph samples, indicating contamination from older carbon. The amount of contamination appears to be directly related to the age of the petroglyphs: the older the petroglyph, the greater the contamination.

Welsh and Dorn (1997) present mathematical procedures to correct for potential contamination from the host rock, but they note that the correction procedure would be valid only if the abundance and age of organics in the samples from the host panel are representative of the amount of contamination in the petroglyph samples. They also note that host rock samples appear to be heterogeneous.

Of critical importance is that different types of organic materials were observed in the samples from Hedgepeth Hills as well as from Côa (Welsh and Dorn 1997). When "bulk" samples from Côa were split into denser and fibrous particles, the denser particles yielded an age of nearly 30,000 B.P. and the fibrous material yielded an age of 17,500 B.P. Dragovich

(2000) has also found that different types of entombed organic materials yield different ages.

Clearly, different types of organic remains can yield different ^{14}C ages, and weathering rinds and rock varnish do not always prevent contamination from both younger and older sources. As a result, Dorn (1998a) offers strong cautionary notes concerning previous AMS ages on WROS (see also Dragovich 2000). Because "bulk" samples were used, the AMS ages may yield ambiguous results due to a mixture of older and younger organics. Independent data must be used to evaluate the accuracy of such dates. Eleven petroglyphs from the Bighorn and Wind River Basins have AMS ages from WROS. All but one have been based on "bulk" samples, and we evaluate the implications of Dorn's recent findings for the area's chronology later in this chapter.

Recently, AMS dating of WROS has become even more controversial. Beck et al. (1998) note that samples collected by Dorn from petroglyphs in northern Arizona contained two types of organic materials (vitrinite and carbonized woody tissue) that yielded different radiocarbon dates, and they assert that these two materials should not co-occur naturally. Beck et al. (1998) were also unable to isolate organic materials in samples collected by coauthors Malotki (a linguist at Northern Arizona University) and Beck (from the University of Arizona AMS Facility).

Dorn (1998b) responded to these charges by noting that coal-like particles were identified in rock varnish more than three decades ago and that he and other researchers have recognized carbonized woody tissue. Dorn published photographs of carbonized woody tissue entombed in varnish in 1993 (Francis et al. 1993:722). The occurrence of different types of organic material in rock coatings has been well established, and the contemporaneity of such materials has been discussed for more than a decade (Dorn 1994; Dorn et al. 1989, 1992; Nobbs and Dorn 1993). More than 10 years ago D. Tanner independently processed "split samples" and obtained results similar to Dorn's (Dorn et al. 1989). Some of the same samples discussed by Beck et al. (1998) were examined by Dorn and coauthors in Beck et al. (1998) in the 1980s, with different-appearing organic materials interpreted to be the result of reworking of the same material by varnish-forming microorganisms (Dorn et al. 1989), not different types of organics (Dorn 1998b). Dorn has trained other researchers and students in sample collection and preparation techniques. In a yet-to-be-published study these independent researchers at Arizona State University (Arrowsmith et al. 1998) identified vitrinite, fusinite, and carbonized woody tissue in varnish samples from the White Tank Mountains in Arizona.

Dorn has always emphasized the importance of selecting locations on boulders and rock surfaces that preserve layered varnish (see also Liu and Broecker 2000), and he has perfected physical extraction techniques that preserve the varnish, entombed organics, and underlying rock. One of his students, Liu (1994), has developed methods for preparing ultrathin cross sections so that varnish samples can be readily examined.

We believe this controversy over AMS ages is at least partially the result of a fundamental misunderstanding about the nature of rock varnish formation; the use of improper field techniques may also be involved. Questions will be resolved and dating techniques refined only by further research, and we hope Dorn and others will continue to push forward with work on the nature of subvarnish organics and dating techniques.

CATION-RATIO DATING Relative minimum limiting ages for petroglyphs can be obtained through cation-ratio (CR) dating of the overlying rock varnish. Cation ratios have been used in conjunction with numerical dating techniques to derive calibrated minimum limited ages for petroglyph manufacture. CR dating is based on the premise that the ratio of cations (positive ions) of potassium + calcium/titanium ($[K + Ca]/Ti$) in the varnish changes with time. If this ratio is measured for petroglyphs with known exposure ages, generally determined by AMS ages, a calibration, called a cation-leaching curve (CLC), can be constructed. This is a semilog least squares regression of the mean CRs and the mean numerical ages (Figure 5.2). The CRs of samples of unknown age are then compared with the curve, and a CR age is assigned. Because of spatial variation in the chemistry of varnish, airborne fallout, and other environmental factors, CLCs must be constructed for a given geographic region. Since AMS ages from the Bighorn and Wind River Basins have been derived from bulk samples of WROs, the calibrated ages based on the Bighorn/Wind River CLC may have a greater error factor than previously believed. This possibility does not change the relative ordering based on cation ratios, however (see Welsh and Dorn 1997).

The efficacy of cation-ratio dating has been debated (see Dorn 1994 and Francis et al. 1993 for a summary). We have used CR dating to obtain calibrated ages for more than 30 petroglyphs in the Bighorn and Wind River Basins. Although we have found that the CR dating technique has clear limitations and cannot be used to date all petroglyphs, under certain conditions—careful field sampling, the evaluation of sample thin-sections, and integration with independent chronological data—CR dating is useful and accurate.

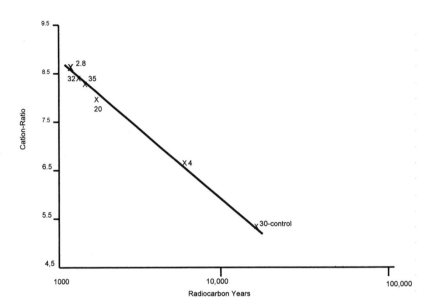

5.2. Preliminary cation-leaching curve for the Bighorn area, Wyoming and Montana, based on 1990 data. Numbers marking points on the curve are sample numbers from Francis et al. (1993) and denote AMS-dated calibration points used to generate the curve.

The first controversy involves the cause of the empirically observed decrease in the ratio of (K + Ca)/Ti over time. The trend of decreasing CRs with time has been duplicated by different groups around the world (Bull 1991; Glazovskiy 1985; Pineda et al. 1988, 1990; Whitley and Annegarn 1994; Whitney and Harrington 1993; Zhang et al. 1990). The question is not whether CRs decrease with time but why. Reneau and Raymond (1991) found no evidence for leaching in the "darkest, best developed" varnishes and have argued that the decline in CRs over time is due to contamination from the rock underlying the varnish rather than greater leaching of mobile cations (K and Ca) as compared with immobile cations (Ti). Nevertheless, clear evidence of leaching has been found by numerous researchers (Dorn and Krinsley 1991; Krinsley and Dorn 1991; Krinsley et al. 1990; O'Hara et al. 1990), and leaching sites or zones can be detected by backscatter electron microscopy (Krinsley and Manley 1989). As discussed by Dorn (1994:26), differences in results of these studies can be explained by the different types of varnishes analyzed (crack and ground-line band varnish versus subaerial varnish continuously exposed to the acidity of rainfall and rock-surface organisms).

The second debate involves the accuracy of techniques used to measure CRs. Three techniques have generally been used to measure the chemical composition of rock varnishes: particle-induced X-ray emission (PIXE), the wavelength dispersive electron microprobe, and inductively coupled plasma (ICP) (see Dorn et al. 1990). Dorn (1994) used PIXE extensively for many CR studies but has used the electron microprobe at Arizona State University since 1989 because of lower costs and the ease of using a local facility.

Bierman and Gillespie (1991) have claimed that PIXE analyses conducted at the Crocker Nuclear Laboratory at the University of California at Davis (UCD), where many of the early CR analyses were carried out, are not accurate because the PIXE misanalyzes titanium by inadvertently adding barium to it. This claim implies that CR age estimates based on UCD PIXE analyses are inaccurate. As outlined by Dorn (1994:26–27), Bierman and Gillespie sent nine samples of "artificial varnish" of known composition to the Crocker Nuclear Laboratory (CNL) for analysis. According to Cahill (1992), Bierman and Gillespie were informed that because of the lack of particle size data and proper standards, the analyses would be qualitative only. Bierman and Gillespie (1991) then published absolute values of the elemental composition of these samples. Cahill (1992) states that Bierman and Gillespie apparently prepared these data from "reduced" and "raw X-ray spectra" provided by CNL, which were labeled incorrect because barium had not been included, and that these data were provided to Bierman and Gillespie for evaluative purposes only and with an explicit prohibition against their publication. Bierman and Gillespie (1992a) dispute these claims.

The relevance of this discussion concerns only the accuracy of CR age estimates of petroglyphs based on PIXE analyses from UCD (Dorn 1989, 1992). First, it is clear that the UCD PIXE does measure barium, as is evident from data cited by Bierman and Gillespie (1992b). Second, the same samples from the Coso Range analyzed by the UCD PIXE were independently analyzed with an electron microprobe and inductively coupled plasma, replicating the results of the UCD PIXE (Dorn 1989; Dorn et al. 1990). Thus, there is little reason to doubt the accuracy of the early chemical analyses of these rock varnishes. We also note that all the CRs from the Bighorn and Wind River Basins are derived from electron microprobe analyses conducted at Arizona State University.

The third debate involving CR dating concerns the methods used to calculate CR ages. Some investigators have used averages and standard deviations of several combined CRs to derive an age estimate (Bierman et al. 1991; Lanteigne 1991). This procedure assumes that all samples from the same surface or petroglyph have the same exposure history. Dorn's (1994) approach, used to obtain CR age estimates in the Bighorn and Wind River Basins (Francis et al. 1993), treats each separate CR from one petroglyph as an independent indicator of age (a minimum of five samples are generally taken from one petroglyph). Each CR is assigned a separate calibrated age based on the cation-leaching curve. These ages are then averaged to assign a mean age for the surface. This procedure assumes only that the calibration curve is the best estimate of CR age and that the CRs are normally distributed. In essence, it keeps the assignment of calibrated ages as close to the raw data as possible, and intersample variability reflects the time-transgressive nature of the growth of rock varnish.

The primary key to the successful application of CR dating is to control factors other than time which influence the development and chemistry of the varnish. As discussed in detail by Dorn (1994:13–15), varnishes differ greatly in structure and chemistry at all scales from microns to kilometers. Varnishes of different colors, of similar colors in subaerial and non-subaerial environments, and in different types of subaerial environments exhibit different characteristics, including stable isotope composition (Dorn and DeNiro 1985), manganese concentrations (Dorn 1990; Jones 1991), micromorphologies (Dorn 1986), degrees of interdigitation with silica skins (Dorn et al. 1992), backscatter textures (Krinsley et al. 1990), and trace element concentrations. Visual characteristics and varnish thickness alone cannot be used as an indicator of relative age (Liu and Broecker 2000; Liu and Dorn 1996).

Additional factors that can influence the CRs obtained from rock varnish include the presence of lichens, fungi, and other organic matter; increased exposure to water from runoff or basin collection; high or low pH values as compared with neutral varnishes; location of the sample site in relation to the soil surface; aspect of the rock surface (northeast-facing surfaces tend to exhibit higher CRs than southwest aspects); locations in rock overhangs and cracks; recent weathering or spalling that exposes a new surface; interdigitation with amorphous silica or oxalates; local anomalies in the amounts of titanium, calcium, and potassium present; and the microtopography of the rock surface (Dorn 1994:27). Rock varnish does not begin to accrete on all parts of a rock surface at the same time. It grows initially in small depressions and microfractures, and sampling the area that was first colonized by rock varnish is critical for obtaining a reasonably accurate minimum limiting age for exposure of that surface (Dorn 1989; Dorn et al. 1992). Erosion of the rock varnish, by either biochemical (e.g., lichens) or mechanical (e.g., wind abrasion) means, can also influence CRs (Dorn 1989; Dorn et al. 1989).

In short, careful determination of the manner and environment in which the varnish originally formed and the factors that affected the varnish after its formation are key elements to the successful application of CR dating. This is entirely analogous to the study of site formation processes and evaluation of the integrity of cultural deposits in archaeological sites. Most of

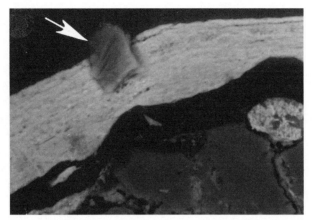

5.3. A fragment of chalk forced evenly into layered varnish from sample WP-90-13, collected from the Legend Rock site. The fragment is almost entirely composed of calcium, reflecting the chalk's calcium carbonate composition. This figure was chalked during the 1950s for photographic enhancement. Photograph courtesy of Ron Dorn.

the sources of variation in CRs can be controlled by careful field sampling and by evaluation of cross sections of the samples in the laboratory. Even when initial field evaluation suggests that a site or the figures within a site are good candidates for dating by CR methods, laboratory evaluation of the cross sections may demonstrate other factors that render them undatable. For example, many of the petroglyphs in the Bighorn and Wind River Basins have been chalked to enhance photography. In some cases, chalk (resulting in the introduction of extraordinarily high amounts of calcium) is still apparent in peck marks when sample cross sections are viewed under a scanning electron microscope (Figure 5.3). Several figures in the initial dating study yielded such high CRs due to the addition of calcium that they were completely undatable by CR methods (Francis et al. 1993:723).

Finally, the use of blind tests and the integration of CR data with other information used to infer age are critical for evaluating the accuracy of CRs and calibrated ages from a given site or region. This is the approach taken by Loendorf (1991b) in the evaluation of CR dates from the Pinon Canyon Maneuver Site in southeastern Colorado, and the one we have taken in the application of CR age estimates to petroglyphs in the Bighorn and Wind River Basins. CR ages from superimposed figures should be consistent with the relative ages of those figures, or CR ages from figures containing horses or other datable items should be consistent with the known ages of those items. In the Bighorn and Wind River Basins we have used CR age estimates from different areas of the same figure to check for internal consistency and overlap of the CRs; we have sampled superimposed figures at several different sites (see Francis et al. 1993:730–731); and we have sampled figures for which we could establish an age based on other criteria. In all cases, the CR age estimates have been consistent within

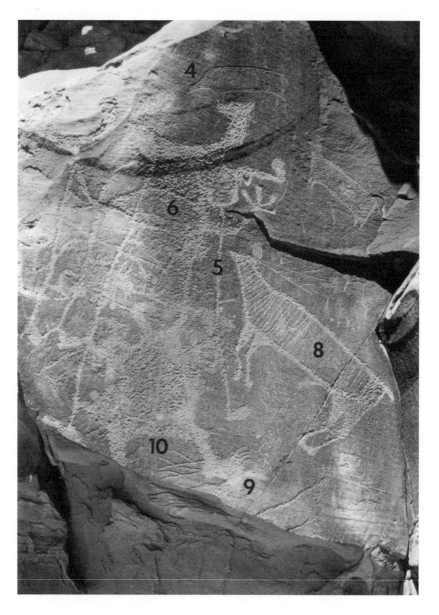

5.4. Panel 48 at the Legend Rock site. The numbers indicate the locations of varnish samples collected from the various figures.

figures, with relative ages based on superimpositions, and with the inferred age of the figure.

For example, at the Legend Rock site, six different samples were taken from different figures on the same panel (Figure 5.4). Samples 90-4a, b are from an outline-pecked bison that appeared to exhibit the greatest degree of varnish development. AMS ages from this figure averaged around 6,000 to 5,700 years B.P. The organic matter in this sample was identified as carbonized woody tissue or charcoal (Francis et al. 1993:722). It is clearly not a mixture of older and younger organic materials and was used as a calibration point for the CLC. This figure yielded the lowest, and therefore oldest, CRs of any figure on this panel. Sample 90-6 was taken from the upper torso of a large Dinwoody composite anthropomorphic figure; sample 90-9 was taken from the right foot of the same figure. This figure exhibits much less varnish development and intuitively should be younger than the bison. This is indeed reflected by the CR age estimates. When the standard deviation of the CR estimates is taken into account, the ages of these samples range from 3,000 to 2,300 years B.P. and 3,000 to 2,600 years B.P., respectively, and exhibit almost complete overlap, as should occur with two ages from the same figure. CR ages from the elk (sample 90-8) to the right of the anthropomorphic figure range from 2,900 to 2,000 years, suggesting direct association with the anthropomorph. Sample 90-5 from the attenuated figure superimposed on the right foot of the anthropomorph averages around 2,200 years B.P., slightly younger than the anthropomorph and consistent with the superimposition. Finally, sample 90-10 was taken from a set of antlers superimposed by the anthropomorph. The CR age estimate for the antlers is approximately 6,200 years, again consistent with the superimposition.

Three other similar tests were incorporated into the initial dating study in the Bighorn and Wind River Basins (Francis et al. 1993). All yielded similar results, with calibrated CR ages consistent with superimpositions and internal consistency within the same figure. Multiple sampling and CR age estimates from several other figures that had clearly showed several episodes of manufacture also yielded internally consistent results (Francis 1994).

CORRELATIVE METHODS   A third approach that can be used to infer ages of petroglyphs is correlative, that is, it uses events to make statements of equivalency in age (Dorn 1998a). Conceptually, this approach is identical to stratigraphic correlation, used by geologists to date sedimentary deposits across large areas or by archaeologists to date strata between sites. A detailed analysis of the stratigraphy of the rock varnish is necessary for this approach, and as is the case with both AMS and CR dating techniques, only layered varnish that shows no evidence of disturbance can be used (see Dorn 1998a).

More detailed discussions of this approach can be found in Dorn 1998a and Liu and Dorn 1996. It is summarized here as it relates to some of the early AMS ages from petroglyphs in the Bighorn Basin and in the Green

River Basin of southwestern Wyoming. Briefly, in an analysis of subaerial varnish from some 2,900 microbasins on rocks from late Pleistocene and Holocene surfaces in Death Valley, California, Liu (1994; Liu and Dorn 1996) found consistent patterning in the micromorphology and micro-chemical composition of varnish layers across the Great Basin and into Wyoming. When viewed in ultra-thin section (which permits the prepara-tion of normally opaque material into sections thin enough to transmit light, allowing more detailed microscopic analysis [Liu 1994]), the varnish lamellae consistently exhibit orange-yellow layers (manganese-poor lamel-late varnishes) overlying black layers (manganese-rich botryoidal varnishes).

Several models have been developed to explain manganese enhancement in rock varnish (Cremaschi 1996; Dorn and Oberlander 1981; Drake et al. 1993; Hooke et al. 1969; Jones 1991; Krumbein and Jens 1981; Moore and Elvidge 1982; Nagy et al. 1991; Palmer et al. 1985; Whalley 1983). All these models suggest that various biotic or abiotic factors contribute to the formation of manganese-rich varnishes. But regardless of the model, black subaerial varnishes form in relatively wet environments and man-ganese-poor, orange-yellow subaerial varnishes grow in desert settings (Dorn 1986, 1990; Fleisher et al. 1999; Liu and Broecker 2000). Thus, the alternating layers of black and orange-yellow subaerial varnish record fluctuations in climatic conditions.

Twenty-six independent age controls for the different surfaces were established using a variety of techniques: conventional ^{14}C; uranium-series measurements of tufa on shorelines of paleolakes; cosmogenic ^{3}He (helium), ^{10}Be (beryllium), and ^{26}Al (aluminum) ages; and ^{14}C ages on WROS. It should be noted that the ^{14}C ages of WROS are from varnishes overlying volcanic rocks, which do not contain organic carbon and are therefore not subject to potential contamination from older organic carbon in the host rock (Welsh and Dorn 1997).

These data allowed Liu and Dorn (1996:193) to build a preliminary stratigraphic sequence of varnish layering units dating back to the Pleistocene (Figure 5.5). Furthermore, the timing of these relatively wet and dry episodes appears to correlate well with what is known about the timing of climatic changes in the western United States over the last 24,000 years (Liu and Dorn 1996:193). The uppermost orange-yellow layer (unit 1) formed during the last 10,000 years when the climate is known to have been quite arid (COHMAP 1988). The two black layers in unit 2 correlate with wet episodes between 10,000 and 11,000 years ago (the Younger-Dryas interval) (Benson et al. 1992; Elliott-Fisk 1987; Gosse, Evenson et al. 1995) and another wet pulse about 14,000 years ago (Benson et al. 1992). Unit 3 likely correlates with the glacial retreat and warming at the

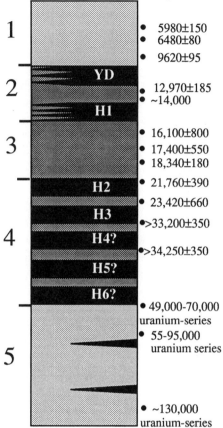

Unit   Laminae   Age Control

1 — 5980±150
— 6480±80
— 9620±95

2 — YD
— 12,970±185
— ~14,000
— H1

3 — 16,100±800
— 17,400±550
— 18,340±180

— H2 — 21,760±390
— 23,420±660
H3
4 — H4? — >33,200±350
— H5? — >34,250±350
— H6?

— 49,000-70,000
uranium-series
5 — 55-95,000
uranium series

— ~130,000
uranium-series

5.5. Stratigraphic correlation of rock varnish microlaminations for the Pleistocene (Liu and Dorn 1996). The gray shading represents orange-colored, manganese-poor varnishes formed under dry conditions. The black bands represent black, manganese-rich varnishes formed under wetter conditions. YD = Younger Dryas; H1–6 = Heinrich events.

end of the Pleistocene (Cerling et al. 1994), and the uppermost black layer in unit 4 most likely reflects the last glacial maxima between 20,000 and 21,000 years ago (Gosse, Klein et al. 1995; Phillips et al. 1990).

The stratigraphic sequence observed in rock varnish in Death Valley and the Great Basin appears to be replicated by varnish sequences overlying petroglyphs in at least two sites in western Wyoming (Liu and Dorn 1996:205). Both Wyoming samples exhibited a thin layer of black varnish overlain by a thick unit of orange varnish. AMS ages of subvarnish organic matter from these petroglyphs suggest that the black layer may correlate with the Younger-Dryas interval and that the thicker orange unit corresponds to the Holocene. With only two samples analyzed in this manner, additional examination of the stratigraphy of varnish microlaminations in Wyoming is clearly needed. Varnish microlaminations offer great potential as a climatic recorder in arid regions (Liu and Broecker 2000) and have direct application to the dating of petroglyphs.

Dating the Prehistoric Imagery of the Bighorn and Wind River Basins

In 1990, working primarily with the Wyoming Bureau of Land Management, we began a cooperative, interdisciplinary research program to obtain numerical age estimates from a variety of petroglyph and pictograph sites across the Bighorn and Wind River Basins. We were able to bring pioneering experts on dating techniques, including Ronald Dorn and Marvin Rowe, to Wyoming and Montana on several occasions to collect samples.

This research has served many different purposes. Building on our previous archaeological excavations and traditional dating, the program has provided the baseline data to develop a chronology and refine classification schemes for the wide variety of petroglyphs and pictographs found in the study area. It has helped our colleagues in other disciplines refine and improve sample collection and dating techniques. And it has provided valuable information to the land-managing agencies for the evaluation and protection of a class of little-understood cultural resources. The program has evolved to include not just dating but also detailed recording, data collection, and analysis of sites throughout the study area.

As a result of these efforts, petroglyphs and pictographs in the Bighorn and Wind River Basins must be considered among the most well dated in the world. As of 2001, we have 14 AMS ages on WROS, 49 CR ages from petroglyphs, and 3 AMS ages from pictographs. Of these, 2 AMS ages and 7 CR age estimates from petroglyphs are considered unreliable because of contamination by chalk and other modern recording techniques (Francis et al. 1993). If multiple sampling from the same figure is taken into account, the total comes to 11 AMS and 37 CR dated petroglyphs and 3 AMS dated pictographs from 14 different sites in the Bighorn and Wind River regions, with all but the most recent age estimates published in Francis et al. 1993, Francis 1994, and Liu and Dorn 1996. The ages range from Paleoindian to the Protohistoric and Historic periods (see Chapter 6).

As discussed earlier in this chapter, both AMS and CR age estimates are controversial. The AMS ages we have thus far obtained are based on bulk sampling of WROS and could include different types of carbon. In some cases, however, we have been able to identify the specific type of organic material being dated: charcoal applied to the petroglyph after its manufacture (Francis et al. 1993:722). AMS ages from this type of material are not subject to the same types of uncertainties as ages from "bulk" samples of unknown material. The AMS ages are also consistent with analyses of varnish microstratigraphy developed with independent age controls. Since the inheritance of older carbon is time-transgressive and increases with age, and the vast majority of petroglyphs in the Bighorn and Wind River Basins are relatively young (mid to late Holocene), the effects of older carbon in "bulk" samples may be fairly small for our study area. We believe the currently available AMS ages from petroglyphs in the Wind River and Bighorn Basins are reasonably accurate age estimates.

With regard to the CR ages, no one has disputed that CRs decrease over time. Because of the ability to identify specific factors that yield unreliable CR age estimates, the tests built into the dating program, and the internal consistency of the CR sequence, the CR age estimates from the Bighorn and Wind River Basins most certainly constitute an accurate relative sequence. More important, however, is the fact that calibrated CR estimates are consistent with independent age controls provided by traditional archaeological techniques. Thus, the relative sequence can be anchored to independently derived ages. CR age estimates have a greater degree of uncertainty than other dating techniques, but since as prehistorians we deal with variation on the scale of thousands of years, the CR age estimates provide valuable chronological data.

Our results have yielded a far more complicated picture of prehistory in the Bighorn and Wind River Basins than previously imagined. Rather than a simple series of ages indicating that one type of figure was sequentially replaced by another type throughout the study area (as is often the case with other classes of archaeological remains such as projectile points or architectural features), a complex pattern of concurrent traditions in different portions of the Wind River and Bighorn Basins has emerged (Francis et al. 1993). When coupled with ethnographic data, our findings highlight the role of this area as a boundary between aboriginal groups of the Great Plains and Great Basin. These results also provide new insights into the function and use of the imagery and the spiritual and ceremonial aspects of different cultural systems throughout prehistory.

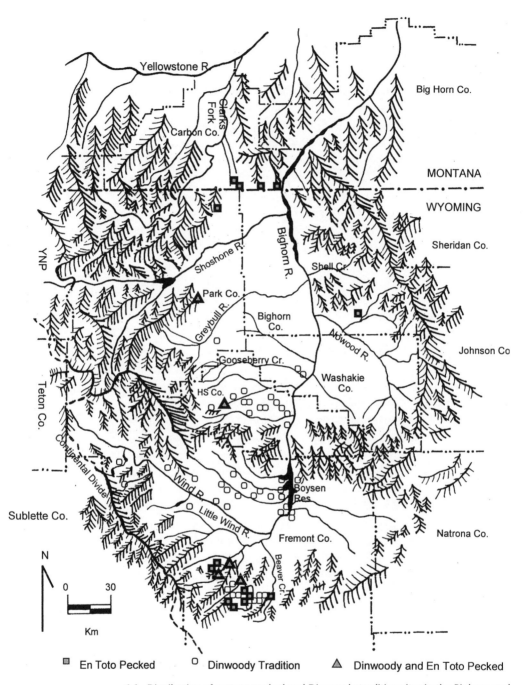

6.1. Distribution of en toto pecked and Dinwoody tradition sites in the Bighorn and Wind River Basins.

SIX

On the Western Front

The Dinwoody Tradition

NAMED FOR THE WELL-KNOWN TYPE SITE ADJACENT TO
Dinwoody Lake on the Wind River Indian Reservation, the highly
distinctive and widely recognized Dinwoody tradition dominates the western side of the Bighorn and Wind River Basins (Figure 6.1). Photographs
of the Dinwoody type site have been widely published both in scholarly
works (Hultkrantz 1987:50; Wellmann 1979:Color Plate 30; Vander
1997:Plate 14) and in commercial calendars and coffee-table books. The
Dinwoody locale is among the most sacred of places for the Wind River
Shoshone people, and because it was becoming widely known and vulner-
able to increased vandalism, the tribal government closed the site to
nontribal members. Out of respect for the the Shoshone people, who do
not wish the site to be further publicized, we have chosen not to include
photographs of the Dinwoody type site in this book. Because it has been
used in many previous publications, however, we retain the term
Dinwoody for this highly distinctive tradition of rock imagery.

As we define the Dinwoody tradition, it encompasses an entire complex
of pecked anthropomorphic, zoomorphic, and abstract descriptive figure
types, including the large, elaborate, and sometimes frightening anthropomorphic or therianthropic images termed the Interior Line style by
Gebhard (1969). Also found throughout the western side of the Bighorn
and Wind River Basins from the southern front of the Pryor Mountains to
the southern tributaries of the Wind River are much simpler, solidly
pecked, and easily recognizable human figures. These occur with solidly
pecked animal forms and occasional abstract figures and were called en
toto pecked by Loendorf and Porsche (1985).

Settings

Sites containing Dinwoody and/or en toto pecked imagery occur
along the Wind and Bighorn Rivers and their western-flowing tributaries,
from the upper reaches of these drainages near the peaks of the Wind
River Range to the arid interior Bighorn Basin. Key Dinwoody tradition
sites in the upper Wind River valley include major complexes adjacent to
Ring and Trail Lakes along Torrey Creek and adjacent to Upper Dinwoody Lake on Dinwoody Creek, some of the most breathtaking settings
in the region. At elevations above 2,200 m, elaborate Dinwoody tradition
anthropomorphic figures occur on outcrops of Tensleep sandstone or
large sandstone talus boulders that face glacial lakes formed when
moraines dammed the creek valleys. Views upvalley from these sites
look directly on mountain slopes now used as critical winter range for
bighorn sheep or onto the glaciated peaks of the Wind Rivers. Views
downvalley open across the Wind River to the peaks of the Absaroka
Range (Figure 6.2).

Downstream from the mouth of Torrey and Dinwoody Creeks, the
Wind River and its tributaries drain the central portion of the present-day
Wind River Indian Reservation. With the exception of the Dinwoody type
site and several other localities recorded by Sowers (1939, 1940, 1941b),
relatively little documentation has occurred on the reservation. Most
research has been conducted on lands adjoining the reservation or those
withdrawn from it for agricultural development and reclamation in the
early twentieth century. As a result, the apparent "concentrations" of sites
around the reservation near Boysen Reservoir in the central Wind River
Basin (see Figure 6.1) reflect the intensity of fieldwork rather than true site
distributions.

Site settings in this area provide a startling contrast to those in the
upper Wind River valley. Except for irrigation agriculture, the central
Wind River Basin is nearly barren of vegetation. Downcutting by the Wind
River and its tributaries through Tertiary deposits has exposed faces of soft
Eocene sandstones along the margins of valleys. Many of these faces were
used to render nearly life-sized Dinwoody tradition anthropomorphic
figures. Panels often directly face the adjacent valley and are sometimes
located on highly unusual outcrops or isolated monoliths visible for kilometers in nearly all directions (Figure 6.3).

The Bighorn Basin presents still another site setting for Dinwoody
imagery. Images occur on Late Cretaceous sandstone surfaces exposed by
downcutting of western-flowing tributaries of the Bighorn River through

6.2. The Absaroka Range viewed from the upper Wind River area. Petroglyphs occur on boulders and ridges overlooking the glacial lakes.

6.3. Looking northwest toward the Owl Creek Mountains. Panels of Dinwoody petroglyphs occur on all sides of the monolith.

6.4. Looking west up the Cottonwood Creek valley toward the Legend Rock site. Dinwoody trad6ition panels occur for nearly 800 m along the Frontier sandstone cliff on the right side of the photograph.

the hogbacks and minor uplifts at the foot of the Absaroka Range. The rocky sandstone outcrops of the hogbacks often support stands of juniper and other foothill vegetation, in contrast to the sparse desert scrub of the interior basin. Some sites, such as Legend Rock along Cottonwood Creek, one of the major Dinwoody complexes of the Bighorn Basin, occur in extremely open settings (Figure 6.4). Many smaller sites occur in more sheltered and secluded areas in the broken topography of the hogbacks, often on heavily varnished surfaces. Both cliff faces and talus boulders strewn along the slopes of sandstone outcrops form the backdrop for representations, and in many cases figures have been pecked on multiple faces of the same boulder or wind around curves of a vertical face, creating striking three-dimensional qualities.

Petroglyph Canyon, in extreme southern Montana in one of the most arid and harsh parts of the Bighorn Basin, is one of the key en toto pecked sites in the region. A concentration of small, fully pecked anthropomorphic and zoomorphic figures occurs along a portion of a now-dry wash flowing southeasterly into the Bighorn River off the south slope of Big Pryor Mountain. Heavily varnished sandstone surfaces were chosen for these representations. Considerable occupational debris and archaeological deposits occur in the canyon and may be associated with the manufacture and use of the imagery.

Manufacturing Techniques

Pecking removes the upper layers of varnish and rock, exposing the nearly white, underlying stone and often creating highly visible and sometimes startling images. Experiments in the manufacture of pecked figures suggest they were made more easily than one might predict (Bard and Busby 1974). In some cases, the artist scratched or incised a groove to form the outline of the body, which was subsequently filled in by pecking. Many other images were executed by simply pecking out a form, as either an outline or the entire body, without using an underlying pattern. Bodies or torsos were filled with widely spaced peck marks, creating a stippling effect, or were entirely pecked away.

Many figures throughout the Bighorn and Wind River Basins exhibit several different types of pecking with variation in the size and depth of peck marks. Large dint marks suggest freehand percussion whereas more refined pecked areas may have been made by using indirect percussion (Loendorf 1984). Excavations at the Legend Rock site have provided the only evidence to date for the types of tools used to make these pecked images. Waterworn pebbles found at the base of one panel at this site may have been used in the manufacture of Dinwoody tradition figures (Walker and Francis 1989).

Future excavations are likely to recover additional evidence of tool kits, and most likely a variety of tools were used. Evidence from southeastern Colorado (Loendorf et al. 1988) suggests that rough pecking could have been accomplished by a fist-sized pointed chopping tool and that smaller flakes or spalls resembling a pick could have been used for finer work.

A stone tool assemblage recovered from a site in northern New Mexico provides an excellent example of a tool kit for the manufacture of pecked figures. Moore (1994:168) recovered 83 lithic artifacts from the base of a panel of pecked petroglyphs. Twenty-four were tools, and the remainder represented debitage or waste from the manufacture and the resharpening or reshaping of the tools. One tool was a corner-notched projectile point much older than the estimated age of the petroglyphs in the panel. It was interpreted as an heirloom or offering that was either in the possession of the makers of the petroglyphs or brought to the site at a later date. Other tools were an array of cobble choppers and abraders, flake choppers, flake abraders and pounders, and hammerstones, with considerable variation in size. Made from siltstone, basalt, and fine-grained quartzite, the choppers had an average length of 76.9 mm, an average width of 68.9 mm, and an average weight of 272.4 g; the flake abraders and pounders had an average length of 43.7 mm, an average width of 36.3 mm, and an average weight of 41.7 g. The tools displayed relatively smooth edges "with microscopic short linear striations parallel to the edges and microscopic pitting of the rounded edges" (Moore 1994:172). These use-wear patterns have been replicated by experimental studies in the manufacture of pecked images (Moore 1994:177) and sandstone manos and metates (Dodd 1979).

En Toto Pecked Figure Types

Loendorf (1984) first recognized the unusual nature of small, solidly pecked human and animal figures at the Petroglyph Canyon site in the Pryor Mountains of extreme southern Montana. Loendorf and Porsche (1985:69–70) later designated these figure types as the en toto pecked style, based on their limited spatial distribution in Montana and what was presumed to be a fairly restricted temporal duration. Subsequent studies have revealed a much wider spatial distribution throughout the Bighorn and Wind River Basins of Wyoming, however, and indicate a much longer temporal range for these figures as well (Francis et al. 1993). En toto pecked figures co-occur with Dinwoody images at many sites throughout the region, suggesting a very close relationship. Thus, we have dropped the term *style* from the designation and consider these to be descriptive figure types.

Small human forms are the most common en toto pecked figure type. Because of the relatively small sample of en toto pecked sites that have been intensively investigated, we consider human images one general descriptive figure type, with a fairly wide range of variation. With further documentation and additional chronological studies, it may be possible to designate more carefully defined figure types within the general anthropomorphic category.

En toto pecked human forms are generally no larger than 25 cm in height and are most often depicted in frontal view. Long, thin torsos (Figure 6.5) constitute the most common body shape, with a few occurrences of round-bodied figures. Images often include male genitalia. Arms can be represented as downturned or extended above the head. Legs are often bowed. When hands and toes are represented, they are often exaggerated in size and out of proportion with the rest of the figure (Figure 6.6), in a manner similar to that observed on innumerable Dinwoody figures.

Human images almost always lack headdresses. Heads are generally small and round, and eyes are rarely shown. A few occurrences of flattened heads (Figure 6.7), reminiscent of a "hammerhead," have also been documented. This head shape also occurs fairly frequently on Dinwoody

6.5. En toto pecked
human images from
the Petroglyph Canyon
site in the Pryor
Mountains. Photo by
Dennett, Muessig,
Ryan, and Associates.
Courtesy Bureau of
Land Management,
Montana.

6.6. Exaggerated
hands on an en toto
pecked anthropomor-
phic figure at the
Petroglyph Canyon
site. Ron Dorn is col-
lecting a varnish
sample from another
human figure at the
lower edge of the
panel.

tradition anthropomorphic figures (Francis 1989:177). At Petroglyph Canyon a fan-shaped headdress has been added to a much older pecked stick figure (Figure 6.8). This headdress form is identical to an extremely common design element observed on Dinwoody tradition anthropomorphs (Stewart 1989). These aspects of head shape, along with exaggerated hands and the fact that en toto pecked human figures also occur at Dinwoody sites, suggest close cultural relationships between the two general groupings of pecked imagery in the Bighorn and Wind River Basins.

Multiple human figures form a dominant theme for many en toto pecked panels. Figures are often placed side by side on cliff walls, in portrait fashion, showing little or no action. Rarely do the human figures hold bows or other tools. Only two "hunting" scenes, one from Petroglyph Canyon and another from Legend Rock, are known.

Many en toto pecked animals were not carefully executed and are not readily identifiable to species (Figure 6.9). As a result, they are often best described as unidentifiable quadrupeds. Some figures have antlers or horns, but they are usually not sufficiently distinct to infer species. The most common identifiable depictions are bighorn sheep, deer or elk, canids, small mammals, and possibly small bears. At least one bird form occurs at Petroglyph Canyon, along with an extremely well executed bison (see Figure 3.2), which appears to be in the throes of a nasal hemorrhage. Snakes and possibly insects may also be recognizable (Loendorf and Porsche 1985:70).

En toto pecked panels only rarely incorporate geometric or entoptic design elements such as meandering lines or cross-hatch patterns. At the Crooked Creek site near Bighorn Canyon a series of dots trails away from a line of animal figures (Loendorf and Porsche 1985:15).

En toto pecked imagery occurs from the southern slopes of the Pryor Mountains in the northern portion of the study area to the foothills of the Wind River Mountains at the southern extreme of the Wind River Basin (Figure 6.1), largely along streams that drain the west side of the basins. En toto pecked co-occurs with and has a slightly wider spatial distribution than the Dinwoody tradition. Sites that contain only en toto pecked figures occur at the northern and southern peripheries of the Wind River and Bighorn Basins, giving the impression that en toto pecked imagery outlines a core area in which Dinwoody is the predominant expression.

En toto pecked sites are not particularly common in the Pryor Mountains, where only four sites, including Petroglyph Canyon, are known. These sites mark the northern extent of pecked figures in Montana. Sites with en toto pecked figures have been documented by James Stewart along Twin Creek and the Popo Agie River in the extreme southern Wind River

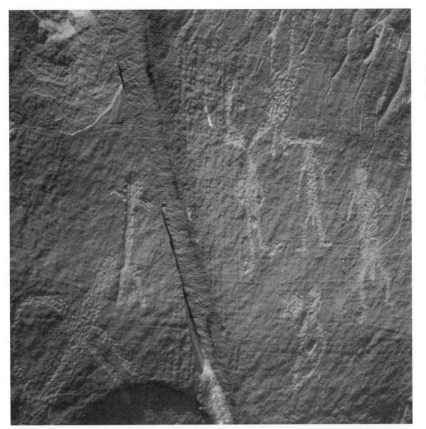

6.7. "Hammerhead" en toto pecked figures from the Legend Rock site.

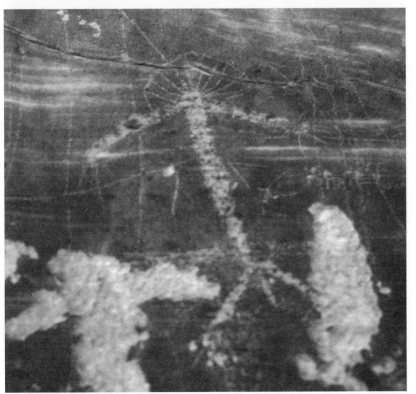

6.8. Fan-type head-dress added to an en toto pecked human figure at the Petroglyph Canyon site.

6.9. En toto pecked zoomorphic figures.

Basin (site forms are on file at the SHPO Cultural Records Office, Laramie). We have yet to conduct intensive documentation at these localities, and it is difficult to say how this imagery compares with that of the northern portion of the study area.

A few Dinwoody tradition sites also occur in the southern portion of the Wind River Basin along many of the same drainages as en toto pecked sites. Furthermore, both en toto pecked human figures and Dinwoody images can be found at some sites throughout the Wind River and Bighorn Basins. Such is the case at 48PA28 in the Oregon Basin, at the Legend Rock site, and at two sites recorded by Stewart in the southern Wind River Basin. Many of the zoomorphic forms at Dinwoody sites could easily be considered en toto pecked.

Test excavation at locations near panels in Petroglyph Canyon produced abundant occupational debris from two cultural levels, radiocarbon dated to 1,270 ± 125 and 850 ± 50 years B.P. (Loendorf 1984:113–115). Although these levels were not directly associated with or burying en toto pecked images, the ages are consistent with the occurrence of the bow and arrow in en toto pecked imagery and were used to suggest tentative ages between 1,250 to 850 years ago for the en toto pecked class.

Results of AMS and cation-ratio (CR) dating of en toto pecked figures at three different sites are consistent with these age estimates and also suggest that manufacture of en toto pecked figures may range from the Late Archaic to near Historic times (Francis et al. 1993). Ages for 12 en toto pecked images from the Petroglyph Canyon, Bear Shield, and Legend Rock sites are available (Table 6.1). The two oldest ages are from unidentifiable quadrupeds at Petroglyph Canyon and suggest that use of the site began about 2,500 years ago. One of the youngest AMS ages, approximately 300 radiocarbon years B.P., is from the well-known rabbit figure at the Legend Rock site (Figure 6.10). AMS and CR ages from the bison, the "blood" at the bison's mouth, and the bird image at Petroglyph Canyon fall between these two extremes. Taken as a whole, these ages suggest that en toto pecked animal figures were manufactured for nearly 2,000 years. An approximate 500-year age differential between the bison and the much fresher appearing "blood" (Figure 3.2) also provides evidence that these sites were visited and used over the course of thousands of years.

Based on available dates, most anthropomorphic images may be slightly younger than the oldest animal figures. The oldest AMS age suggests that one of the en toto pecked human images from the Bear Shield site was made around 1,500 years ago, in the early portion of the Late Prehistoric period. Ages from the other four anthropomorphs cluster between 1,300 and 1,100 years ago and are entirely consistent with conventional ^{14}C ages from occupational debris near the panels.

As noted in Chapter 5, the AMS ages were obtained from bulk samples, which could contain some contamination from either older or younger organic materials. It should also be recalled that CRs from rock varnish provide a relative age sequence. A relative ordering of mean CRs from each sample (data from Francis et al. 1993:727) is completely consistent with a relative ordering of the same figures based on AMS ages (Table 6.2). In conjunction with subject matter (i.e., the occurrence of bows and arrows) and the independently derived ages from nearby cultural deposits, these data suggest that any error factor of AMS ages is fairly minimal. In addition, multiple samples from the same figure at the Bear Shield site yielded evidence consistent with superimpositions. Sample 90–35 was taken from the left leg of an en toto pecked human figure (Figure 6.11). A CR age (sample 90–36) from the right leg of this same figure is consistent with the AMS age and with a younger CR age from the finely incised bear superimposed over

Table 6.1. Chronometric Ages for En Toto Pecked Figures in the Bighorn and Wind River Basins

Sample	Site #	Description	Age	Type[a]	Lab #	Reference
90-7	48HO4	Anthropomorphic figure	1100 ± 200	CR		Francis et al. 1993
90-17	48HO4	Rabbit	295 ± 55	AMS WRO	AA-6542	Francis et al. 1993
90-26	24CB601	Anthropomorphic figure	1300 ± 100	CR		Francis et al. 1993
90-27	24CB601	Unidentified quadruped	2500 ± 250	CR		Francis et al. 1993
90-28	24CB601	Anthropomorphic figure	1250 ± 65	AMS WRO	AA-6544	Francis et al. 1993
90-29	24CB601	Anthropomorphic figure	1000 ± 150	CR		Francis et al. 1993
90-30	24CB601	Bird figure	<1000	CR		Francis et al. 1993
90-31	24CB601	Anthropomorphic figure	1300 ± 100	CR		Francis et al. 1993
90-32	24CB601	Bison	1470 ± 75	AMS WRO	AA-6539	Francis et al. 1993
90-33	24CB601	"Blood" at mouth of bison	<1000	CR		Francis et al. 1993
90-34	24CB601	Upside-down quadruped	2600 ± 350	CR		Francis et al. 1993
90-35	24CB1090	Left leg, anthropo-morphic figure	1595 ± 60	AMS WRO	AA-6543	Francis et al. 1993
90-36	24CB1090	Right leg, anthropo-morphic figure	1400 ± 200	CR		Francis et al. 1993

[a]AMS WRO: AMS age from weathering rind organics embedded in varnish; CR: cation-ratio age.

6.10. En toto pecked rabbit at the Legend Rock site.

Table 6.2. Comparison of Relative Ages Based on CRs with AMS Ages for En Toto Pecked Figures from the Bighorn and Wind River Basins

Sample	Site #	Description	Mean CR	AMS Age
90-34	24CB601	Upside-down quadruped	7.70 ± .13	
90-27	24CB601	Unknown quadruped	7.76 ± .10	
90-35	24CB1090	Left leg, anthropomorphic figure	8.21 ± .08	1596 ± 60
90-36	24CB1090	Right leg, anthropomorphic figure	8.34 ± .13	
90-32	24CB601	Bison	8.38 ± .08	1470 ± 75
90-26	24CB601	Anthropomorphic figure	8.41 ± .08	
90-31	24CB601	Anthropomorphic figure	8.42 ± .08	
90-28	24CB601	Anthropomorphic figure	8.54 ± .09	1250 ± 65
90-7	48HO4	Anthropomorphic figure	8.55 ± .11	
90-29	24CB601	Anthropomorphic figure	8.62 ± .08	
90-30	24CB601	Bird	8.79 ± .09	
90-33	24CB601	"Blood" at mouth of 90-32	8.81 ± .07	
90-17	48HO4	Rabbit	Undatable	295 ± 55

Source: Francis et al. 1993.

6.11. Panel 1 at the Bear Shield site in the Pryor Mountains, where fine-line incised figures are superimposed over en toto pecked figures. Varnish samples collected from the left and right legs of the left anthropomorphic figure yielded early Late Prehistoric ages of around 1,500 B.P. The finely incised bear yielded the youngest CR age of any figure yet dated in the Bighorn and Wind River Basins, suggesting manufacture during the Historic period.

the en toto pecked figure (see Francis 1993:731). Thus, we are confident in stating that some en toto pecked imagery dates to the Late Archaic period but that the majority appears to have been made throughout the Late Prehistoric period.

The Dinwoody Tradition

Dinwoody tradition petroglyphs have long been recognized as distinctive to the Wind River and Bighorn Basins (Gebhard 1969; Wellmann 1979), largely because of the occurrence of elaborate, near-life-sized anthropomorphic or therianthropic figures. These images often have complex patterns of interior lines or secondary figures incorporated into the body of the larger figure (Figure 6.12). Limbs and heads are frequently found in bizarre orientations, and horns or headdresses are always present. Feet and hands are depicted in several ways. Some figures exhibit extreme lifelike detail; others show a series of lines, most closely resembling claws for the feet, and in some cases both arms and hands are depicted as short wings. Wavy lines and danglers often radiate from the hands, feet, or heads, and occasionally concentric circles or arcs surround the head, creating an aura-like effect (Francis 1991:409, 411).

Gebhard (1969) considered these figures to be so distinct that they warranted their own stylistic designation, the "Interior Line style," separate from other styles in which zoomorphic and other human figures were more common. This separation has led to perception that "Dinwoody" consists only of large, interior-lined anthropomorphic figures. Tipps and Schroedl (1985) recognized that zoomorphic figures were often associated with the "Interior Line style." After intensive investigations at the Legend Rock site (Walker and Francis 1989), however, it became clear that interior-lined anthropomorphs were coterminous with a variety of human and zoomorphic forms and were simply one type of anthropomorphic figure in a complex of closely related imagery with considerable time depth.

Dinwoody panels are quite simply striking, and the large, distorted anthropomorphic figures often have eerie, ghost-like qualities. Panels are quite variable in size, complexity, and composition. Single anthropomorphic figures, often with one or two associated animal figures, can be unexpectedly encountered on canyon walls. In other places prominent and highly visible rock faces are covered with tens of images of different types (Figure 6.13), giving the appearance of a scene or composition. Our current evidence, however, indicates that many of these panels are palimpsests, in which figures have been manufactured and altered over the course of thousands of years. The visibility of these panels is often enhanced by the large size of the anthropomorphic figures, coupled with the contrast between the white sandstone of a newly pecked image and the backdrop of a heavily varnished rock face. The near-life-sized anthropomorphic figures dominate the panels, with significantly smaller animal images occurring at the sides or bottom of the presiding images.

For most all Dinwoody imagery, pecking is the only apparent manufacturing technique. A few animal figures have details such as antlers or feet, rendered by very fine incising or scratching. In addition, there are intriguing hints that paint may have been added to some images. On one image at the Legend Rock site, cross sections of varnish samples revealed small pieces of charcoal sandwiched between the rock surface and the overlying varnish (Francis et al. 1993:722), suggesting that the figure, an outline-pecked bison (see Figure 5.4), may have once been painted or outlined in black. In Sinks Canyon a few Dinwoody images show faint signs of red paint (Reiss and Rosenberg 1998). Whether the paint was part of the original manufacturing process or a much later addition has yet to be determined.

Descriptive Figure Types

Based on the work at Legend Rock, Francis (1989:157–189) first identified three anthropomorphic and two zoomorphic figure types within the Dinwoody tradition. Subsequent work at several other sites in the Bighorn Basin resulted in the refinement of these categories and the definition of two additional human and one zoomorphic type (Francis 1994). The principal criteria for type definitions are the method of manufacture, body shape, and the occurrence of distinctive design elements.

ZOOMORPHIC TYPES   Zoomorphic figures are an integral part of the Dinwoody tradition. Animal figures occur in combination with anthropomorphic images as part of the same panel, occasionally as panels composed only of animal figures, and as single isolated figures. Unlike the human images, the animals are often depicted with a great degree of realism and detail.

Outline-pecked/interior-lined animals are among the most distinctive and striking of the Dinwoody zoomorphic figure types (Figure 6.14). They are not particularly common, and the best examples have been documented at the Legend Rock site (Francis 1989:157, 168). The distinguishing characteristic is a pecked line forming the outline of the body. On some figures the interior of the body has been left completely unpecked. On others fine vertical lines have been pecked into the torso. Stipple pecking covers the torso of still other figures. Heads are often fully

6.12. Dinwoody tradition anthropomorphic figures from the Thermopolis area. The right-hand image is nearly two meters tall and stands on top of a rattlesnake.

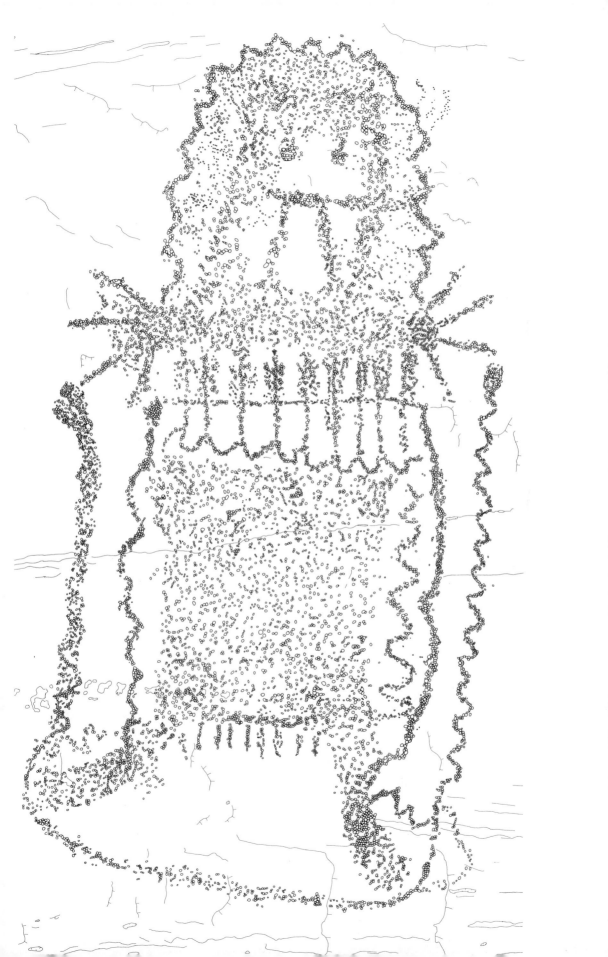

6.13. Panel 1 at 48FR372. CR ages from the fully pecked figure at the left of the panel suggest manufacture around 1,200 years ago whereas the interior-lined figure on the right side of the panel was made about 400 years earlier. Drawing from Tipps and Schroedl 1985.66

pecked, and the animals are shown in profile, with either two or four legs represented. Hooves, when present, are rendered as fully pecked or outline-pecked circles. Horns and antlers are fine, almost incised, and carefully executed, and many figures exhibit detailed depictions of genitalia. Compared with other zoomorphic types, these figures are large. At Legend Rock they have a mean height of over 26 cm and a mean width approaching 34 cm (Francis 1989:157). Large artiodactyls, including bison, elk, and possibly deer, are the predominant creatures depicted. Of the 29 such figures documented at Legend Rock, 20 were identified as large artiodactyls, and the remainder were one possible canid and eight unidentified.

Fully pecked animals are the most common Dinwoody zoomorphic type. As the name implies, this type is identified by the occurrence of fully pecked, often realistic figures (Figure 6.15). Although these figures are very similar to en toto pecked animals and could be considered the same descriptive figure type, there appear to be some subtle differences. Fully

6.14. Panel 35 at the Legend Rock site. Figure D is typical of Dinwoody tradition outline-pecked animal figures. Other animal figures on this panel are less representative and have yielded possible Paleoindian AMS and CR ages. Redrawn from a photograph by Mary Helen Hendry. Handprint is about the size of an adult human hand.

6.15. Fully pecked canine figures occur on the lower right side of the panel at the base of a large anthropomorphic figure. Note the small size of the animals in relation to the anthropomorph, which is over 1 m tall.

pecked animals associated with Dinwoody anthropomorphs tend to be more representational and carefully executed than similar figures at sites without Dinwoody anthropomorphs. Thus, we have tentatively distinguished between en toto pecked and fully pecked Dinwoody zoomorphs. Clearly, further study is necessary to clarify relationships between the two.

Fully pecked animals tend to be significantly smaller than outline-pecked animals. They are also dwarfed by anthropomorphic figures on the same panel. The animals typically appear at the base of or around the sides of the principal human figure, but explicit hunting scenes are not apparent. At Legend Rock, the fully pecked figures have a mean height of less than 18 cm and a mean width of 23 cm (Francis 1989:168). Creatures are shown in full profile with either two or four legs represented, often as straight lines. In some cases, the animals appear to be running. Antlers or horns are rendered with special attention.

As compared with the outline-pecked type, a much wider range of species is depicted and includes large artiodactyls, medium-sized artiodactyls, birds, rabbits, felines, turtles, and lizards. Medium artiodactyls, with clear representations of bighorn sheep, deer, and pronghorn, are most common. Canids are also common and have ears, pointed snouts, and extended tails.

A final zoomorphic type has been termed fine-line pecked by Francis (1994:43–44). These figures, which may not even be animals, are formed by a series of finely pecked lines radiating from a central point or line (Figure 6.16). Sometimes appendages are present. No specific body shape is apparent, and certainly no species is identifiable. The overall shape is one of a fan or possibly some sort of an insect. These figures are not particularly common and have been documented in the Coal Draw area of the Bighorn Basin and at sites surrounding Boysen Reservoir.

FULLY PECKED ANTHROPOMORPHIC FIGURES The fully pecked anthropomorphic figure type is distinguished by solidly pecked torsos and horns, horned headdress, or other form of head decoration (Figure 6.17). This type was first defined at the Legend Rock site and is one of the more common figure types there.

These anthropomorphic forms tend to be fairly large, with a mean maximum height of 46.63 cm and a mean maximum width of 30.03 cm (Francis 1989:176). Bodies are generally rectangular-shaped and squat, although there are a few examples of more elongated forms. In many cases, the neck and head are not depicted; instead, the head is formed by the horns or headdress and is an extension of the torso with little indication of a neck. The head may have a single set of horns, horns surrounding

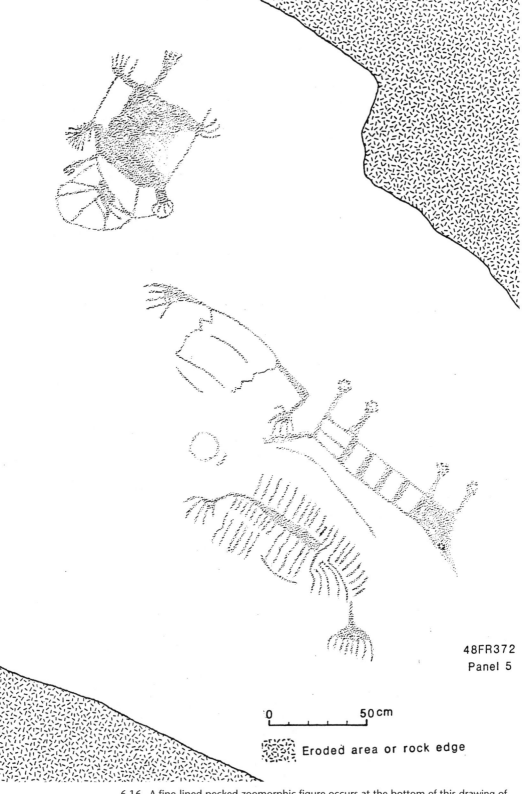

48FR372
Panel 5

0   50 cm

Eroded area or rock edge

6.16. A fine-lined pecked zoomorphic figure occurs at the bottom of this drawing of panel 5 at 48FR372. The panel occurs on a slab that has broken off the monolith and rolled downslope. AMS ages suggest the figure was manufactured around 1,800 years ago.

6.17. Dinwoody fully pecked anthropomorphic figure, approximately 35 cm tall, at the Legend Rock site.

6.18. Dinwoody composite figure from the Legend Rock site. The unusual headdress, secondary figure, and multiple limbs give the impression that the entire image is upside-down. The figure is nearly 2 m tall.

some other type of headdress, or a helmet or fan-like representation. Arms are typically extended and have a variable number of fingers and toes. Legs, when present, are short. Frequently, only the feet at the bottom of the torso have been pecked, giving these petroglyphs the appearance of a spread-legged, sitting position. The number of toes is also variable. The view is always frontal, and sex is rarely indicated.

COMPOSITE ANTHROPOMORPHIC TYPE   The composite anthropomorphic type was originally considered part of the general interior-lined anthropomorphic category (Francis 1989:178), but figures of this type are sufficiently different from true interior-lined figures to warrant a separate designation (Francis 1994:40). The distinguishing characteristic of composite figures is the presence of at least one small, secondary human or animal figure pecked into the torso of the principal image (Figure 6.18).

Most commonly, the torsos of composite figures are fully pecked or lightly stipple-pecked, and the secondary figures are placed on an open or unpecked spot, often in the lower portion of the body. The arms and legs of the secondary figures often protrude from the body of the primary figure. Thus, at first glance these figures give the appearance of having multiple sets of arms and legs and of being upside-down. Hendry (1983:36, 61) called this type of figure either the double composite or host satellite design. Body shapes are generally rectangular. The arms of the main figure are sometimes extended and have a variable number of fingers. The feet of the main figure are often fully pecked and have no toes.

These figures are generally quite large. Examples from the Legend Rock and Amazon sites (48HO39) are more than a meter tall. Heads tend to be more clearly represented, as compared with the fully pecked figures, and a headdress or some type of hairstyle is always present. Horns are the most common type of head treatment. One unusual example from the Legend Rock site is a head treatment that is reminiscent of the "squash blossom" hairstyle.

ELONGATE INTERIOR-LINED ANTHROPOMORPHIC TYPE   The elongate interior-lined anthropomorphic figure type is the hallmark of the Dinwoody tradition. Distinguishing characteristics are pecked interior lines in the torsos and an overall body shape in which the length is greater than the width (Francis 1994:41). Most of these anthropomorphs are quite large, averaging well over 1 m in height, and they illustrate striking characteristics associated with full-blown hallucinations (see frontispiece). One unusual example from 48HO469 depicts two heads and body trunks connected to one set of legs (Figure 6.19). Finely pecked vertical lines fill the

6.19. Elaborate interior-lined Dinwoody anthropomorphic figures from 48HO469. Both figures approach 1 m in height. The bifurcated body is extremely unusual and holds an unusual plant. AMS ages from this figure suggest a very recent manufacture date of around 300 years ago. Drawing courtesy of Linda Olson and the Bureau of Land Management, Worland Field Office.

heads and bodies, and the legs are stipple-pecked with intricately detailed, four-toed feet. The figure's right foot is completely pecked, and the left has interior lines. A second set of arms encircles the head of the right body, and the left holds what appears to be a plant.

Interior-lined figures are always shown in frontal view in what appears to be a standing posture. Many figures have lines, resembling fringe, at the base of or forming the torso (Figure 6.20), and it is tempting to suggest that this feature represents some type of clothing. Hands, arms, legs, and feet are often distorted, with variable numbers of fingers and toes often having the appearance of claws. Arms depicted as wings are also quite common among these figures. Thus, many interior-lined figures are in fact

therianthropic. One important characteristic of the interior-lined figures is the occurrence of wavy lines dangling from the hands or feet. Such lines sometimes completely surround the figure. The combination of human and animal characteristics, impressions of auras, possible depictions of internal organs, and suggestions of flying or "out-of-body" phenomena give Dinwoody imagery a surreal character that has no parallel in the Plains.

ATTENUATED ANTHROPOMORPHS   One of the more unusual types of Dinwoody anthropomorphic forms is a class of figures in which the body is formed by a long, single, wavy line (Figure 6.21). These attenuated figures are known from the Legend Rock site and one or two other locali-

6.20. This interior-lined figure at 48HO469 has an AMS age of about 225 years B.P. Note the projectile point below the figure's left hand. The 1.5-m-tall figure holds a bow and arrow and possibly a rattle. The head appears to emerge from the rock. Drawing courtesy of Linda Olson and the Bureau of Land Management, Worland Field Office.

ties in the Bighorn Basin. They are generally quite tall, with a mean height of nearly 1 m. The head consists solely of a horned headdress formed by bifurcation of the body line. Arms tend to be stubby, and hands have a variable number of fingers. Like the headdress, legs are formed by bifurcation of the body line. Feet and toes are often carefully pecked, with minute details represented. In a few cases, a single foot has been pecked at the base of the body line.

At Legend Rock the attenuated figures are associated with composite or interior-lined glyphs and are rarely found in isolation. Often the body lines weave around rock surfaces or other anthropomorphic figures in what appears to be an integral part of the overall panel. Occasionally, the arms and legs of the main figure in the panel are formed by an attenuated figure. The single lines representing the arms or legs curve around rock surfaces with bizarre orientations and terminate in a horned headdress.

WIDE-BODY ANTHROPOMORPHIC FIGURES   The final type of Dinwoody anthropomorphic figure is termed wide-body (Figure 6.22) because of its distinctive body shape (Francis 1994:42). The height and width of the torso are nearly equal, or width may exceed height. The head is incorporated into the body, and the base is flat, imparting a squat appearance. Facial features are occasionally represented at the top of the body, and head-dresses are rare. These figures may be either fully pecked or interior-lined. Hands and feet are depicted as lines resembling wings or claws. Legs are rarely present, giving the impression of sitting figures. Overall, these figures tend to be shorter than other types of Dinwoody anthropomorphs. One example from 48HO354 in the Bighorn Basin is only about 50 cm tall.

ABSTRACT DESIGNS   Abstract or geometric designs occasionally occur as discrete figures or elements within Dinwoody panels. At the Legend Rock site these designs generally consist of amorphous pecked areas with no discrete form (Francis 1989:184). They also include isolated lines (sometimes meandering), V-shaped figures, and circular areas. Clearly identifiable grid lines, spirals, and other geometric forms, commonly found in the western Great Basin, are extremely rare in Dinwoody tradition imagery.

Temporal Parameters
As noted earlier in this chapter, clearly identifiable Dinwoody tradition imagery can be securely dated to at least the Archaic period. There is evidence that a few pecked images in the Bighorn Basin may be much older, however. Weathering rind organics and varnish samples collected from three pecked figures at the Legend Rock site in 1995 by Dorn yielded

6.21. The attenuated figure on the left side of this panel at 48HO692 yielded a CR age of less than 600 years B.P. AMS ages from the heavily varnished, fully pecked mountain sheep at the bottom of the panel indicate manufacture during the Late Archaic period, about 2,500 years ago. The interior-lined figure at the right side of the panel yielded a CR age of less than 450 years B.P. These ages demonstrate long-term use and modification.

6.22. Wide-body Dinwoody figure from 48HO354, with a CR age suggesting manufacture less than 1,000 years ago. The figure is about 50 cm in height and width.

Paleoindian ages. The figures from which these ages were obtained are all outside the range of variation for typical Dinwoody figures, and they cannot be readily classified into any of the Dinwoody descriptive figure types.

All three figures are located on what was identified as panel 35 (Figure 6.14) by Walker and Francis (1989). Several outline-pecked animals, two fully pecked animals, one human handprint, and one unusual outline-pecked human figure make up this panel. The animals have horns and antlers and appear to represent artiodactyls, including at least one bison and several elk or deer. The human figure lacks any indication of a headdress or interior lines within the torso. The highest figure, a possible bison, is approximately 4.35 m above the present ground surface; the human is the lowest figure at about 3.1 m above the ground. Panel 35 was specifically selected to sample because of its height above the ground surface and heavy coating of varnish, suggestive of greater antiquity than many other panels. Four figures on this panel were dated: three are possibly Paleoindian, and the fourth appears to be Early Archaic.

Sample 95–4 was collected from the neck of figure C (as identified by Walker and Francis 1989:158), a small, outline-pecked animal. There is no pecking on the interior of the body. Stipple pecking occurs on the neck, however, and the figure has what seem to be ears rather than antlers. The small size of this figure and lack of finely executed antlers distinguish it from typical Dinwoody zoomorphic figures. Weathering rind organics yielded an AMS age of 10,660 ± 50 years B.P. (Liu and Dorn 1996:205).

Analysis of the varnish microstratigraphy provides supporting evidence for the early age of this figure. The varnish has a thin layer of black, manganese-rich varnish sandwiched between the underlying rock and base of the manganese-poor varnish. Liu and Dorn (1996:205) interpret the lower, manganese-rich layer as possibly representing the wet Younger-Dryas climatic episode, dating to the terminal Pleistocene. This sequence is consistent with varnish microstratigraphy observed throughout the arid western United States, and the same microstratigraphic sequence has been observed on at least one petroglyph in the Green River Basin that has an AMS age of 11,650 ± 50 years B.P. (Liu and Dorn 1996:205).

Two other figures on panel 35 yielded CR ages that may be in the Paleoindian range. Sample 95–6 was collected from the palm of the fully pecked hand and yielded an age of 10,700 ± 1,400 years B.P. Sample 95–7 from the outline-pecked human at the base of the panel yielded an age of 11,000 ± 2,500. The CR ages have very large associated error factors. We do not consider a pre-Clovis age to be likely at all. Similarity in pecking techniques and varnish development between these two figures and the AMS-dated animal support similar ages for all three figures, however.

A fourth figure, a large outline-pecked animal with stipple pecking in the body (designated figure E by Walker and Francis 1989), yielded a CR age of 6,800 ± 1,800 years B.P. This figure is much more typical of other Dinwoody zoomorphic forms, and its numerical age overlaps with ages obtained from similar figures on other panels. We consider this representation to be one of the earliest Dinwoody images yet documented.

A total of 37 age estimates are now available from figures clearly identifiable as Dinwoody tradition (Table 6.3): 7 AMS ages on weathering rind organics, 28 CR ages (Francis et al. 1993; Francis 1994), and 2 conventional radiocarbon ages from charcoal overlying a partially buried figure at the Legend Rock site (Walker and Francis 1989). The 37 ages represent 31 different petroglyphs from nine different sites in the Bighorn and Wind River Basins. Multiple samples from different portions of five different figures were collected to monitor internal consistency and to ascertain temporal differences between manufacturing episodes.

This sample of ages should be considered judgmental. Sites were chosen because other types of chronological data were available, because unusual artifacts had been found in association with the images, or to obtain ages for specific descriptive figure types. Within sites, only those petroglyphs with well-preserved varnish were selected for sampling, and because of the deleterious effects of chalking on varnish chemistry, not all the figures sampled proved to be datable. The undatable figures are reported in Francis et al. (1993) and are not included in this analysis. All other available ages are reported here. We also note that although the overall sample of ages is relatively large, far fewer figures within each descriptive type have numerical age estimates. Thus, the available ages may not necessarily encompass the entire range of chronological variation within one type.

Of the 31 ages, 5 are Early Archaic (8,000–4,500 B.P.), and 8 occur within the 3,000 to 2,400 B.P. range, spanning the Middle and Late Archaic periods. Six ages fall into the latter portion of the Late Archaic period, and 3 others overlap the latter portion of the Late Archaic and early portion of the Late Prehistoric periods. Eleven are clearly Late Prehistoric in age, and only 4 are Protohistoric. This distribution may well be due to some sampling bias and differential preservation rather than to variation in the intensity of manufacture. For example, at the Legend Rock site (which has yielded all the oldest dates) there was a concerted effort to sample "old-looking" petroglyphs with heavy varnish development. In addition, the low frequency of Protohistoric figures may be attributable to the fact that varnish suitable for dating has simply not had time to develop.

Analysis of this series of dates yields several notable patterns. First, the oldest ages are clearly from the outline-pecked zoomorphic type, all from

Table 6.3. Chronometric Ages for the Dinwoody Tradition, Bighorn and Wind River Basins

Sample	Site #	Description	Age	Type[a]	Lab #	Reference
Zoomorphic Figure Types						
95-5	48HO4	Outline-pecked quadruped	6800 ± 1800	CR		This volume
90-10	48HO4	Antlers, outline-pecked animal	6200 ± 800	CR		Francis et al. 1993
90-4a	48HO4	Outline-pecked bison	6005 ± 105	AMS WRO	AA-6552	Francis et al. 1993
90-4b			5775 ± 80	AMS WRO	AA-6536	
90-8	48HO4	Outline-pecked elk	2500 ± 350	CR		Francis et al. 1993
90-14	48HO4	Fully pecked canine	5400 ± 800	CR		Francis et al. 1993
95-17	48HO692	Fully pecked mountain sheep	2510 ± 290	AMS WRO		This volume
95-22	48HO39	Fully pecked canine	1100 ± 200	CR		This volume
95-21	48HO39	Fully pecked turtle	1000 ± 100	CR		This volume
90-20	48FR372	Fine-line pecked	1820 ± 65	AMS WRO	AA-6538	Francis et al. 1993
90-3	48HO660	Fine-line pecked	<1000	CR		Francis et al. 1993
Anthropomorphic Figure Types						
91-4	48HO354	Fully pecked	2512 ± 272	CR		Francis 1994
95-15	48HO691	Fully pecked	2500 ± 400	CR		This volume
90-15	48HO4	Fully pecked	2400 ± 400	CR		Francis et al. 1993
	48HO4	Fully pecked	2180 ± 130	C[14] exc	Beta-27384	Francis 1989
			1920 ± 140	C[14] exc	Beta-27383	
95-9	48HO691	Fully pecked	1300 ± 250	CR		This volume
95-12	48FR372	Fully pecked	1200 ± 150	CR		This volume
90-6	48HO4	Composite, torso	2700 ± 300	CR		Francis et al. 1993
90-9	48HO4	Composite, foot	2800 ± 200	CR		Francis et al. 1993
90-11	48HO4	Composite, lower right torso	1400 ± 100	CR		Francis et al. 1993
90-12	48HO4	Composite, left foot	1500 ± 200	CR		Francis et al. 1993
91-2-1	48HO354	Elongate interior-lined	2500 ± 30	CR		Francis 1994
91-2-2		Repecked section of 91-2-1	1700 ± 200	CR		
90-18	48HO4	Elongate interior-lined	2100 ± 200	CR		Francis et al. 1993
95-24	48FR372	Elongate interior-lined	1600 ± 300	CR		This volume

Table 6.3. *(Continued)*

Sample	Site #	Description	Age	Type[a]	Lab #	Reference
91-3-1	48HO354	Elongate interior-lined	1500 ± 200	CR		Francis 1994
91-3-2		Repecked section of 91-3-1	<1000	CR		
95-10	48HO691	Elongate interior-lined	1300 ± 200	CR		This volume
95-20	48HO39	Elongate interior-lined	970 ± 50	AMS WRO	Beta-84415	This volume
95-19	48HO692	Elongate interior-lined	<450	CR		This volume
90-2	48HO469	Elongate interior-lined	325 ± 70	AMS WRO	AA-6536	Francis et al. 1993
90-1	48HO469	Elongate interior-lined	225 ± 60	AMS WRO	AA-6536	Francis et al. 1993
90-5	48HO4	Attenuated	2200 ± 200	CR		Francis et al. 1993
95-16	48HO692	Attenuated	<600	CR		This volume
90-19	48FR194	Wide body	<1000	CR		Francis et al. 1993
91-1	48HO354	Wide body	<1000	CR		Francis 1994

[a]AMS WRO: AMS age from weathering rind organics embedded in varnish; CR: cation-ratio age; AMS paint: AMS age from organics extracted from paint; ^{14}C exc: conventional radiocarbon age from deposits and associated cultural materials burying a figure or panel.

the Legend Rock site. The oldest age for this type is the 6,800 B.P. CR age estimate from the large antlered animal on the right side of panel 35 (Figure 6.14). The remaining ages are all from panel 48 (see Figure 5.4). The bison and a set of finely executed antlers, morphologically similar to antlers found on complete figures, yielded Early Archaic ages. The AMS age from the bison (sample 90–4) is from charcoal that had been applied to the figure (Francis et al. 1993). The large elk at the right side of panel 48 yielded a CR age estimate of 2,500 years ago. Thus, the age range for the outline-pecked zoomorphic type appears to span much of the entire Archaic period, a time frame of more than 4,000 years.

Manufacture of the fully pecked zoomorphic type also appears to span thousands of years. A heavily varnished, fully pecked canid at the base of panel 74 at Legend Rock yielded an Early Archaic age of about 5,400 years old. A possible bighorn sheep at 48HO692 (Figure 6.21) yielded an AMS age of around 2,500 years ago, and a canid (Figure 6.15) and turtle at 48HO39 (Figure 6.23) both appear to have been made about 1,000 years ago. The two available dates for the fine-line pecked type indicate ages of less than 2,000 years.

The anthropomorphic types generally appear to be younger than the zoomorphic types, with the vast majority postdating 2,500 B.P. The com-

6.23. Panel 1 at 48HO39, Water Ghost Woman and her spirit helper Turtle. AMS and CR ages from these two figures overlap completely and indicate manufacture around 1,000 years ago. The female figure is about 1.5 m tall.

posite anthropomorphic type appears to be slightly older than the other types, although only two figures of this type have numerical age estimates. Two overlapping CR ages from the composite figure on panel 48 at Legend Rock (Figure 5.4) suggest manufacture between 3,000 and 2,300 years ago. These ages also overlap the CR age from the outline-pecked elk to the immediate right of the anthropomorphic figure and clearly demonstrate the association of anthropomorphic figures with the outline-pecked zoomorphic type. The youngest composite image (Figure 6.24) yielded two overlapping CR ages suggesting manufacture between 1,700 and 1,300 years ago.

Six ages are now available for the fully pecked anthropomorphic type. CR ages from figures at three different sites all cluster around 2,500 years ago. These early figures have some differences from younger examples of the fully pecked type. For example, the line surrounding the head and wavy lines dangling from the arms seen on the dated figure from 48HO354 (Figure 6.25) are uncommon. The 1988 excavations at Legend Rock pro-

6.24. Panel 57 at the Legend Rock site. This figure has a "squash blossom" headdress and is about 2 m tall. Varnish samples from the torso and one foot of this figure yielded overlapping CR ages, suggesting manufacture between 1,700 and 1,300 years ago.

vide age estimates for more typical examples of the type. A test unit placed to expose a partially buried figure (Figure 6.26) yielded charcoal and prehistoric artifacts from nearly all excavated levels. Charcoal from the excavated level burying the base of the figure yielded an age of 1,920 ± 140 B.P., and charcoal from levels well below the base of the figure was dated to 2,180 ± 130 B.P. (Francis 1989), unquestionably demonstrating manufacture of the figure by around 2,000 years ago. Two other ages are available from fully pecked figures at 48FR372 (Figure 6.13) and 48HO691 (Figure 6.27); both fall into the early portion of the Late Prehistoric period.

Nine of the hallmark elongated interior-lined figures now have numerical age estimates. Only two figures can be ascribed to the Late Archaic period. One of these, from 48HO354, demonstrates the repecking and alteration of images common at Dinwoody sites. One varnish sample collected from a heavily varnished portion of the lower torso yielded a CR age of about 2,500 years. The thumb of the figure's right hand clearly had been repecked, revealing much fresher sandstone, and yielded a CR age of around 1,700 years ago.

Manufacture of two other figures, including the interior-lined figure at the far right of panel 1 at 48FR372 (Figure 6.13), spans the boundary between the Late Archaic and Late Prehistoric periods. The remaining five age estimates extend from the latter portion of the Late Prehistoric period into the Protohistoric. These include the female figure holding a bow and

On the Western Front: The Dinwoody Tradition

6.25. This fully pecked figure from 48HO354 yielded a CR age of about 2,500 years B.P. It has webbed feet and is about 80 cm tall.

6.26. 1988 excavation unit before a partially buried, fully pecked figure at the Legend Rock site. ^{14}C ages from charcoal recovered in sediments burying the base of the figure suggest manufacture around 2,000 years ago.

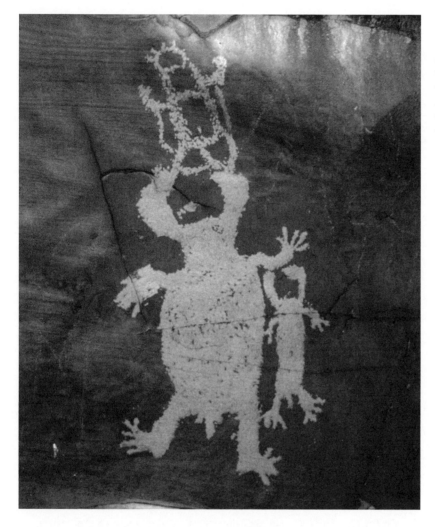

6.27. Late Prehistoric fully pecked figure from the Thermopolis area. The principal figure is about 50 cm tall.

arrow on panel 1 at 48HO39 (Figure 6.23), the finely pecked figure with oversized hands at 48HO692 (Figure 6.21), and two figures in the Coal Draw area at 48HO469 (Figures 6.19 and 6.20)

CR age estimates are now available for two attenuated figures. One from panel 48 at Legend Rock (Figure 5.4) yielded an age of 2,200 years. This figure was superimposed on the composite anthropomorph, and the CR ages from both the attenuated and composite figures are consistent with the superimposition. The second attenuated figure (Figure 6.21), at 48HO692, returned an age of less than 600 years. Finally, two ages are also available for the wide-body figures (Figure 6.22); both are less than

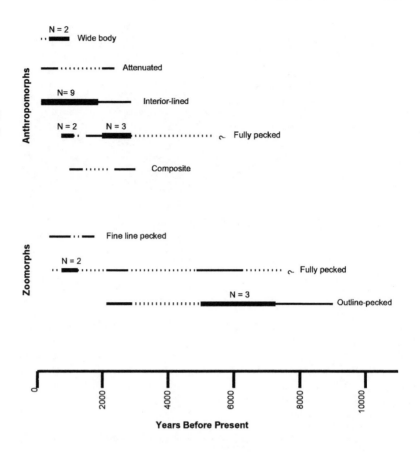

6.28. Distribution of ages for Dinwoody descriptive figure types. The thin vertical lines represent a single date; the thicker vertical lines represent multiple overlapping dates from the same figure type. The sample size is indicated next to the line.

1,000 years old, suggesting that this figure type is among the most recent in the Dinwoody tradition.

Figure 6.28 updates the analysis of temporal trends first presented by Francis (1994). The initial analysis was based on 25 ages. The inclusion of 12 additional ages from the 1995 investigations does not substantially change the initial conclusions but fills some gaps in the temporal extent of several figure types.

As noted in the 1994 analysis, outline-pecked zoomorphic figures appear to be the oldest figure type, beginning about 7,000 years ago. Outline-pecked zoomorphs appear to be most common during the Early Archaic period, but their manufacture extends to nearly 2,000 years ago, overlapping the ages of different anthropomorphic types by at least 1,000 years. Fully pecked zoomorphic figures appear to span the entire age range of the Dinwoody tradition, beginning possibly as early as 6,000 years ago and continuing throughout the Archaic and Late Prehistoric periods. The fine-line pecked figures thus far appear to be no older than 2,000 years.

Manufacture of anthropomorphic figures possibly begins by at least 3,000 years ago and certainly by 2,000 years ago. We suspect that some fully pecked anthropomorphic figures may be much older, possibly Early Archaic in age. This inference is based on the close spatial associations and similar, extremely heavy varnish development on the same panel as the fully pecked canid dated to the Early Archaic (Figure 6.29). Unfortunately, the anthropomorphic figures on this panel proved to be undatable because of the effects of chalking (Francis et al. 1993). Nevertheless, manufacture of the fully pecked figures appears to have been most common during the Late Archaic and early portions of the Late Prehistoric, between 3,000 and 1,000 years ago. The age range for the composite figures is nearly identical to that for the fully pecked figures.

The temporal distribution of the interior-lined figures presents a slightly different pattern. A few interior-lined figures appear to have been manufactured during the Late Archaic. They become much more common during the Late Prehistoric period, however, with manufacture extending into Protohistoric and Historic times, and they appear to be the predominant figure type during this time range. The age range of the attenuated figures generally mirrors that of the interior-lined type. The two available dates for wide-body figures suggest that these are extremely recent. Pecked horses and riders occur in direct association with Dinwoody anthropomorphs (Figure 6.30), providing a link with Shoshone oral tradition and supporting the Protohistoric AMS dates and our inference that Dinwoody petroglyphs continued to be made into Historic times.

As noted previously, most of the AMS radiocarbon ages are based on bulk samples and thus may be subject to some error due to contamination (the exception being sample 90–4, which was identified as charcoal). As is the case with en toto pecked, the relative sequence based on cation ratios is consistent with AMS ages (Table 6.4, 1990 and 1991 dating studies). The Dinwoody CR and AMS sequence is also completely consistent with the en toto pecked CR and AMS ages (Table 6.2). We note that the AMS ages from the 1995 investigations complement the age ranges for figure types established from the earlier studies and are consistent with subject matter. For example, sample 95–20 (Table 6.3) yielded an age of about 970 B.P. for a human figure holding a bow, consistent with other archaeological data. Thus, error factors for AMS ages appear to be minimal, and we are confident that the AMS and associated calibrated CR ages can be used to establish general time frames for the manufacture of the different figure types.

6.29. Panel 74 at the Legend Rock site, photographed by William Mulloy. Figures on this panel are almost completely revarnished. Most proved undatable because of heavy chalking, but one of the animal figures at the lower right yielded an Early Archaic age. Similarity in varnish development over the entire panel suggests that some of the human figures may have a comparable age.

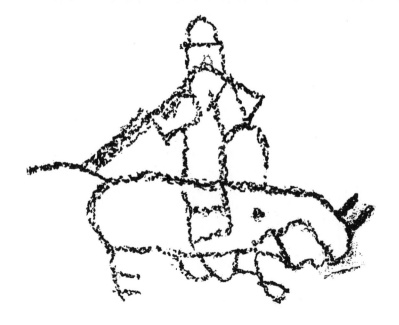

6.30. Dinwoody figures and pecked horse and rider from the Boysen Reservoir area documented by Sowers (1940) and Walker (1994b).

Table 6.4. Comparison of Relative Ages Based on CRs with AMS Ages for Dinwoody Tradition Figures in the Bighorn and Wind River Basins

Sample	Site #	Description	Mean CR	AMS Age
90-10	48HO4	Antlers, outline-pecked animal	6.86 ± .12	
90-4	48HO4	Outline-pecked bison	6.87 ± .08	5775 ± 80; 6005 ± 105
90-14	48HO4	Fully pecked canine	6.94 ± .09	
90-15	48HO4	Fully pecked anthropomorph	7.61 ± .14	
90-9	48HO4	Composite anthropomorph, torso	7.64 ± .06	
90-6	48HO4	Composite anthropomorph, foot	7.68 ± .10	
91-2-1	48HO354	Elongate interior-lined	7.71 ± .09	
91-4	48HO354	Fully pecked anthropomorph	7.74 ± .12	
90-8	48HO4	Outline-pecked elk	7.76 ± .13	
90-5	48HO4	Attenuated anthropomorph	7.78 ± .08	
90-18	48HO4	Elongate interior-lined	7.90 ± .08	
90-20	48FR372	Fine-line pecked zoomorph	7.97 ± .11	1820 ± 65
91-2-2	48HO354	Repecked section of 91-2-1	8.14 ± .10	
90-12	48HO4	Composite, left foot	8.25 ± .12	
90-11	48HO4	Composite, lower right torso	8.30 ± .07	
91-3-1	48HO354	Elongate interior-lined	8.34 ± .07	
90-2	48HO469	Elongate interior-lined	8.80 ± .09	325 ± 70
90-3	48HO660	Fine-line pecked zoomorph	9.04 ± .24	
90-1	48HO469	Elongate interior-lined	9.05 ± .09	225 ± 60
91-3-2	48HO354	Repecked section of 91-3-1	9.05 ± .17	
90-19	48FR194	Wide body	9.12 ± .14	
91-1	48HO354	Wide body	9.12 ± .17	

Sources: Francis et al. 1993; Francis 1994.

Spatial Distributions

One of the more unusual aspects of the Dinwoody tradition is its circum-scribed spatial distribution (Figure 6.1). It does not occur outside the Bighorn and Wind River Basins, and within the basins its occurrence is limited to the valley system of the Wind River and the western portion of the upper Bighorn River drainage system (Gebhard 1969:20). In the Bighorn Basin, nearly all Dinwoody sites occur south of the Greybull

River, along tributaries of the Bighorn River draining the Absaroka and Owl Creek Mountains, and west of the Bighorn River. In the Wind River Basin, sites are found along tributaries draining the eastern slope of the Wind River Mountains and the south side of the Owl Creek Mountains and adjacent to the Wind River. Dinwoody sites do not occur in the eastern Wind River Basin.

Spatial patterning also occurs within the Dinwoody area. Descriptive figure types are not evenly distributed, and sufficient quantitative data are now available to permit some preliminary observations. For example, the relative frequencies of anthropomorphic, zoomorphic, and abstract figures vary across the Dinwoody region (Table 6.5). These data are derived from analyses at the Legend Rock site (Francis 1989), descriptions and figure counts from several sites in the Boysen Reservoir area (Tipps and Schroedl 1985; Wheeler 1957), and panel forms from sites in the Thermopolis area in the Bighorn Basin and near Ring Lake Ranch on the upper Wind River completed as part of recent recording projects by the authors. The figure counts exclude obvious historic figures and graffiti.

The Legend Rock site, near the foothills of the Owl Creek Mountains, exhibits the highest relative frequency of zoomorphic figures, including both outline- and fully pecked types. The relative frequency of zoomorphic representations decreases in the Thermopolis area. Tipps and Schroedl (1985:28) recorded relatively few zoomorphs around Boysen Reservoir, just above the entrance to Wind River Canyon, termed here the lower Wind River area. Many of the sites originally documented in the Boysen pool area are now inundated, however, and Wheeler's (1957) pre-reservoir data may provide a more accurate indication of the relative occurrence of zoomorphic figures. Nearly 30 percent of the figures observed by Wheeler (1957:273) are zoomorphs and include both outline- and fully pecked types. Zoomorphic figures are extremely rare in the Ring Lake Ranch vicinity of the upper Wind River.

Large artiodactyls (bison and elk), medium-sized artiodactyls (deer, bighorn sheep, and pronghorn), canids, and unknown quadrupeds are most common at the Legend Rock site (Francis 1989:157, 168). Three birds or bird-like figures and single examples of a rabbit, feline, lizard, and bear paw also occur at Legend Rock. The large artiodactyls are outline-pecked whereas smaller animals tend to be rendered by completely pecking out the body. A similar suite of creatures is represented in the lower Wind River area with the notable addition of bears. Sowers (1940) recorded a large outline-pecked bear with interior parallel lines near what is now Boysen Reservoir (Figure 6.31). Bears also occur at 48FR13 and 48FR99, and bear claws at 48FR34 and 48FR86 (Walker 1994b).

Table 6.5. Comparison of General Dinwoody Figure Types from Sites and Sub-Areas of the Bighorn and Wind River Basins

Site/Sub-Area	Anthropo-morphic		Zoomorphic		Abstract/Geometric	
	n	%	n	%	n	%
48HO4	91	38	104	43	44	18
Thermopolis area						
48HO39	12	36	9	27	12	36
48HO660	20	39	16	31	15	29
Lower Wind River						
Tipps and Schroedl 1985	57	60	10	11	27	29
Wheeler 1957	93	57	44	27	25	15
48FR311, 5 panels only	26	79	1	<1	6	18

6.31. Large outline-pecked bear from the Boysen Reservoir area recorded by Sowers (1940). Drawing by Berta Newton.

Canids are also common in the lower Wind River and Thermopolis areas, and often they are attached to a human-like form by a line (see Sowers 1940:Plate 33 for one example). At 48FR43 (Walker 1994b:150) one animal figure has a long linear body, pointed snout, and upraised tail of moderate length. The short, straight legs end in four pointed toes or claws. This animal is attached by a string or thong to a squat human figure with upraised arms and legs splayed to the sides of its lower body. At sites 48HO39 and 48HO660 near Thermopolis, canids are most common, followed by unknown quadrupeds, three small insect-like figures and one larger fine-line pecked image, two birds, one turtle, and one feline.

Clear variation can be seen in the distribution of anthropomorphic figures. For sites in the Bighorn Basin, anthropomorphic figures (including all the Dinwoody descriptive types as well as en toto pecked figures at these same sites) constitute slightly under 40 percent of the pecked imagery (Table 6.5). At Legend Rock the short, squat, fully pecked type significantly outnumbers interior-lined and composite figures and attenuated images; en toto pecked figures are also common. In the Thermopolis area interior-lined figures, many of which are surrounded or enveloped by wavy lines, dominate. Although rare in the Bighorn Basin, wide-body figures, along with short, squat, fully pecked representations, are concentrated in the lower Wind River area (see illustrations in Walker 1994b).

Finally, interior-lined figures clearly dominate in the upper Wind River area. Some are typical interior-lined representations, but most are winged, with some panels in the vicinity of both Ring and Dinwoody Lakes composed largely of such images (Figure 6.32). Childers (1984:16) recognized two types of these images: smaller figures that more closely resembled birds, and larger winged representations with more "human-like" characteristics.

Ethnographic Perspectives and Interpretations

Extensive research by Whitley (1988, 1992, 1994a, 1994b, 1994c) unequivocally demonstrates that petroglyphs and pictographs throughout western North America, including the Bighorn and Wind River Basins, were created to graphically depict the visions received and experienced by many different individuals during altered states of consciousness. Whitley (1994b) provides dozens of ethnographic references that directly or indirectly link paintings and engravings with the visionary imagery experienced during trance.

More specifically, for the Shoshone and other Numic-speaking groups throughout the Great Basin, ethnographic evidence suggests that the manu-

6.32. Bird-like figures from the upper Wind River area. Drawing by Ann Phillips.

facture and use of paintings and engravings was directly related to the activities of the religious specialists, or shamans, and shaman initiates. Such areas were used for vision questing by these individuals to acquire knowledge and supernatural power for the purposes of curing, thereby earning elevated social position, income, and status within the community (Shimkin 1986a:311, 315–316). Hultkrantz (1987:52–53) reports that the Tukudika, or Sheep Eaters, and other Shoshone frequently experienced visions at sites in a ritual called *puhawilo,* or "sleeping at medicine-rock." Visions were commonly sought by young men, who went to the sites, bathed in a nearby stream or lake, and then sat facing the panel while they waited for several days for a visit from a supernatural power. Once the being or power arrived, its form might change throughout the experience. As one shaman reported to Hultkrantz, he had a vision "of a lightning spirit that changed its shape; it was first like a body of water, then like a human being, then like an animal, and finally it faded away" (Hultkrantz 1987:53). For the Shoshone, the visionary experience was perceived as an intense, dangerous ordeal invoking fear, anxiety, and aggression, and shamans were often considered dangerous, aggressive, and sexually preda-tory individuals who were avoided whenever possible (Whitley 1998b:29).

Engravings and paintings were created the morning after a vision was received in order to preserve it, as forgetting the details of a vision could result in death or illness. Previously created panels were consulted to refresh the shaman's memory and to renew the connection to the supernat-ural (Applegate 1978:50–51; Gayton 1948:109, 240; Hultkrantz 1987:55; Kelly 1932:190, 194; Kelly 1939:152).

Documented vision questing areas in the Wind River and Bighorn Basins include locales around Bull Lake, Crowheart Butte, Dinwoody Canyon, Medicine Butte, Cedar Buttes, Sage Creek, Willow Creek, and Owl Creek (Whitley 1994a). Well-known sites often occur in direct association with many of these locales, and many Dinwoody tradition images are concentrated in the vicinity of such places. Concentrations of engravings also occur in areas that have not been ethnographically documented as vision questing locales, such as surrounding glacial lakes, around hot springs, and on unusual and striking rock outcrops.

Petroglyph and pictograph sites are known as *poha kahni,* or "house of power" (Shimkin 1986a:325). These places are believed to hold great supernatural power and are thought of as portals to the supernatural and home to a variety of dangerous, if not deadly, supernatural beings (Liljeblad 1986:652; Whitley 1994b:7). The distribution of supernatural power followed the distribution of permanent water sources, high peaks, rock outcrops, and caves (Miller 1985:58–59), and spirits are often described as emerging from cracks in the rocks or from the water (Steward 1938: 187–188; Whitley 1992; Zigmond 1977:33–34, 1980:177–180).

A variety of supernatural persona and spirits, including ghost beings, little people, water babies, rock babies, mountain trolls, mountain dwarfs, or dwarf spirits, could be encountered during the vision. The Shoshone report that the spirits themselves draw their images on the rock, usually during winter; when a Shoshone approaches a site, he or she can hear the spirits pecking on the rock (Hultkrantz 1987:49). Whitley comments: "The art was metaphorically denoted as made by these spirits for one simple reason: no distinction was made, semantically, epistemologically, linguistically, or otherwise, between the actions of a shaman, his spirit helper, and his dream. To say that the art was made by a water baby, in other words, was simply to affirm that it was engraved by a shaman" (1992:97).

The distribution of supernatural power is not uniform. For example, among Numic-speaking groups the Coso Range of eastern California is acknowledged as the center of weather-control shamanism (Whitley 1994c:363), whereas the Dinwoody region is home to a variety of ghost beings who hold different types of supernatural knowledge and power. Mountains are the home of ogres and evil giants, water babies live in lakes and hot springs, and white water buffaloes can be found in Bull Lake (Hultkrantz 1986:633). Furthermore, shamans are both general practitioners and specialists (Liljeblad 1986:644) and are known to have traveled extremely long distances outside their home territory to acquire specific types of supernatural power (Whitley 1994b:7). Shimkin (1986a:325) reports that many of the images in the Dinwoody area represent water ghost and rock ghost beings. Thus, it is reasonable to assume that variation in the spatial distribution of specific figure types reflects the different types of beings encountered in different places during the shamans' vision quests and that some figure types may be interpretable with reference to Shoshonean beliefs about the spiritual world. The most striking examples occur in the upper Wind River and Thermopolis areas.

Upper Wind River

Wokai mumbic, a giant cannibalistic owl, is an important Shoshone spirit. *Wokai mumbic* talks and behaves like a human being but resembles an owl or sometimes an enormous dragonfly. When it flies, the earth shakes and there is noise like thunder. The monster grabs hold of children, flies away with them, and eats them and is said to be identical with the evil spirit of the night, *toxabit narukumb,* whose sounds—"tchi-tchi-tchi-tchi"—may be heard at night. These shrieks frighten many people, for the Shoshone believe the owls predict evil. Hooting owls, including Great Horned and Great Gray owls, as well as screech owls are common in the region. *Wokai mumbic* and *toxabit narukumb* mimic hoot and screech owls, respectively, and may be the supernatural spirits associated with these creatures (Hultkrantz n.d.; Nabokov and Loendorf 2000).

Steward (1943:390) notes that the hooting sounds of owls are said to foretell an event. He relates the story of a man who had owl power and who was said to be in a hunting camp when an owl flew into a tree, spoke to him, and warned him that an enemy war party was approaching. This account suggests that the primary power obtained from *wokai mumbic* was prophecy. Individuals who have this sort of power are usually also capable of traveling into the past to find lost objects or to learn the facts about a past event (Hultkrantz 1981:32).

Other birds also play important roles in Shoshone spiritual belief. A small, hummingbird-like creature is believed to be the Thunderbird, and eagles are thought to shoot lightning by flashing their wings (Hultkrantz 1986:632). Eagles are also regarded as messengers to the sky realm (Hultkrantz 1986:633), as evidenced by the placement of an eagle nest on the top of the Sun Dance pole. Curiously, it is small birds such as blackbirds and hummingbirds that are most often referred to as collecting water in the clouds and making them thunder (Hultkrantz 1987:46; Vander 1997: 228). One consultant told Hultkrantz (1987:46) that the *tongwoyaget* ("crying clouds") is like the hummingbird but even smaller and faster.

Although other types of anthropomorphic figures that probably depict ghost beings occur in the upper Wind River area, flying or winged creatures dominate the imagery, and it is apparent that many of the figures are

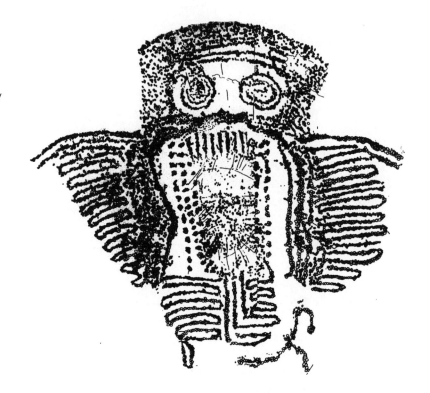

6.33. Owl-like figure from the upper Wind River area. Drawing by Linda Olson.

related to creatures and forces of the sky (Figure 6.32). Significantly, the figures can be divided into two groups (Childers 1984). Many of the larger ones are quite owl-like, recognizable because they have concentric circles around their eyes and three toes prominently displayed on their feet (Figure 6.33). These figures may indeed be representations of *wokai mumbic* or *toxabit narukumb*. The smaller figures have propeller-like wings, possibly a conceptualization of the rapid movement of humming-bird wings, and may depict the supernatural associations of hummingbirds (Figure 6.32 L).

Also significant is the occurrence of zigzag or wavy lines in many of these depictions. These may be metaphorical representations of lightning, which is clearly associated with several supernatural birds. Furthermore, *wokai mumbic* also makes noise like thunder. *Enga gwikwizopu*, lightning or "red flashing," is a powerful and superior force that resides in the sky and blesses only medicine men (Steward 1943:390).

Thermopolis Area
Numerous interior-lined figures in the Thermopolis area appear to depict a dangerous class of supernatural creatures known as *pan dzoavits,* or water

ghosts. Lowie (1909b:234) describes a *pan dzoavits* as "a giant with enormous hands and feet, who lives in the water." Water ghosts are closely related to another class of creatures known as *pa:unha*, "water babies" or "children of the water." Like water ghosts, these creatures live in creeks, rivers, and lakes. They are usually only one to one and a half feet tall, however, and so heavy that one cannot move them (Hultkrantz 1987:49). Water babies sound like crying babies and, like water ghosts, are said to have long hair.

Water ghosts and water babies are said to be the cause of the boiling water in the hot springs and geysers (Hultkrantz 1986:633) and are extremely dangerous. If a person is successful in meeting and surviving an encounter with them, that individual is given special powers. Water ghosts and water babies cause a variety of illnesses, including rheumatism, pneumonia, and heart attacks, by shooting victims with magical arrows (Shimkin 1986a:325).

Curing these illnesses and others caused by the intrusion of an object or spirit was effected by sucking, blowing, brushing, or other means of expelling the object (Hultkrantz 1986:636). Shimkin (1947b:192) indicates that the power from the water ghosts both caused and cured epilepsy, a catch-all term used for various maladies and mental disorders during the late 1800s. Most medicine men feared to attempt cures for these afflictions, but those who were brave would try with some success (Shimkin 1947c: 337). Shoshone "wound doctors" also specialized in sucking out tainted blood and removing arrow points from warriors (Steward 1943:285). If medicine men refused to attempt cures or failed to cure the afflicted, they were often suspected of witchcraft and ran the risk of being killed (Hultkrantz 1986:636).

Steward (1943:283) reports that the power of water ghosts also made men hardy in war. Furthermore, some Shoshone warriors could not be hurt by bullets or arrows. Lowie (1909b:224) reports that arrows simply grazed or passed harmless by individuals with this power. Shoshone warriors often used arrow points as talismans (Markley and Crofts 1997:17), perhaps a symbolic representation of the protection conferred by the power of water ghosts.

After the introduction of firearms this power was transferred to bullets: "Many years ago four Shoshoni went to a place within the Reservation where there are rock-drawings. They stopped and slept there. One of them got a vision. The power told the Indian that he would become invulnerable to fire weapons, no bullet would be able to pierce his body. The man got encouraged, and when he then went fighting the bullets dropped off from his body just like mud" (Hultkrantz n.d.). This account may refer to the visionary experiences of Norah, a Wind River Shoshone, who was blessed with invulnerability to bullets at the rock drawings of Medicine Butte. Norah was instructed by the spirit to jump into greasy mud, which turned out to be melted lead (Hultkrantz n.d.). The greasy mud may be a metaphorical reference to the bubbling mud of thermal "paint pots" or other hot springs that can resemble molten lead.

A particularly outstanding example of a water ghost image occurs at 48HO39. Two figures on panel 1 are believed to represent a female known as *pa waip,* or Water Ghost Woman, and her spirit helper, Turtle (Figure 6.23) (see Hultkrantz 1987; Shimkin 1947c). The dominant anthropomorphic representation is over 1.4 m tall (Figure 6.34). The figure holds a bow in its left hand. A small quadruped is attached to the bow, as is another, much smaller, acephalous anthropomorphic figure with an ovoid body and vertical parallel lines running the length of its body and extending beyond the top of the figure. Both the large and the small anthropomorphs have arms that are horizontally oriented with the right arm slightly bent upward at the elbow. The left arm is not bent. Fingers and toes are shown on the figures in an exaggerated display, with the exception of the right leg of the major figure, whose toes are hidden because the foot is truncated by a crack in the rock face. The large figure has long hair, perhaps braids, hanging down on both sides of its head. Its face is formed in a concave area of the rock; it has eyes, a mouth, and a nose that was made on a natural protrusion of the sandstone surface. Tear streaks are evident from the eyes. The entire body of the figure is pecked except for two circular areas on the chest that may represent breasts. The complete pecking makes the figure appear as though it is wearing a garment wrapped around its lower body, obscuring the area from the waist to below the knees. Short vertical lines protrude from the bottom of this garment.

To the left of the water ghost woman is a circular form that has short stubby arms and legs with fingers and toes. Measuring 35 cm across its maximum dimension, it has a U-shaped line attached on one side for a head. Pecked dots, two well made and a third poorly made, are found immediately above the figure. The petroglyph resembles a turtle. Small flecks of charcoal were noted in the body of the figure, apparently added later to enhance it.

Pa waip, or Water Ghost Woman, lives in the water. Turtle is her assistant, significant for its liminal nature, allowing it to do chores for her on land. *Pa waip* is said to have long hair (Hultkrantz 1987:49), as depicted by the braids in the petroglyph. People know she is around because they hear her crying, demonstrated in the petroglyph by the tear streaks below the eyes. Like other water ghosts, *pa waip* is dangerous and powerful,

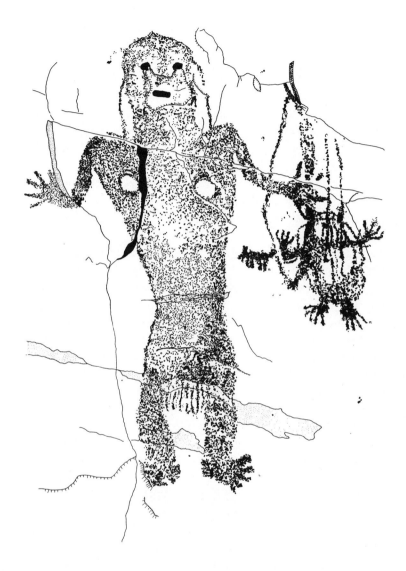

shooting people with invisible arrows that cause illness. The bow in the petroglyph's hand may be a sign of Water Ghost Woman's evil activities.

Among other practices, Water Ghost Woman can grab people through holes in the ice, but more often she entices men into sexual encounters before devouring or drowning them. John McAdams, a Wind River Shoshone, described an encounter with her to Shimkin (1947b:306): A man was enticed into Bull Lake by a pretty woman. As he was alongside her, making love, "some Indians come along, spearing fish, and [he] jumped out like a trout, thus saving [his] life but losing the girl." The story suggests that the man almost wishes he had not been interrupted, though one wonders what would have happened had he been allowed to continue the tryst.

Although not as detailed, many other figures in the Thermopolis area share characteristics with the Water Ghost Woman at 48HO39. Several have projectile points hanging from their arms (Figure 6.35), which may depict either the illness-causing evil nature of these beings or the invincibility against arrows conferred on some warriors. Most of the figures have exaggerated fingers and toes. Although Shimkin suggests these are emanations of power, many of the figures are encased in or encircled by wavy lines as though they are underwater (Figures 6.15, 6.25). The hands often protrude from these lines, as though the creature were lurking, prepared to grab any mortal who strayed too near.

Archaeological materials recovered from this area strongly reinforce the shamanistic associations of these figures. Twelve complete and fragmentary steatite and sandstone sucking tubes or pipes have been found in deposits at the base of the image shown in Figure 6.20 (Frison and Van Norman 1993). This number includes six broken and refitted tubes, one complete tube, and fragments of five others. Based on the identification of impact fractures, Frison and Van Norman (1993:170) inferred that the specimens had been deliberately broken. At least one specimen was packed with red ochre, and none showed any evidence of having been used for smoking. One tube is carved with finely incised bird images; another exhibits a figure somewhat similar to the interior-lined anthropomorphic rock images (Frison and Van Norman 1993:172). Because the refittable pieces of these tubes were found in very close proximity to one another, Frison and Van Norman (1993:170) inferred that the pipes had been stored in some sort of container, such as a pouch. This inference is supported by the ethnographic observation that shamans sometimes stored their paraphernalia in petroglyph or pictograph sites, or inside the supernatural (Gayton 1948).

Further ethnographic research may enable identification of other representations such as the two-headed image shown in Figure 6.19 and the ribbed anthropomorph depicted in the frontispiece. Both these figures hold some type of plant, possibly native tobacco or the deadly *doyatowura*, which may be *Datura* (Lowie 1924:297; Shimkin 1953, 1986a:325). Many of the anthropomorphic figures in the Thermopolis area appear to emanate from cracks in the rock: vaguely defined heads appear to flow out of cracks into intricately detailed bodies, and fingers or limbs are often truncated by cracks and fissures. These are certainly metaphorical representations of travel between the natural and supernatural worlds. Such figures may also represent specific beings, such as rock ghosts, about which we know very

6.35. One of several water ghost figures with projectile points dangling from their arms. This panel is several meters above the modern ground surface and is nearly 2 m in height. Drawing courtesy of Linda Olson and the Bureau of Land Management, Worland Field Office.

little. The large, intricately pecked water ghost figures present a stark contrast to the short, squat, fully pecked anthropomorphs and wide-body figures common at Legend Rock and in the lower Wind River area. It is tempting to hypothesize that such figures represent the potent dwarfs, or little people. We have not yet studied ethnographic references to these figure types, however.

On a more general level, just as the distribution of engravings at least partially reflects the distribution of supernatural power, the variation seen in the occurrence of Dinwoody descriptive figures types reflects the sacred geography and cosmography (Irwin 1996) of Numic-speaking people who have likely inhabited the Bighorn and Wind River Basins for thousands of years. A common feature of religions based on visionary experiences is the structuring of the supernatural world into at least three different strata: the above realm, the middle realm, and the below realm, all inhabited by a variety of dream spirits. These worlds, along with the natural world and human perception, form a continuum with no separation between them (Irwin 1996:27–32).

The cosmography of the Shoshone and other Numic-speaking groups exhibits this tripartite division of the supernatural world. This structure is at least partially expressed in the account of a visionary experience first given to Rev. John Roberts, founder of the Episcopal church and school on the Wind River Reservation in 1881, and later told by Roberts to Culin (1901). The account explains how a Shoshone shaman had gone to the mountains to pray: "At the end of some days three animals appeared to him: an eagle, a bear, and a badger. The eagle addressed him and, taking off one of his claws, gave it to him that by means of it he could command all the powers of the air. Then the bear addressed him and, taking off one of his claws, gave it to him and told him that by means of it he could command all the powers of the earth. Finally the badger addressed him and, taking off one of his claws, gave it to him and told him by means of it he could command all that was under the earth" (Culin 1901:17). To support his claim, the shaman showed Roberts the three claws, which he wore around his neck. Roberts further reported that there were "pictured rocks" that the Indians visited to obtain their power (Culin 1901:17).

More important, however, is the shaman's description of the supernatural realms: the sky, the earth, and the underworld. Closely related to the underworld is the underwater environment, a place that is known to hold special significance for the Shoshone (Vander 1997:112–117). Research by Vander (1997) elucidates the various plants, animals, and forces that inhabit the realms, and along with the work of Shimkin (1947a, 1947b, 1947c, 1986a), Hultkrantz (n.d., 1960, 1961, 1966, 1966–67, 1970, 1981,

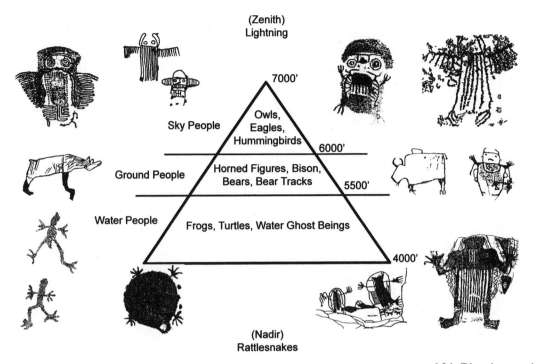

6.36. Tripartite organization of Shoshonean cosmography with some of the beings and creatures that inhabit each of the spiritual realms.

1987), Lowie (1909b, 1924), Culin (1901), Steward (1943), and Liljeblad (1986), can be used to compile a hierarchy of spirit powers and beings and their placement in the Shoshone cosmography (Figure 6.36).

The sky world is occupied by powers such as lightning, thunder, and a variety of birds, and the terrestrial world is inhabited by four-legged creatures, rock ghosts, and little people. The underwater world is filled with liminal amphibian and reptile species, water ghosts, and the water buffalo, and the underground realm is the home of rattlesnakes.

Physically, the highest portion of the Wind River Shoshone homeland along the upper reaches of the Wind River is filled with bird images and creatures of the sky. We also note that these sites are directly associated with lakes, and they also contain many possible water ghost images. The lower Wind River, in the middle of the Shoshone homeland, features many more terrestrial species, unidentified quadrupeds and what could be depictions of little people, or *ninimbi,* whereas sites near Thermopolis in proximity to the hot springs are distinguished by numerous images of water ghost beings. This organization clearly mirrors the natural world, and the distribution of petroglyphs, along with the beings and creatures depicted in these sites, becomes a metaphorical expression of the natural world and the continuum between the natural and supernatural realms.

Temporal Considerations

When combined with the available chronological evidence, the spatial distributions of Dinwoody figure types offer powerful testament to the dynamic qualities of the Shoshone spiritual world. For example, the oldest images tend to be animals, which are also concentrated in the Legend Rock and lower Wind River areas, whereas the much younger water ghost figures dominate in other areas. Although we do not yet have any numerical ages for the bird-like figures in the upper Wind River area, the general appearance and light varnish development of most of these figures suggest a relatively recent age. Thus, different portions of the Shoshone homeland may have acquired different types of supernatural power over the course of thousands of years.

The chronological evidence also suggests some evolutionary trends in the development of both anthropomorphic and zoomorphic figure types. For the anthropomorphic figures, the smaller fully pecked type thus far appears to be the oldest figure type, dating predominantly to the Archaic period. These figures are firmly dated to the Late Archaic, and a few may well date to the Early Archaic. The frequency of these figures appears to decrease in the latter portion of the Late Prehistoric period. Manufacture of the composite and interior-lined figures begins during the Late Archaic, about 3,000 years ago, and the elaborate interior-lined figures become the dominant image throughout the entire Late Prehistoric. Although these composite and interior-lined figures are easily distinguished, they have a common characteristic: features on the interior of the torso are illustrated in some fashion, whether with a small secondary figure or a complex pattern of interior lines. A relatively straightforward sequence, beginning with simple fully pecked figures, changing to multiple interior figures, and changing again to complex patterns of interior lines, is entirely plausible.

The development of the fine-line pecked zoomorphic type seems to parallel that of the interior-lined anthropomorphs. Nevertheless, the major zoomorphic types follow a much different pattern than the anthropomorphic figures. In one sense, the outline-pecked animals are far more elaborate than the fully pecked animals. They are larger and more realistic and often have fairly complex interior-line characteristics. They appear to be older, dating to at least the Early Archaic, and their manufacture spans a much shorter period of time, ending in the Late Archaic. Manufacture of the fully pecked animals begins in the Early Archaic and apparently continues fairly steadily through the Late Prehistoric. In other words, for the predominant zoomorphic figure types, the trend is from complex to simple, a pattern exactly opposite the one observed for the anthropomorphic figures, which become the primary figure type during the Late Prehistoric.

This contrast in development strongly suggests that the relationships between human visionaries and the supernatural world changed through time and that the role of specific types of animal figures in the spiritual world changed as well. The belief system surrounding *ninimbi* and animal inhabitants of the supernatural realms appears to be the most ancient, dating to at least the Early Archaic. It is important to note that the extremely intricate interior-lined figures, most of which probably represent ghost beings, are quite recent, dating primarily to the latter part of the Late Prehistoric and the Protohistoric. This relatively recent complexity may mean that shamanistic practices reached their zenith immediately before Euro-American contact, at which time Native American cultures experienced a crisis from which they have yet to recover (Whitley 1994c).

The Dinwoody tradition survived for at least 7,000 years up to the Historic period. It exhibits a great deal of internal cohesion: the symbolism and beliefs expressed in the imagery were seemingly uninfluenced by the introduction of new forms (shield-bearing warriors, V-necks, and the like) around 900 to 1,000 years ago. These new forms, which we explore in the next chapter, are very different from Dinwoody in both manufacturing techniques and symbolism, yet are also clearly related to religious practices and visionary experiences.

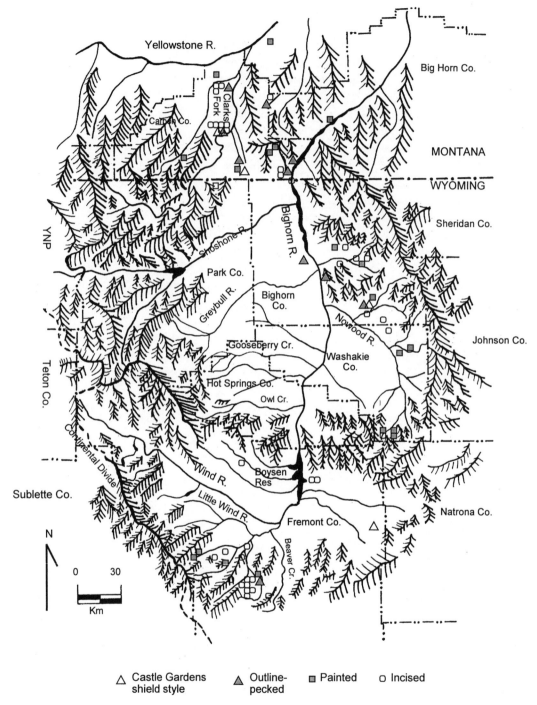

7.1. Distribution of outline-pecked, incised, and painted classes in the Bighorn and Wind River Basins.

SEVEN

Looking East

Incised, Painted, and Outline-Pecked Imagery

INCISED, PAINTED, AND LESS COMMONLY, OUTLINE-
pecked figures dominate the imagery east of the Bighorn River
into the Bighorn Mountains, on the eastern side of the Wind River Basin
east of the Wind River, and along the southernmost tributaries of the Wind
River (Figure 7.1). In the Pryor Mountains incised and painted sites occur
along drainages flowing north into the Yellowstone River. Significantly,
incised and painted images generally do not occur at the same sites as the
en toto pecked images at the southern front of the Pryors. And incising and
painting only rarely occur at the same sites as Dinwoody tradition and en
toto pecked figures at the southern margin of the Wind River Basin.

In the eastern portion of the Bighorn and Wind River Basins all different types of incising and painting can and do occur within the same sites.
Indeed, some images were executed using incising, abrading, and painting
in combination. It is clear that all these manufacturing techniques were
used concurrently to depict the same general figure types. There may be
specific cultural or ethnic preferences for the use of certain techniques versus others, but if so, these preferences cannot be identified at present.
Recognizing this overlap in manufacturing techniques and cultural affiliation is essential to any understanding of the imagery in this area.

Settings

Incised and painted images occur in several types of settings from
the interior basins to the higher elevations of the Bighorn Mountains. Sites
range from solitary images on cliff faces to thousands of figures painted or
engraved on the same rock surface.

Castle Gardens is one of the more unusual settings in the Wind River and Bighorn Basins (Figure 2.4). The site is located on a prominent and unique outcrop of Paleocene and Cretaceous sandstones in the interior Wind River Basin (Walker and Todd 1984:5) that jut out above the basin's Tertiary fill. The setting is extremely dry, with the nearest permanent water occurring several kilometers away. Yet the sandstone cliffs support stands of limber pine (*Pinus flexilus*) and Rocky Mountain juniper (*Juniperus scopulorum*), forming a biological island in the basin (Knight et al. 1976: 183 cited in Walker and Todd 1984:5). The site contains thousands of incised images, including the hallmark shields of the distinctive Castle Gardens shield style, on the massive sandstone bedrock. Although some artifacts occur at the base of panels and sparse occupational debris has been documented in the near vicinity (Walker and Todd 1984), the imagery at Castle Gardens does not appear to be associated with a major human habitation site.

The key sites of Trapper Canyon, Medicine Lodge Creek, and Pictograph Cave illustrate important attributes of many other incised and painted sites. These three localities are all found in foothill settings in caves or rockshelters and are directly associated with significant habitation sites occupied for thousands of years. Both Trapper Canyon and Medicine Lodge Creek occur at the mouths of major streams draining the western face of the Bighorn Mountains, in sheltered, ecotonal settings between the interior basin and the mountains. Medicine Lodge Creek contains the greatest diversity of imagery of any site in the region, with outline-pecked representations of a variety of animals, outline-pecked and incised shield-bearing warriors, stick figures, and painted human figures. The images are all found on an overhung cliff face of Tensleep sandstone above deeply stratified sediments reflecting at least 10,000 years of human occupation (Frison 1978). Trapper Canyon is dominated by deeply incised figures. It has not been excavated, but thick charcoal levels, features, and artifacts exposed in the cutbanks adjacent to the shelter attest to intensive occupation.

Pictograph Cave (Figure 7.2) is the largest of three caves at the head of a side canyon on the south side of the Yellowstone River valley. The valley provides access to both the Yellowstone River and the grasslands of the Montana plains, as well as to the northern slope of the Pryor Mountains. Pictograph Cave contains a variety of red and black painted images, some of which clearly date to the Historic period. Like Medicine Lodge Creek and probably Trapper Canyon, Pictograph Cave was intensively occupied throughout the last 10,000 years. Indeed, the Works Progress Administration (WPA)–sponsored excavations at Pictograph Cave directed by William

7.2. Pictograph Cave, outside Billings, Montana. Intense occupation over thousands of years, along with thousands of painted images, make this site one of the key localities in the Northwestern Plains.

Mulloy (1958) provided the initial basis for the Northwestern Plains cultural chronology.

The canyon country on the west slope of the Bighorn Mountains south of the town of Tensleep is one of the most spectacular settings in the entire Bighorn Basin. In this rugged foothills environment dominated by juniper and Ponderosa and limber pine, Canyon Creek and its tributaries have carved deep canyons through thick exposures of Tensleep sandstone, forming thousands of rockshelters and caves, many of which contain a variety of painted images. One of the most breathtaking sites is a huge rockshelter on Canyon Creek that was partially excavated in 1970 (Mack 1971). Known locally as Powwow Cavern, the Amphitheater, or the Alcove (Figure 7.3), this rockshelter measures 62 m front to back and 215 m side to side. At its maximum this large cavern is nearly 50 m in height. Intensive recording of the paintings in the cave has been completed by Mike Bies of the Worland Bureau of Land Management. A series of red-painted figures occurs along the back wall and is concentrated at the upstream end of the shelter, where it is partially protected by a huge mound of rockfall. Many of the figures are only a few centimeters above the present ground surface, suggesting that deposition inside the shelter has buried an unknown number of other paintings. Smaller rockshelters in the area are also dominated by a variety of red-painted figures, and a few sites such as Little Canyon Creek Cave show evidence of several different episodes of painting, with red paint superimposed by black charcoal and manganese figures.

7.3. The Amphitheater, or Alcove, in the Canyon Creek drainage of the southern Bighorns.

Manufacturing Techniques

Two different techniques were used to execute incised figures. In the first, called "deep-line incising" (Loendorf and Porsche 1985:88), the incisions form deep, rounded grooves. Because of the lack of historic items made with this technique, deep-line incised figures are thought to be mostly from the Late Prehistoric period. Fine-line incised figures (Loendorf and Porsche 1985:64–69) were made by scratching the rock surface and appear to date almost exclusively to the Protohistoric and Historic periods.

Incised petroglyphs could have been made with a variety of stone, bone, or antler tools, depending on the hardness of the rock surface being worked. A rounded implement, such as an antler tine, could have been used to create the deep wide grooves seen in some of the incised figures throughout the Bighorn and Wind River Basins. Sharper instruments, such as flakes or perhaps even metal awls or knives, could have been used for V-shaped incisions and many of the fine-line incised or scratched designs. Abrasion to smooth the surface of the rock face could have been accomplished with sandstone blocks.

A variety of painting techniques, including solid monochrome, outlining, bichrome, and polychrome, were used. In the Bighorn and Wind River area the most frequently used colors are red, black, white, yellow, and green. Red is decidedly the most common, with more than half the paintings executed in a shade of red. Various paint colors are associated with power or natural phenomena in Plains Indian cultures.

Wissler (1907:42–43) describes a ceremony among the Lakota in which the paint acquired supernatural power through heating, changing the color of the pigment from yellow to red. Red paint is specifically identified in the traditions of the Crow, among whom its popularity is linked to a battle among four supernatural beings in heaven. Their blood fell to the earth, and the people "dabbled in it so as to become godlike. Thereafter red was the favorite color. It strengthened both the soul and the body" (Marquis 1928:195). Crow warriors often received red paint in visions, and a chapter in the Tobacco Society was named Red Paint, *awaxuwemice*. Indeed, the fact that there is a separate word in the Crow language for red paint attests to its importance.

Paints are made of pigments (sometimes increased by adding crushed minerals known as extenders) and binders. The main pigments are derived from colored clays or minerals; red ochre or red hematite and yellow ochre or yellow hematite are the most popular. White is usually obtained from a white clay, by pulverizing gypsum crystals, or by using another white earth material such as diatomaceous earth. Black often has a manganese base, although charcoal is also used. The latter is significant because it allows direct radiocarbon dating of the pigment. Green and yellow pigments are thought to be derived from copper oxides, but they have not been extensively studied and have seldom been identified through the use of any scientific techniques.

Scanning electron microscopy and X-ray diffraction are two techniques that have been used to identify the minerals in paints (Ford et al. 1994; McKee and Thomas 1973; Scott and Hyder 1993). Red pigment at Valley of the Shields, a site on the northern border of the study area, was identified as finely ground hematite through electron microscopy (Loendorf 1990:47), and a green pigment from a Finnegan Cave pictograph in Montana, to the northwest of the study area, was identified as celadonite, a fairly rare mineral that forms in the cavities of basalt or other igneous rocks (Loendorf 1994a:127). An X-ray diffraction study revealed that aragonite, gypsum, and an alum (halotrichite-pickeringite) were used for white pigments in pictographs from central Nevada (Koski et al. 1973). These mineral extenders were also found mixed in the red, orange, and yellow paint. Elsewhere in the world, crushed talc and pulverized feldspar have been mixed with pigment to produce larger volumes of paint (Clottes 1994:5–6).

Good sources of pigment were highly prized. The Flathead, for example, speak of a pigment source in a cave near Helena, Montana, where they obtained red ochre:

> A famous spot for obtaining red paint in the Flathead Country was at *a'pel yu'tsamen* ("possessing red paint") near Helena. The paint was obtained from a large, long cave under a cliff. As the paint rock was at the head of the cave and it was quite dark inside, a rope was tied to the waist of the man who went in, so he might readily find his way back. When the head of the cave was reached the searcher felt with his hands and pulled down blocks of the decomposing rock, returning with as much as he could carry. When he came out he divided the paint among the people, who put it in hide sacks. Long ago the best quality paint rock from this place was exported by the Helena people (Helena Flathead Indians) to neighboring tribes. After the introduction of horses, parties of Flathead and their allies gathered paint at this place when passing or hunting near there. It is said that several men lost their lives or were injured in this cave by rocks falling on them. There was also a belief that this cave could open and shut at will, and that several men had been killed by it. (Teit 1930:340)

The Blackfoot Indians waged battles with the Flathead over access to this well-known paint cave which were as "furious as battles for the buffalo" (Johnson 1969:205–206).

Yellowstone National Park is specifically mentioned as a source of pigments used by the Wind River Shoshone. Apparently, the dried pigments surrounding the hot springs known as "paint pots" were used for paint. Because many of these colors are algae-based, these paint pigments are organic rather than inorganic. Captain William Jones described the paint used by his Shoshone guides: "The material employed was usually an ocherous ore, and much of the earthy hematite from the Green Springs locality on Pelican Creek was collected and used for this purpose. The green slimy cryptogamic vegetation from the same spot was also daubed in stripes and patches on the horses in some instances" (Jones 1875:278). Thus, the Shoshone collected and used both inorganic and organic materials for pigments, and these materials were gathered from the same general source area. Curiously, there are no recorded pictographs in Yellowstone National Park, where they might be expected if pigments are abundant. That is unusual because, as described below, it is relatively common to find pictographs near sources of pigment. Perhaps the park's heavy snowfall and abundant rain prevent the preservation of pictographs or perhaps organic pigments do not preserve as well as inorganic pigments.

Place names such as Paintrock Creek on the eastern side of the Bighorn Basin area indicate that the presence of pigments may have been used as an identifying feature before the early Historic period when these locations received their Euro-American names. The Wind River Shoshone also used paint names for streams. For example, the Ham's Fork of the Green River was called Black Paint, and Gooseberry Creek, a stream that flows easterly into the Bighorn River to the north of Thermopolis, was named White Clay or White Paint (Shimkin 1947a:251).

It is not unusual to find pigment sources within the boundaries of a pictograph site itself. At Frozen Leg Cave, in south-central Montana near the Wyoming border, there is a limonite source that almost certainly was used for some of the yellow pictographs in the cave. Natural deposits of both hematite and limonite occur in Lookout Cave in north-central Montana. A cache of limonite powder was found under a large boulder in the cave (Conner 1995), suggesting that the yellow pigment was ground for use as paint in the yellow paintings found on the walls (Barnier 1969). Red paintings are also found in Lookout Cave, and they may be derived from the hematite. Keyser (personal communication 1996) noted that he had observed chunks of red pigment at the Valley of the Shields site.

These mixed minerals and pigments need a binder to hold them together. Binders, believed to be organic materials such as plant oils, rendered animal fats, or blood, made the paint fluid so it could be applied to the rock. Binders are poorly understood. Recent research has been directed toward identifying the DNA in binders with promising results (Hyman and Rowe 1992), and thus far, animal fats or oils have been identified.

Relatively little is known about the manufacturing process for most paints. Apparently, different shades of red could be obtained by heating lighter-colored ochre until it turned to a desirable color. This process was discovered at a pictograph cave in southeastern Colorado where a seam of yellow ochre was found in direct association with the remains of a hearth along with fired chunks of the material, converted through the heat to a red color (Loendorf and Kuehn 1991). In a series of experiments carried out after the discovery of this site Galindo heated some of the chunks of limonite in an open campfire. Within a few hours they had turned red (Loendorf 1994b:96). She then pulverized and ground some of the pigment and mixed it with rendered kidney fat to make experimental pictographs.

Paints were applied with the fingers, and in some pictographs it is possible to see the whorls of fingerprints. Brushes made of hair and frayed sticks were also apparently used. Frayed wooden brushes that Mulloy (1958: 118–119) believes may have been used for painting were recovered in the deposits of Pictograph Cave. In some instances, the rock surface is smoothed or prepared before the paint is applied. Sandstone abrading blocks used to create these smooth palettes have been recovered at the base of pictograph panels (Loendorf 1990).

Shield-Bearing Warriors and V-Shouldered Anthropomorphs

The shield-bearing warrior and V-shouldered anthropomorph are two of the most widely recognized figure types throughout the Great Plains (Wellmann 1979:130). Shield-bearing warriors are most common east of the Continental Divide from Alberta, through eastern Montana and into Wyoming, western South Dakota and Nebraska, southeastern Colorado, central Kansas, and into New Mexico and Texas (Schuster 1987:31). In some areas of the Great Plains shield-bearing warriors constitute more than half of all figures. These figures also occur in lower Idaho, Utah, Nevada (Aikens 1966, 1967; Cole 1990; Wormington 1955), and Oregon (Keyser and Minthorn 1998), but they are rare. V-shouldered figures are restricted to the Great Plains. Given their extremely wide spatial distribution, it is clear that shield-bearing warriors were made by many different ethnic groups speaking a variety of languages and that this figure type cannot be ascribed to a single cultural affiliation.

The shield-bearing warrior (Figure 7.4) was originally defined as a distinctive type or motif by William Mulloy (1958), based on his research at Pictograph Cave. Mulloy's description still serves to begin the discussion of this figure type as it occurs in the Bighorn and Wind River Basins. At Pictograph Cave, Mulloy notes, the shield-bearing warrior is depicted as the

front view of a man almost entirely obscured by a large circular shield. There are fifteen such figures. Most prominent is the shield from which the head, which is circular or ovoid, projects at the top and the legs at the bottom of the shield. In only two cases are the arms shown. [One] looks as though it might have a shield on his back as well as in front. Five have some object which expands upward obliquely on the right side from behind the shield. It might be a spear or club and it always has something on its end. Legs are standardized and shown in profile or three-quarter view. A peculiar stylized way of representing the knees consists of adding a projection to the front or curving them in a peculiar way. Six have horned headgear or hair arrangement and six are phallic. (1958:121)

The human heads often display eyes, nose, and mouth in addition to the headgear noted by Mulloy. The shields themselves are often decorated, with fringe or interior images of animals, other human figures, and abstract designs (Loendorf and Porsche 1985:79). At a few sites in Alberta, Montana, Wyoming, and South Dakota, shield-bearing warriors are depicted with V-shoulder or V-necked figures showing through the shield or similar figures on the shield as a decoration (Conner 1980; Keyser 1984; Magne and Klassen 1991; Mulloy 1958; Schuster 1987:33).

Most shield-bearing warriors are thought to date to the Late Prehistoric and Protohistoric periods (Magne and Klassen 1991:410). This inference is supported by all the current dates on shield-bearing warrior figures from the Bighorn and Wind River Basins (Table 7.1). The frequency of their occurrence diminishes during the Historic period, as indicated by their relatively rare associations with historic items such as horses and guns. Only a few such examples are known from the Writing-on-Stone site in Alberta and at scattered sites in Montana and northwestern South Dakota (see Magne and Klassen 1991:411), and only one site with mounted shield-bearing warriors is currently known from the Bighorn Basin. Shield-bearing warriors are also closely associated both temporally and spatially with a variety of V-shouldered and rectangular-bodied anthropomorphic forms (Magne and Klassen 1991:411), whose manufacture clearly continues into the Historic period.

The widespread geographic occurrence of the shield-bearing warrior, which laps over into the Great Basin, has led to great speculation about the figure's cultural origin. In diffusionist-migration models a single point of origin is ascribed to a particular type of figure, followed by spread to other areas. Thus, Morss (1931) and Wormington (1955) considered shield-bearing warriors to be diagnostic of the Fremont in Utah. Aikens (1966, 1967) suggested that this figure type was associated with southward-moving Athapaskan-speaking groups, and Gebhard (1966), Grant (1967),

7.4. Deeply incised shield-bearing warriors from Trapper Canyon in the Bighorn Mountains.

Table 7.1. Chronometric Ages for Outline-Pecked and Painted Figures in the Bighorn and Wind River Basins

Sample	Site #	Description	Age	Type[a]	Lab #	Reference
95-1	48BH92	Outline-pecked shield figure	750 ± 50	AMS WRO	Beta-84414	This volume
95-2	48BH92	Outline-pecked bear claw	760 ± 200	CR		This volume
90-21[b]	48BH499	Outline-pecked elk	325 ± 70	AMS WRO	AA-6541	Francis et al. 1993
—	24BH501	Solid, red-painted anthropomorph	840 ± 50	AMS paint	AA-8843	Chaffee, Loendorf et al. 1994
	24CB1094	Castle Gardens shield figure	950 ± 80 870 ± 80	^{14}C exc ^{14}C exc	GX-13791 I-15130	Loendorf 1990
	24YL1	Black-painted turtle	2300 ± 60 2120 ± 190 2010 ± 130	AMS paint AMS paint AMS paint	TAMU-24YL1.3M152 TAMU-24YL1.3M160 TAMU-24YL1.3M172	This volume
98-1	48WA323	Black-painted lines	550 ± 40	AMS paint	CAMS-62936	This volume

[a]AMS WRO: AMS age from weathering rind organics embedded in varnish; CR: cation-ratio age; AMS paint: AMS age from organics extracted from paint; ^{14}C exc: conventional radiocarbon age from deposits and associated cultural materials burying a figure or panel.

[b]Because of modern damage to the figure, its age was not considered reliable by Francis et al. 1993.

and Schaafsma (1971) hypothesized a Great Basin origin and a subsequent spread onto the Plains. Keyser (1975, 1977) also postulated a Shoshonean origin.

In a more recent analysis of anthropomorphic forms at Writing-on-Stone, one of the major complexes of the northern Plains, Magne and Klassen (1991) argue convincingly for cultural continuity between shield-bearing warriors and the variety of V-shouldered, hourglass, and rectangular-bodied anthropomorphic forms, despite the fact that shield-bearing warriors were not manufactured to any great extent during the Historic period. Magne and Klassen (1991) note the close association between shield-bearers and V-shouldered figures, even occasionally on the same figure; the complete lack of V-shouldered figures west of the Continental Divide; strong formal continuities in Late Prehistoric, Protohistoric, and Historic classic V-shouldered figures and other rectangular body forms; and the fact that a variety of Plains groups, as opposed to the Shoshone, painted V-shouldered and shield-bearing warriors on hides during the Historic period.

Magne and Klassen (1991:413) relate the lack of Historic shield-bearers to the acquisition of horses and guns and the change from pedestrian to mounted warfare. As noted by Ewers (1955:203), shields used by mounted warriors were about half the size of those used by pedestrian warriors. Furthermore, numerous accounts of the Piegan, Hidatsa, and even the Plains Apache indicate that the large shields were used as full-body shields by pedestrian warriors (Loendorf and Porsche 1985:80–83). In a mounted attack such shields would have been extremely cumbersome, if not a tactical disadvantage. As the importance of the horse culture increased, material culture also changed and is reflected in the imagery (Magne and Klassen 1991:413). Magne and Klassen (1991:416) conclude that the anthropomorphic forms at Writing-on-Stone are the products of a single cultural tradition, reflecting continuity in use of the site by the Blackfoot and related groups during Late Prehistoric, Protohistoric, and Historic times.

The widespread distribution of the shield-bearing warrior and associated V-shouldered figures east of the Continental Divide is strong evidence that these figure types were manufactured by a variety of cultural groups primarily of Great Plains origin rather than Great Basin origin. This conclusion has implications for the imagery of the Bighorn and Wind River Basins, especially in view of the diversity in manufacturing techniques used to render these images. Shield-bearing warriors and other associated Late Prehistoric anthropomorphic figures could well have been manufactured by any number of Plains cultural groups using the area.

There is strong ethnographic evidence from many different Plains groups, such as the Cheyenne, Sioux, Crow, Gros Ventre, Blackfoot, and even Comanche, to support the visionary experience as the origin for the imagery seen on warrior shields and, by extension, shields depicted on stone throughout the area. The visionary experience and process by which shield imagery was acquired and subsequently depicted is entirely analogous to the visionary experience for the manufacture and use of pictographs and petroglyphs. According to Irwin (1996:228), the most important aspect of a warrior's shield was its religious symbolism; it was painted with images evoking the dream spirits of the individual's vision. Generally, the only one empowered to make the shield was the visionary who had the experience, often accomplished by fasting to enter an altered state of consciousness. Among the Cheyenne (Grinnell 1923), unpainted shields were used by those without dream power whereas painted shields were created and cared for by the original visionary. Shields under the care of a particular group were inherited from the original visionary. The primary purpose of the imagery on the shield was spiritual protection and power over enemies. Obtaining a sacred shield was seen as indicative of the path of the shaman-warrior (Irwin 1996:229).

The Castle Gardens Shield Style

The oldest recognizable examples of the shield-bearing warrior figure type are elaborate and carefully made figures in what Loendorf (1995) has named the "Castle Gardens" shield style, after the type site Castle Gardens in the southeastern Wind River Basin. This is one of the few taxonomic groupings defined for the Bighorn and Wind River Basins which we feel meets the spatial and temporal criteria to warrant designation as a distinct style. The temporal duration appears to be quite short, and there is a wide-spread spatial distribution for figures rendered in this style.

The Castle Gardens shield style combines several different manufacturing techniques that serve to distinguish the style as unique in the Bighorn and Wind River Basins. The style is also unique in that it depicts shields alone as well as shield-bearing warriors.

As a first step in an elaborate manufacturing process, the prehistoric artist prepared the rock surface by abrading it to a smooth finish, removing the less-consolidated, weathered layer of surface sandstone to reveal a harder, inner layer for incising and painting. Surface preparation was accomplished with fist-sized angular sandstone blocks, as shown by the recovery of such artifacts from the base of panels at the Valley of the Shields site in the Pryor Mountains (Loendorf 1990:47). One of these abraders exhibited small splotches of the same paint used in the paintings, positively associating these artifacts with the panels.

Next the artist deeply incised the pattern of a circular shield or shield-bearing warrior on the prepared rock surface. Frequently, the shield was divided into quadrants or pie-shaped sections by deeply incised geometric or animal forms (Figure 7.5). One example (Figure 7.6) uses four human heads to divide the shield. The four round heads are attached by their necks to a central circle. They have short spiked hair, round weeping eyes, semi-round ears, and chevron designs on the necks.

With the incised pattern complete, the artist apparently filled in the figure with several shades of paint. Circles on the interior of the shield are often stenciled. Apparently, some round object, such as a circular rawhide cutout, was placed on the rock surface to protect it from paint. Paint was then applied over and around this object, leaving a negative image of the circle once the protective sheet was removed. We do not know how the paint was applied, but it is evident that it was done carefully, with sufficient precision to stay within the outlines of the incised pattern. Brushes may have been used, although none has thus far been recovered from excavations.

The pigment colors are varied and include two shades of red (one more purple than the other), two shades of orange (one more yellow than the other), black, white, and green. Polychrome painting and the use of green paint are both extremely rare in Wyoming and serve as distinguishing characteristics of the Castle Gardens shield style. We do not yet know the source or the specific types of pigments used to create paintings in this style.

The "Great Turtle" figure from the Castle Gardens site (Figure 7.7) exemplifies many of the hallmarks of the Castle Gardens shield style. This striking figure, which is now housed at the Wyoming State Museum in Cheyenne, was removed from the site between 1932, when E. B. Renaud first visited the area, and 1940, when Ted Sowers (1941a:6) was at the site. It was donated to the museum in 1941 by means of the "vigilante justice" of local residents who were irate about vandalism of the figure (see Loendorf 1995). Renaud's (1936:12–13) original description of the shield, which is 42 cm in diameter with short fringe lines around its exterior, conveys its intricacy:

> [The turtle] . . . is neatly engraved and carefully colored in three shades, the same as the other drawings, green, orange-yellow and purplish-red. No instance was observed of the pigment ever running over the line from the division which it was intended to cover. There are 60 such

7.5. Castle Gardens style shield from the Castle Gardens site in the southeastern Wind River Basin. Bear paws are used to divide the shield into pie-shaped sections.

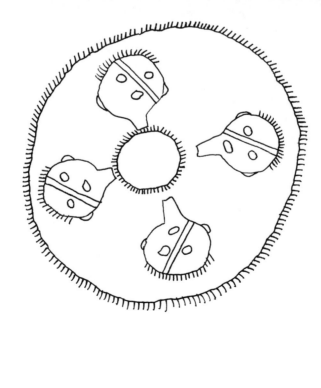

7.6. Castle Gardens style shield decorated with multiple human heads, Castle Gardens site. The heads have spiked hair like that of human figures at Pictograph Cave in Montana.

sections, 46 on the elliptical carapace, 13 for the legs, and one for the triangular head. The ensemble forms a very attractive polychrome mosaic, with four legs similarly colored but not rigidly symmetrical in design. The tail in characteristic position and an isolated curve on either side of the turtle complete the design and fill up the open space together with two zig-zag lines, lightning-like, connecting the animal with the upper part of the framing circle.

Other large bichrome and polychrome shield-bearing warriors found throughout south-central Montana may also be related to the Castle Gardens shield style. These figures lack evidence of surface preparation, incising of the design before painting, and the use of green paint. Nevertheless, some of the specific decorative design elements on the shields bear an uncanny similarity to some of the decorations seen on unquestionable Castle Gardens shield style images. The lack of depiction of Historic period items also suggests a temporal equivalency with the Castle Gardens shield style.

An excellent example of these possible related shield-bearing warriors occurs at Pictograph Cave (Mulloy 1958:127). Although the black-and-white shield-bearing warrior (Figure 7.8) is missing its feet, the extant painting measures more than 1 m in height. The figure has a round head, round eyes with weeping streaks beneath them, semi-round ears attached to each side of the head, spiked hair, and a long neck with chevron designs. The attributes of the head on this particular figure have a striking resemblance to representations of human heads at the Castle Gardens site (Figure 7.6).

SPATIAL PARAMETERS   Elaborate shield-bearing warriors (Figure 7.9) manufactured using the same series of techniques as those seen at Castle Gardens occur about 200 km north at the Valley of the Shields site in the Pryor Mountains at the northern edge of our study area (Loendorf 1990). A few sites between these two extremes, such as the Prepared Shield and Paul Duke sites in the Weatherman Draw area near Valley of the Shields and the Medicine Lodge Creek site in the foothills of the Bighorn Mountains, contain occasional shields rendered in the Castle Gardens style. Unfortunately, we do not know if some of the large shield figures in Pictograph Cave were painted on prepared surfaces, but these designs are sufficiently similar to those at Castle Gardens and Valley of the Shields to suggest some sort of affinity. The weeping eye motif also occurs on a deeply incised shield-bearing warrior at the Ellison's Rock site on Rosebud Creek northeast of the Bighorn Mountains (Conner 1984).

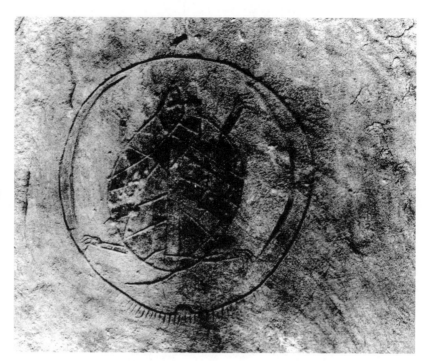

7.7. The Great Turtle from the Castle Gardens site. The carapace is polychrome-painted in varying shades of red, orange, black, white, and green. The figure was removed from the site by vandals between 1932 and 1940 and now resides at the Wyoming State Museum in Cheyenne. Photo courtesy of the Smithsonian Institution.

7.8. Black-and-white-painted shield figure from Pictograph Cave, Montana. This figure has the spiked hair of some human figures at the Castle Gardens site as well as the distinctive "weeping eye" design element. At the right side of the panel, note the V-shouldered figure superimposed by guns, which are painted in red.

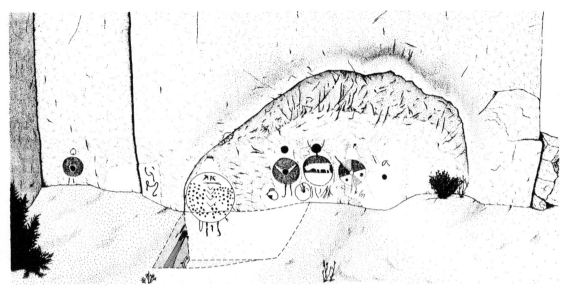

7.9. Main panel from the Valley of the Shields site in the Pryor Mountains of Montana (from Loendorf 1990). Excavation beneath the figures yielded tools used in the manufacture of the rock images, along with a hearth and small amounts of lithic debris. Radiocarbon dates from these excavations indicate that the elaborate Castle Gardens shield style images were manufactured during the early to middle Late Prehistoric period, beginning about 900 years ago.6

Beyond the Bighorn and Wind River Basins a few prepared shields done in the Castle Gardens style occur at the Bear Gulch site near Lewiston, Montana—some 200 km north of Valley of the Shields (Loendorf 1995: 12). There are also some striking similarities between the Castle Gardens shield style and some shield paintings found in Arizona and New Mexico (Loendorf 1995:13).

TIME CONSTRAINTS   Because they are the most elaborate and complex of the shield-bearing figures, Gebhard et al. (1987a) suggested that the Castle Gardens style shields are the most recent, with suggested manufacturing dates sometime after A.D. 1600. We are fortunate to have radiocarbon dates (Table 7.1) from cultural materials directly associated with a panel of Castle Gardens style shield-bearing warriors at the Valley of the Shields site (Loendorf 1990). As already noted, sandstone abraders, one stained with pigment used in the paintings, were found at the base of the main panel of shield-bearing warriors. These tools were recovered from a cultural level containing fragments of burned log, burned and unburned bone, and a small amount of lithic debitage. Charcoal in this level yielded two radiocarbon ages of 950 ± 80 and 870 ± 80 B.P., corrected to a range between approximately A.D. 1000 and A.D. 1250 (Loendorf 1990). These ages are about 450 years older than the estimates given by Gebhard et al. (1987a).

Images at the Castle Gardens site have not yet been directly dated by any means. The only available radiocarbon ages from sites in close proximity to the petroglyphs suggest occupation of the immediate area during the same general time frame as Valley of the Shields. Excavations at site 48FR1398 along an access road to Castle Gardens yielded evidence of two primary cultural levels with burned bone intermixed with hearths, chipped stone, and ground stone tools, including sandstone abraders. The age of the lower level was established by three radiocarbon dates: 780 ± 110 B.P., 750 ± 100 B.P., and 660 ± 100 B.P. (Walker and Todd 1984). These dates average about 100 years more recent than the dates at Valley of the Shields but clearly overlap.

Unlike the case at Valley of the Shields, at Castle Gardens there is no obvious reason to relate the radiocarbon dates to the shield paintings. The area from which the radiocarbon dates were obtained is about 500 m from the nearest petroglyphs. Although sandstone abrading tools were found in the excavation, there is no direct evidence to indicate that they were used for manufacture of the images. Nonetheless, consistency in the radiocarbon ages from Castle Gardens and Valley of the Shields serves as secondary support for the age of this style.

CULTURAL AFFILIATIONS   Tribes living in or controlling portions of Wyoming during the Historic period are unlikely candidates for authorship of the Castle Gardens shield style (Loendorf 1995). In the case of both the Crow and the Northern Arapaho, oral tradition and archaeological evidence indicate that these groups arrived on the high plains of Wyoming several hundred years after the Castle Gardens shield style. Shoshonean groups have likely occupied western Wyoming for several thousand years, but current evidence indicates that this style is not part of their tradition.

Tribes not living in Wyoming during the Historic period must therefore also be considered potential authors of the Castle Gardens shield style. Primary among these are the southern Athapaskans and the Tanoan-speaking Kiowa, whose oral traditions and linguistic distributions indicate that they once had territories far north of their present homelands in the American Southwest.

Although Lowie (1956:365) originally dismissed a northern origin for the Kiowa because of their linguistic association with Tanoan-speaking Pueblo groups, their oral tradition speaks of a homeland near the headwaters of the Missouri River, where they developed an alliance with the southward-moving Kiowa-Apache. These two groups then apparently moved east to the Yellowstone River valley and allied with the Crow during pre-horse times. Subsequently, they moved to the Black Hills and then southward after A.D. 1750, ultimately controlling a territory in northeastern New Mexico, western Oklahoma, northern Texas, and western Kansas by 1830.

A variety of other evidence consistent with Kiowa oral tradition suggests a northern homeland. Archaeologically, Schlesier (1994:309–316) links the Kiowa with the Late Archaic Pelican Lake complex of the Northern Plains. More recent linguistic research suggests that the split between Kiowa and other Tanoan languages occurred as much as 2,600 to 3,000 years ago (Hale and Harris 1979). Thus, it is possible that the Kiowa were living in Montana at the same time as the Castle Gardens shield style images were being made (Loendorf 1995:38).

Finally, large elaborate shields were an important part of Kiowa material culture (Powell 1904). Kiowa religious tradition, through the actions of the culture hero Poor Sore-Eyed Boy, imbues great supernatural power to shields (Mooney 1897).

It has long been recognized that the southern Athapaskans, including the Navajo and all the Apache groups, once had a homeland in northwestern Canada. The Avonlea complex of the Northern Plains and the Beehive Technocomplex in Wyoming and Montana (Fredlund 1988; Frison 1988; Greiser 1994), dated to the early part of the Late Prehistoric period and overlapping with the manufacture of the Castle Gardens shield style, have been linked with southward-moving Athapaskans (Kehoe 1966, 1968; Wilcox 1988).

The exact route and timing of the Athapaskans' arrival into the American Southwest has been the subject of considerable debate (see Schaafsma 1996:23–24; Towner 1996). One school of thought argues for a route through the mountains and valleys of Colorado and Utah with arrival on the Colorado Plateau by no later than A.D.1350–1400. The other hypothesis suggests a slightly later arrival in eastern New Mexico via the High Plains, with subsequent movement into the mountains of northwestern New Mexico. Both the Navajo and Apache have been linked to large elaborate shield images (Loendorf 1995:42–43) and the Gobernador style in New Mexico and Arizona (Schaafsma 1980). These images are remarkably similar to the Castle Gardens shield style in the use of abraded and prepared surfaces, polychrome painting (including green), and a predominance of circular designs. Schaafsma (1980) has suggested a manufacturing date of sometime after A.D.1600 for these images.

The striking parallels between the Castle Gardens and Gobernador styles, in terms of the unusual combination of manufacturing techniques, provide some convincing evidence for a cultural link between the two styles. And regardless of the particular routes or exact dates of the Athapaskan arrival in the American Southwest, all the suggested scenarios allow several centuries for these groups to have moved from the Montana/Wyoming area into the Southwest (Loendorf 1995:43). Loendorf (1995:45) concludes that Athapaskan-speaking groups or the Kiowa are more likely to have made the Castle Gardens shield style than groups living in Wyoming during Historic times.

Other Painted Shield-Bearing Warrior Figure Types

Monochrome outline-painted figures form a second shield-bearing warrior figure type. These are much smaller than Castle Gardens shield style and other polychrome paintings. Red, yellow, or black are the most common colors, and a rectangular or V-shoulder body sometimes appears to be "behind" the shield. As demonstrated by sites such as 24CB407 in the Pryor Mountains and Little Canyon Creek Cave in the Bighorn Mountains, these figures often occur in protected settings such as small rockshelters. Occasionally, they occur at the same sites as polychrome shield-bearing warriors and Castle Gardens shield style.

The monochrome shield-bearing warriors appear to be slighter younger than the polychrome paintings. At Little Canyon Creek Cave the same charcoal-based paint was used for a black-painted shield-bearing warrior and three lines painted immediately below this figure. A sample from the three lines yielded an AMS age of 550 ± 40 radiocarbon years B.P. (CAMS-62936, Table 7.1) and can be used to approximate the age of the shield-bearing warrior.

At other sites, such as on the Nature Conservancy holdings in the southern Bighorn Mountains, there is strong evidence to suggest that manufacture of monochrome shield-bearing warriors continued into the Historic period. At one site small shield-bearing warriors are painted in a charcoal-based black pigment. These figures have human bodies with parallel sides showing through the shields. They have straight legs, but only rarely are their arms depicted. Heads are small and either pointed in a triangular shape or rounded and attached to the tops of the shields without necks. These figures are made in the same black pigment as nearby horses and riders, V-shouldered anthropomorphs, circular forms, and other lines, suggesting contemporaneity. Horses indicate a post–A.D. 1750 age, and more likely during the 1800s. This same type of shield-bearing warrior also occurs at Pictograph Cave (Mulloy 1958:128).

Other sites offer indirect evidence of younger ages for monochrome paintings. Three 70-cm-tall, eroded, and faint polychrome shield-bearing warriors rendered in shades of red and black occur on one panel at the Hilej site near Joliet, Montana (Conner and Conner 1971; Wellmann

1979). On a nearby panel is a much smaller monochrome shield-bearing warrior that stands only about 25 cm in height, painted in orange outline. Because this figure has a different location than the polychrome ones, is in a different color of paint, and is not as faint as the large figures, we suggest it is younger than the polychrome paintings.

Outline-Pecked Shield-Bearing Warriors
Shield-bearing warrior petroglyphs were executed by pecking the outline of the shield, legs, and head. Outline-pecked shield-bearers have many of the same attributes as the painted figures, including arms and hands hidden behind the shield, and spears, clubs, or rakes protruding from behind the shield somewhere along its upper perimeter. This descriptive figure type is not common; within the Bighorn and Wind River Basins good examples are known only from the Medicine Lodge Creek site, the Castle Gardens site, and the Greybull South site. These figures are less common in and around the Pryor Mountains, with a single figure at the Joliet site on Rock Creek, two figures at the Crooked Creek site, and a single figure at the Krause site east of the Clarks Fork (Loendorf and Porsche 1985). Outline-pecked shield figures have also been recently documented at a single site west of Cody, and a few examples occur east of the Bighorn Mountains and in the southern Black Hills (Sundstrom 1990:195).

Outline-pecked shield-bearing warriors are nearly always shown in relatively static poses. Shield designs are not as elaborate as those of the painted figures. A few designs show animals, such as the one at the Joliet site (Figure 7.10), and others display bear claws. Such examples are rare, and simple patterns in which the shield is divided into halves or quarters by crossed lines are more common. Only rarely are the interior units filled or adorned with other designs such as dots and circles (Figure 7.11). Other pecked figures, such as animals, tracks, or arrows, commonly occur next to the shield-bearing warriors. Similarity in the manufacturing techniques and varnish development on these nearby figures suggests ages equivalent to those of the shield-bearing warriors.

A single example of the outline-pecked, shield-bearing warrior figure type has been dated at the Greybull South site (Figure 7.12; Table 7.1). An AMS age on weathering rind organics yielded an age of 750 ± 50 years B.P. (Beta-84414) or, when the error factor derived from organics in the control sample is included, 750 ± 300 years B.P. Another outline-pecked, shield-bearing warrior at the Medicine Lodge Creek site could not be dated because the figure had been chalked. Nevertheless, the cation-ratio samples from portions of this figure that did not contain chalk were consistent with an age of less than 1,000 years (Francis et al. 1993:733). In the single

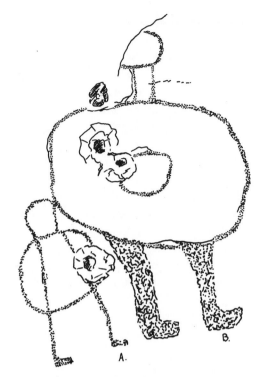

7.10. Outline-pecked shield-bearing warrior from the Joliet site. The figure is an unusual example of this descriptive type because the shield has been decorated.

7.11. Outline-pecked shield-bearing warrior from the North Fork of the Shoshone River, west of Cody. The panel has been damaged by bullet holes. Drawing by Berta Newton and Suzanne Warner.

7.12. Outline-pecked shield-bearing warrior at the Greybull South site. This particular figure has been AMS-dated to about 750 ± 300 years ago. In conjunction with other chronological data, the AMS age suggests that this figure type was made beginning about 750 to 800 years ago.

known example of superimposition, an outline-pecked shield-bearing warrior was placed over an en toto pecked human figure at the Krause site. Based on the estimated age for en toto figures, the outline-pecked figure most likely postdates 840 B.P. These two rough age estimates are consistent with the ^{14}C age at the Greybull South site and can be used to tentatively suggest a beginning date for outline-pecked shield-bearing warrior figures at 750 to 800 years ago. A lack of Historic period motifs associated with these figures suggests that the majority are Late Prehistoric. The inferred age estimates for outline-pecked shield-bearing warriors overlap with age estimates for the Castle Gardens shield style.

Incised Shield-Bearing Warriors

Deep-line incising was used to render shield-bearing warriors and a variety of other figures throughout the Bighorn and Wind River Basins. The basic manufacturing technique is the same as that used to incise designs in the Castle Gardens shield style: the resulting grooves are deep and round in cross section. There is no evidence whatsoever of surface preparation or painting. Numerous examples of these simple incised shield-bearing warriors occur at the Castle Gardens site, Medicine Lodge Creek and Trapper Canyon in the Bighorn Mountains, at several sites in the Pryor Mountains, and in the Red Canyon area in the extreme southern portion of the study area. Such sites are often located at the mouths of major canyons where streams empty into the interior basin. Deeply incised shield-bearing warriors have the same suite of attributes as their outline-pecked and painted counterparts: a lack of arms, slightly bent knees on the legs, and a spear protruding from the shield.

Although there are no direct dates on deeply incised shield-bearing warriors within the study area, most figures executed in this manner are thought to date to the Late Prehistoric period, based on the lack of Historic period items associated with the engravings. This inference is supported by radiocarbon dates from Ellison's Rock, where the deeply incised shield-bearing warriors occur in a rockshelter along with a variety of domestic debris including surface hearths, chipped stone, butchered bone, groundstone, and two pieces of incised sandstone. Radiocarbon ages on charcoal associated with these remains range between 860 ± 150 and 1,150 ± 50 years B.P. (Herbort and Munson 1984:117, 120). Although contemporaneity between the occupation and the engravings cannot be conclusively demonstrated, the radiocarbon ages are entirely consistent with other chronological evidence from shield-bearing warriors.

Finely incised or scratched shield-bearing warriors also occur in the Wind River and Bighorn Basins and are common in the Pryors and at

Castle Gardens as well as in the Red Canyon area. Most of these figures appear to date to the Historic period and differ from the earlier figures by their occurrence in action-related scenes. These figures are typical of what Keyser (1984) calls the "Biographical" style.

Several of the finely incised shield-bearing warriors in the Red Canyon area differ from typical figures in that they have square or rectangular shields. One has a nearly square shield with fringe around its outer perimeter and the usual "rake" sticking out from behind it (Figure 7.13). This figure has a round head with what appear to be two feathers protruding from it. There is no design on the shield. Another figure has a rectangular shield with vertical parallel lines down its front and a spear with a triangular point protruding from behind the shield. This figure has a head with feathers much like the one with the square shield. The square and rectangular shield-bearing warriors are found with the more typical round shields and almost certainly are contemporaneous.

V-Shouldered Anthropomorphs

The V-shouldered anthropomorph, termed by Mulloy (1958) the "V-necked warrior," is less common in the Bighorn and Wind River Basins than the shield-bearing warrior. Based on the seven figures recorded in Pictograph Cave, Mulloy described V-shouldered anthropomorphs (Figure 7.14) as having rectangular-shaped bodies with "characteristic shoulders formed of oblique lines extending downward medially. Legs are straight, usually being extensions of the straight sides of the body. Heads are round above a straight neck. There is usually a lack of detail. Two are phallic" (1958: 122). Arms generally begin at the point of the shoulders and are outstretched with a bend at the elbow. Simple, straight lines are used to depict hands with a variable number of fingers. Only rarely do the human figures hold spears or other objects. The torso is not often decorated. When decoration is present, it consists of simple designs and, rarely, a distinctive "herringbone" design.

No V-shouldered figures have yet been directly dated, but based on their association with shield-bearing warriors, we can surmise that at least some date to the Late Prehistoric period. V-shouldered figures also commonly occur with horses, guns, and other historic trappings. Furthermore, as is the case at Ellison's Rock (Conner 1984), where a V-shouldered figure was incised over a shield-bearer, and at Little Canyon Creek Cave and possibly at Pictograph Cave (L. Olson, personal communication 1992), where they have been painted over other figures, V-shouldered figures often appear to be later additions to sites. These various lines of evidence suggest that

7.13. Finely incised shield-bearing warrior with an unusual square shield. These figures occur in the Red Canyon area at the extreme southwestern portion of the study area and probably date to the Historic period.

7.14. Finely incised V-shouldered anthropomorphic figures from the Beaver Creek area of the Bighorn Mountain foothills.

this figure type, though originating in the Late Prehistoric, becomes more common during the Protohistoric and Historic periods. A similar pattern was observed by Keyser (1977) and Magne and Klassen (1991) at the Writing-on-Stone site in Alberta, a pattern they attribute to cultural changes engendered by the Great Plains tribes' adoption of the horse and gun.

A variety of techniques was used to depict V-shouldered figures (Schuster 1987:34). In the Wind River and Bighorn Basins the techniques include monochrome and bichrome solid painting, outline painting, outline pecking, and incising (both deep-line and fine-line).

Pecked or outline-pecked V-shouldered figures are the least common. A single example is known from the Greybull North site and was pecked within a large outline-pecked bison (Figure 7.15). The human figure stands about 20 cm tall and has a solid-pecked rectangular body with the V-shoulders left unpecked and an outline-pecked head attached atop the shoulders without any neck. This figure has upraised arms with widely splayed fingers. The legs are missing, and the base of the torso terminates at the line used to form the bison's belly.

Although pecked V-shouldered anthropomorphs are rare, incised examples are relatively common at many sites in the Bighorn and Wind River Basins, as demonstrated by the Castle Gardens site. Gebhard et al. (1987a: 57) identified 44 panels that contained both deeply and finely incised V-shouldered anthropomorphs. The Castle Gardens V-shouldered figures are generally small, averaging 8 to 12 cm in height.

One of the most widely recognized figures from Castle Gardens (Figure 7.16) is an excellent example of deep-line incised technique. This exceptionally tall figure is 85 cm in height and has slightly curved body sides that led Gebhard and his colleagues to suggest that the human may be wearing a coat: "The surface of this coat is covered with nine bear claws, arranged in five horizontal bands. The head of the figure bears a single line, perhaps indicating a horn headdress and, as is often the case with V-neck interior line and human outline figures, a single line between the legs probably delineates a penis. The scale of this figure, its bear claw ornamental coat and the large size of the accompanying deer to its right and antelope to the left, make this panel unique in Northern Plains rock art" (Gebhard et al. 1987a:69).

Like other fine-line incised images, V-shouldered anthropomorphs rendered with this technique probably date mostly to the Historic period. Excellent examples of this figure type occur in the Beaver Creek area in the foothills of the Bighorn Mountains (Figure 7.14). The two larger figures in this panel are unusual in that they are holding some sort of object, and the

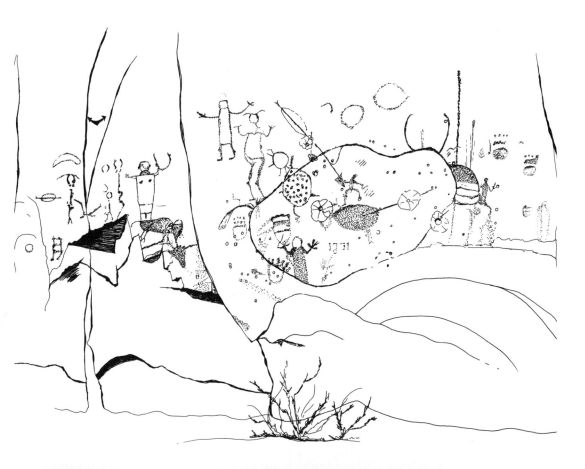

7.15. Outline-pecked V-shouldered anthropomorph on the rump of a large outline-pecked bison at the Greybull North site. Drawing by Berta Newton.

7.16. Deeply incised V-shouldered anthropomorph from the Castle Gardens site. Note the bear claws decorating the torso of the figure, which stands nearly 85 cm high. Photograph by Ted Sowers, courtesy of the American Heritage Center, University of Wyoming.

left-hand figure wears what appear to be fringed leggings. A herringbone design occasionally occurs on the torso on some finely incised V-necks (Figure 7.17). If this design represents a breastplate, it would postdate 1870, as these items did not occur on the Northern Plains until after that time (Ewers 1957a; Schuster 1987:37). Herringbone designs also occur on atypical rectangular-bodied figures in the Red Canyon area, which are discussed in greater detail later in this chapter.

The few examples of decorations on the torso of V-shouldered figures have generally been interpreted as evidence of clothing. Schuster suggests other possible explanations for the herringbone design, including "body decorations, clothing designs, multiple necklaces, or perhaps even ribs, that may symbolically designate the presence of an individual with special shamanic powers" (1987:36–37). In a similar vein, the bear claws on the large Castle Gardens V-neck could represent designs painted on a coat or the transmogrification of an individual to animal form during a vision.

Solid-painted V-necks are not particularly common, though excellent examples are known from the southern Bighorns. At Little Canyon Creek Cave one figure has a solid body done in black manganese-based paint with deep V-shoulders and a long straight line for a neck (Figure 7.18). The head has an inverted teardrop shape, and although the paint is eroded, the head does not appear ever to have had any ears, eyes, nose, or mouth. A darker black-painted line outlines the body, which has a rectangular base. Arms and legs are not shown. An interior white line extends from the base of the V, at the neck of the figure, down into the body, where it terminates as a circular blob of white paint. This "heart line" motif actually ends at the stomach of the figure rather than the heart. This painting is superimposed on older, red-painted figures.

Other V-shouldered anthropomorphs, illustrating a variety of painting techniques, occur on the Nature Conservancy property in the southern Bighorns. One of these figures has a relatively wide body with long out-stretched arms displaying fingers, legs that are made as continuations of the outer body lines, and feet without toes (see drawings in Mack 1971:92, 94). The head is unadorned but appears to have eyes, nose, and mouth. The neck, throat area, and legs are filled with black paint, and the remainder of the figure is made as an outline. Another V-shouldered anthropomorph has a rectangular body, legs as continuations of the body, and outstretched arms and hands. One of the hands may be holding a plant, and the other is shown with fingers. This figure has a long neck and a somewhat unusual head that is shown in profile with an eye and what may be ears. Black pigment was used to enhance the chin and fill the body of this figure.

7.17. Finely incised V-shouldered anthropomorph with an unusual herringbone design on the shoulders from the Legend Rock site. This figure is most likely of historic age and is superimposed on Dinwoody tradition figures.

7.18. Solid, black-painted V-shouldered anthropomorph, trimmed with white, from Little Canyon Creek Cave. This figure has been painted on top of red-painted figures.

Animals Associated with Shield-Bearing Warriors and
V-Shouldered Figures

The animals most often associated with shield-bearing warriors and
V-shouldered figures, either as decorations on the shield or body or on the
same panel as the human figures, are bears, followed by elk or deer and
bison. Less frequently depicted are turtles and birds. Bighorn sheep, antelope, or canids occur only rarely with shield-bearing warriors or V-necks,
and in stark contrast to the Great Basin and American Southwest, as well
as the western side of the Bighorn and Wind River Basins, snakes and
lizards are extremely rare. As yet, only a few animal figures painted in
three or more colors have been recorded, but all other manufacturing techniques used to depict humans were used to depict animals. Similarity in
varnish development, pecking techniques, or paint attributes often suggests
contemporaneity between the human and zoomorphic figures. The size of
the zoomorphic representations varies considerably. Some images of artiodactyls and bears are several meters in length and height, but most are
much smaller, averaging 50 to 70 cm from head to toe. Images of birds,
turtles, and other creatures tend to be smaller still.

Regardless of the size or manufacturing technique, images of elk or deer,
bison, and bears share many characteristics. Figures are shown in profile,
often with a "heart line," and the artiodactyls are generally pierced by
arrows or spears. It is notable that although these creatures are shown as
wounded, explicit hunting scenes with shield-bearers and V-shouldered
figures are quite rare. The projectile points shown in these drawings or
with shield-bearers and V-necks sometimes resemble the common projectile
point types found throughout the region. Side-notched, stemmed, and
unnotched projectile points are represented, and the presence of fletching
on many shafts implies that these are depictions of arrows rather than
spears or darts, supporting the Late Prehistoric age estimate for these
figures. Gebhard et al. (1987a:73) suggested that the types of projectiles
depicted could perhaps be used to date the drawings. Making such a connection is extremely difficult, however, as points are not always illustrated
in any great detail other than a rough outline and the scale of the point is
often out of proportion to the shaft and other elements in the drawing.
Moreover, arrow points were not the only implements hafted onto shafts.
Large bifaces with notching or other types of basal modification occur in
many sites throughout the Northwestern Plains (Frison 1978) and could
just as easily be depicted in rock drawings.

In addition to figures that are relatively easily identified, numerous panels contain nondescript or unidentifiable quadrupeds or figures that have
attributes of more than one species. Conner and Conner (1971:26) call

these figures amorphic because, although they are intended to represent animals, it is impossible to identify them.

BEARS Bears are the most common and usually the most easily recognized animals found with shield-bearing warriors. Prehistoric and historic artists executed large, medium, and small images of these creatures by outline pecking, deep- and fine-line incising, and painting, with the most detail depicted on the larger images. Only rarely are bears shown being pierced by arrows or spears.

As defined by Loendorf and Porsche (1985:77–78), large bears, thought to represent grizzlies, are the most distinctive (Figure 7.19). Six of these images at five different sites are known from the Pryor Mountains; one is known from the Beaver Creek area in the Bighorn Mountain foothills. One large black-and-white bear from the Langstaff site in the Pryor Mountains was painted on a smoothed surface. Only one large bear has been reliably dated (Table 7.1). Cation-ratio age estimates from a fine-line incised bear at the Bear Shield site (see Figure 6.11) indicate an age of less than 1,000 years (Francis et al. 1993:731).

Large bears (approximately 1 m in length) are generally depicted in profile view, showing the right side of the animal. They usually display a hump on the back, just behind the neck, and a dish-shaped face, two well-recognized characteristics of grizzly bears. Artists paid particular attention to the details of the front half of each of these creatures, showing simpler or more diminutive hindquarters. Front legs are usually displayed in an attack position, outstretched and with large feet that have claws bared. The elongated heads have short ears and two eyes. This dual perspective, which shows both eyes when the entire animal is in profile view, distinguishes bears from representations of other animals in the region.

Medium-sized bear images are also common. Little Canyon Creek Cave contains an especially fine bichrome painted bear (see Frison 1978:413). This figure is 70 cm across, its body painted in black manganese-based pigment. It has relatively long ears and a long snout, making it appear pig-like to some, but the characteristic hump on its back and its claws indicate it is intended to represent a grizzly. The claws are painted in black and outlined in white, making them more apparent. The paint is quite similar to that used to depict a neighboring black-and-white V-shouldered anthropomorph, suggesting the two figures are contemporaneous.

Small bear images, usually less than 20 cm in length, are also shown in profile. Some have legs with claws, and heads with mouths and teeth. Compared with the large and medium-sized bear images, they do not as commonly have oversized front legs and front paws with oversized claws,

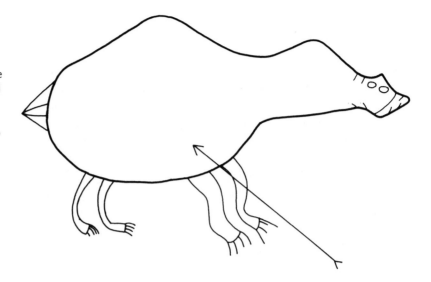

7.19. The big bear from the Joliet site. The hump on the neck and dish-shaped face suggest that this is the image of a grizzly. Also note the attention given the front limbs and the convention of showing two eyes on one side of the head.

or overly large mouths with big teeth. These smaller images are most frequently found in groups, often as decorations on shields.

Bear tracks are also common, either as decoration on human figures or shields or as individual figures. At the Greybull South site a pecked bear claw adjacent to an outline-pecked shield warrior yielded a CR age of 760 ± 200 B.P. (Table 7.1). This date overlaps the AMS age for the shield-bearing warrior and indicates that the two figures are contemporaneous, a conclusion that is supported by macroscopic characteristics of the rock varnish and an identical pecking technique. Bear tracks, very similar to those at the Greybull South site, are also found trailing a large profile view of a bear at the Krause site (Figure 7.20).

Bears have been venerated by many cultures around the world for thousands of years, and judging from their frequent portrayal in the Bighorn and Wind River Basins, they played an important role in the religious and ceremonial life of the area's prehistoric and historic inhabitants. Numerous ethnographic accounts emphasize the power of bears, and descriptions of the ways to enter trance often include references to "acting like" a bear. Thus, it may not be too farfetched to suggest that bear imagery represents more than just clothing decoration or body adornment; it could also represent the connection of bears to the supernatural.

For example, the Blackfoot did not usually hunt bears, unless an adventurous young man hunted one to obtain its claws (Ewers 1958:85). Wissler (1912:131) describes an important Blackfoot medicine bundle that contained "a large dagger-like knife to the handle of which was attached the

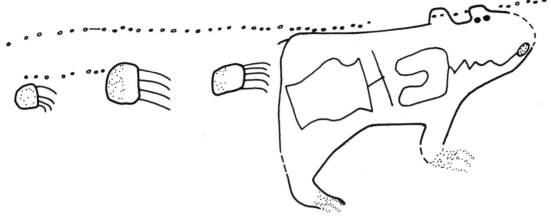

7.20. Bear with trailing bear tracks from the Krause site, southern Montana.

jaws of a bear." The transfer of the bear knife bundle was an elaborate ceremony that included sweating rites and special painted symbols. The owner of the bundle acted like a bear and jumped on the proposed new owner (Ewers 1958:165; Wissler 1912:132–133). The Kiowa had a women's Bear Society in which members "imitated the motions of bears with their hands during dances" (Lowie 1916:849). Among Numic-speaking groups, the Ute believed their ancestors to be bears (Reed 1896:237) and held a 10-day-long Bear Dance directed by a shaman and some helpers every year. In this dance the Ute sought the power of the bear to change winter to spring, to bring fertility and good health, and to ensure successful hunting and gathering (Jorgensen 1964; Lowie 1924:299).

According to Irwin (1996:41), the bear, along with the buffalo, is the most prominent and consistently experienced dream spirit. The bear retreats to its den during the winter and reappears at spring. As an earth power, it is regarded by many Plains people as the animal closest to human beings (Rockwell 1991). The bear rears on its hind legs and gestures in human fashion and is a primary source of a wide variety of medicinal knowledge.

ELK AND DEER Representations of elk and deer alongside shield-bearers and V-shouldered figures are also common. Among the most spectacular are huge outline-pecked animal profiles, such as those found at the Medicine Lodge Creek site. One of the best-known images from this site (Frison 1978:415) almost certainly represents an elk. This massive figure (Figure 7.21), with body pecked in outline form and legs solidly pecked, measures 2.27 m from the tip of its nose to the end of its tail. The image includes backswept antlers, a mouth, an eye that appears to be weeping, a heart line, and genitalia. Four prominent arrows penetrate the animal, in the neck, in the heart/lung area, from the back, and from the rear. Two small pecked human stick figures stand near the head of the animal, and an outline-pecked figure that could be either human or animal hovers over the back. Rectangular-bodied humans and a smaller outline-pecked elk appear to be superimposed over the hind legs. What may be the upper portion of an outline-pecked shield-bearer with a flat headdress touches the arrow that pierces the rump. This arrow is possibly connected to a final unidentified figure. Perhaps because it is so spectacular, this figure has been heavily damaged from chalking and charcoaling for photographic enhancement and the use of latex molds to make a cast. As a result, it is undatable by AMS and CR methods (Table 7.1; Francis et al. 1993:721, 726).

Smaller images of elk or deer are also relatively common at sites where there are shield-bearing warriors or V-shouldered anthropomorphs. Painted examples are found at Pictograph Cave, where one example, executed in black, white, and red, measures 45 cm from its nose to its tail (Figure 7.22). This animal sports tall antlers with inward-turned tines and cloven hooves made as inverted V's. Its black body is broken by a white patch on the rump and a white neck and head that are outlined in black. Beneath the figure there are three spears or arrows with triangular-shaped points aimed at the animal's body. These projectiles appear to be associated with a group of three small human forms standing on a single leg.

Medium-sized incised images of elk or deer are common at Castle Gardens. They likewise exhibit long, branching antlers that both stand up from the head and sweep back over the body, along with cloven hooves depicted by inverted V's. One scene from Castle Gardens (Figure 7.23) includes a similarly depicted elk with a possible vulva-form figure on its rump and what Wellmann (1979:122) interprets as male and female V-shouldered anthropomorphs. He infers female gender for the one figure because of the presence of an extremely broad body possibly representing pregnancy, a dress, and vulva-form design elements. This scene almost certainly has an association with the well-recognized relationship in several Plains tribes between elk and love magic, which gives men magical power over women (Dorsey 1906; Lowie 1918; Wildschut 1975; Wissler 1905, 1912).

BISON   Bison are occasionally rendered as large outline-pecked images similar to the elk at the Medicine Lodge Creek site. A few bison occur at this site, the largest of which is slightly less than 2 m across. Another massive figure of a bison is found north of Greybull, Wyoming (Figure 7.15). Unfortunately, this site is now almost totally destroyed by bullet scars and other defacement.

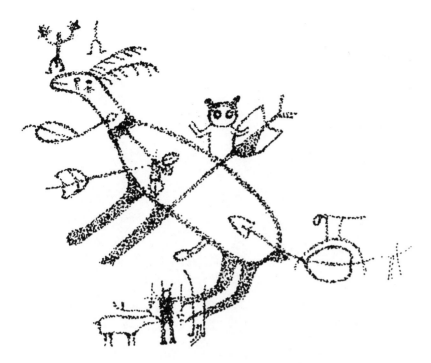

7.21. Outline-pecked elk from the Medicine Lodge Creek site (from Frison 1978:415). This figure is over 2 m long. Unfortunately, because of damage from charcoaling and chalking, it is now undatable with AMS or CR techniques. Original drawing by Mary Helen Hendry.

7.22. Black-and-white-painted elk from Pictograph Cave, Montana. The nose or mouth is painted in red and could represent blood. This figure is only 45 cm long.

7.23. Elk with vulva-forms and associated female figure from the Castle Gardens site. The female has elk teeth on her dress. Photo courtesy of the Smithsonian Institution.

Medium-sized bison images were executed by deep-line and fine-line incising, as well as by solid painting, and are not as common as one might expect. Castle Gardens contains a few incised bison figures, identifiable by double sets of slightly curved horns. Realistic painted images occur in at least one cave in the Pryor Mountains (Conner and Conner 1971) and in Pictograph Cave. Next to the Pictograph Cave bison is an apparent canid. Mulloy thought this painting was exceptionally well made: "Number 39, in particular, showing a wolf at the throat of a buffalo bull, is a most un-usually excellent piece of work, being well proportioned, true to life, and imparting remarkable feeling of motion to the violent action" (1958:124).

TURTLES Turtle images are relatively common at sites where there are also shield-bearing warriors and V-shouldered anthropomorphs (Conner and Conner 1971). They occur both as decorations on shields and as indi-vidual figures. For example, there are several other turtle figures, in addition to the "Great Turtle," at Castle Gardens and two well-known painted figures at Pictograph Cave originally recorded by Mulloy (1958).

The Pictograph Cave turtle (Figure 7.24) has a short pointed head, four legs, and a tail. The design on the turtle's shell is divided by black lines into pie-shaped wedges painted white. This figure, about 15 cm high, was attributed to the Pictograph Cave III stratigraphic unit, thought to date to the Late Prehistoric period, based on the recovery of an incised turtle effigy in Pictograph Cave III deposits and similarities between the two designs.

Because this pictograph has been significantly damaged by recent water seepage through the back wall of Pictograph Cave and will soon be obliterated, it was deemed appropriate to collect a small sample of pigment for dating purposes (Loendorf and Dean 1993). The black pigment was first identified as charcoal by Marvin Rowe and colleagues at Texas A & M University and subsequently dated by AMS ^{14}C methods. Three samples (Table 7.1) have reliable age estimates of 2,300 ± 60 B.P. (TAMU-24YL1.3M152), 2,120 ± 190 B.P. (TAMU-24YL1.3M160), and 2,010 ± 130 B.P. (TAMU-24YL1.3M172). The average of these ages suggests that the figure was manufactured sometime around 2,145 years ago. This turtle is the oldest known painted image from the Northwestern Plains. Its age suggests that similarly painted figures in Pictograph Cave may be of much greater antiquity than the Late Prehistoric and Historic periods.

Mulloy (1958:124) reminds us that turtles are a widespread symbol. They occur as petroglyphs and pictographs throughout western North America and as effigies across the Northern Plains (Figure 7.25). In the early 1970s Conner and Conner (1971:26, 29) questioned the "hunting magic" hypothesis and wondered why hunting and gathering peoples, presumably dependent on big game, would make at least as many images of turtles as they did bison. Cultural symbolism provides one possible explanation. That is, rather than reflect what people eat, paintings and engravings represent culturally important symbols directly related to religious and ideological belief systems. The turtle, a liminal species, can be viewed as a metaphor for travel between the natural and supernatural worlds. The demonstrated antiquity and common usage of this symbol in association with shield-bearing warriors lend strong support to the supernatural power of this animal for many people.

BIRDS   Bird images are commonly found at sites with shield-bearing warriors and V-shouldered anthropomorphs and are made using all the different techniques of incising, painting, and pecking (Figure 7.26). Most bird images are generally 20 to 30 cm in height, but a significant proportion, including those found as the decoration on shields, are smaller. Two birds with outstretched wings in red pigment are placed as decoration on

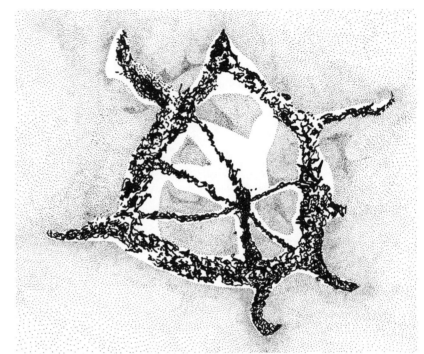

7.24. Artistic rendition of Late Archaic painted turtle from Pictograph Cave, Montana. Three replicate AMS ages indicate this figure was painted in charcoal about 2,100 years ago. Drawing by Linda Olson.

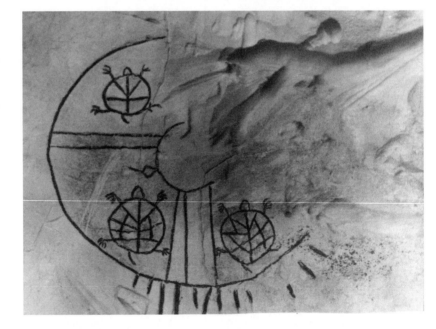

7.25. Shield with turtles from the Castle Gardens site. Photograph by Ted Sowers, courtesy of the American Heritage Center, University of Wyoming.

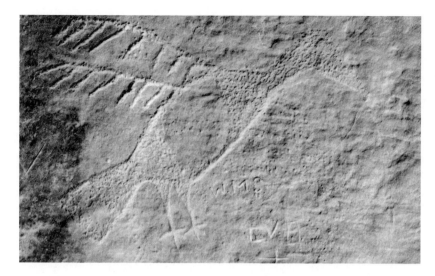

7.26. Bird figure from the Surrell Creek site in the Wind River Mountains.

one of the large shields at the Valley of the Shields site (Loendorf 1990). Two birds with their wings folded are shown on opposing sides of a Castle Gardens style shield (now badly damaged by casting residue) at the Castle Gardens site. These birds, like the ones at the Valley of the Shields, have incised outlines and interiors filled with red pigment. Other isolated figures at Castle Gardens include avian forms as well as typical thunderbird forms (Gebhard et al. 1987a:66–67).

A deeply incised bird with a bulbous head and obvious eyes is found at the Trapper Creek site. This unusual bird image was apparently made by drilling deep holes into the sandstone wall for the eyes. The eyes are so deep they leave a ridge for the beak of the bird, resulting in an owl-like appearance.

Images of birds are commonly associated with visionary experiences (Turpin 1994). They are often used as a metaphor for out-of-body travel and the sensation of flight experienced by individuals during a trance. That they should occur fairly frequently in the painted and incised imagery of the Wind River and Bighorn Basins is not surprising and supports the notion of the visionary and religious nature of this imagery.

Other Human Representations

Although shield-bearing warriors and V-shouldered anthropo-morphs are the most easily recognized human figure types in the Bighorn and Wind River Basins, humans are depicted in dozens of other ways as well. Many figures are simple stick-like renditions of humans with straight bodies, small round heads, and arms and legs that sometimes display hands and feet. Small incised figures with rectangular bodies and crude representations with ovoid-shaped bodies and round heads are also known (Gebhard et al. 1987a). A few appear to be entirely unique, occurring in only one place at one site.

Other human representations occur with sufficient repetition that they likely have some time depth and can be tentatively recognized as specific figure types. They include therianthropic images, solid-painted rectangular-body anthropomorphs, and headdress anthropomorphs.

Therianthropic Images
Several examples of human/animal conflations, including human/bison and human/birds, are known from the Pryor Mountains (Loendorf and Porsche 1985:71). Most distinctive, however, are human/bear representations, which occur at Pictograph Cave and the North Duke site (Loendorf and Porsche 1985:51). Incised images are also known from a site, as yet un-documented, in the Pryors. A few outline-pecked figures with round heads, large eyes, and short "ears" on the top of the head (reminiscent of a teddy bear), such as seen at the Medicine Lodge Creek site (Figure 7.21), may also depict human/bear conflations.

The best example of a "bear dancer" is found at Pictograph Cave (Figure 7.27). This figure is painted in black and white and stands about 40 cm high. It has a rectangular body with a relatively long neck that blends into a round head. The neck has horizontally crossing lines of deco-ration, and the head has eyes with long tear streaks as well as a black streak that is either the mouth or the chin. Its ears are shown as tufts on the top of the head, an important attribute of all the figures in this type. Bear-claw feet give the appearance of bear-claw moccasins. The arms are attached at the shoulders and bent upward with hands and fingers de-picted. The figure holds a bow or bow/lance in one hand and an arrow in the other.

At least two other figures in Pictograph Cave may be similar (Mulloy 1958:130). One is only the head with round eyes that have streak lines radiating beneath them, a mouth with teeth, and tufted ears. This figure, which was also painted in black and white, has a small medallion in the center of its forehead. It is no longer visible on the cave wall. Another figure with a rectangular upper body outline has a round head, round eyes with streaks beneath them, and the telltale tufted ears. This figure, painted as a black outline, is only the torso and head with no other body parts.

As discussed earlier in this chapter, bear ceremonialism, including dances in which the participants dressed in bear-claw feet and decorated

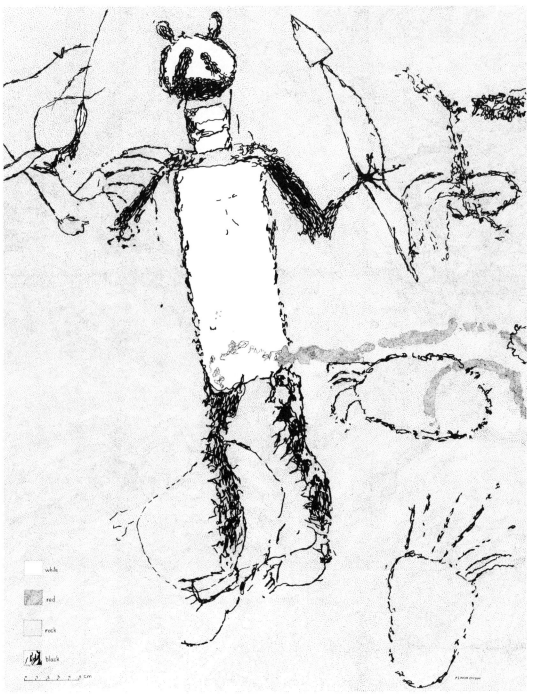

white

red

rock

black

0 1 2.5 5 CM

7.27. Artistic rendition of a bear dancer from Pictograph Cave. Drawing by Linda Olson.

their faces like bears, was important among Plains Indians (Ewers 1967). These ceremonies were performed for three reasons: to honor the bear, to prepare for war, and to heal the sick. The clothing and body decoration of the participants show striking resemblances to the paintings and pictographs. An Assiniboine bear dancer, for example, "shaved the top of his head and rolled some of his hair at each side into a ball resembling a bear's ears. He painted his face red, then made vertical scratches, representing a bear's claw marks, on each side of his face by scraping away some of the paint with his fingernails. He then painted a black circle around each eye and around his mouth" (Ewers 1967:132).

The Crow Indians had a powerful dance, known as the Bear Song Dance, in which the performers prepared their hair, wore bearskin costumes, and imitated the movements of bears (Lowie 1956:267). During the ceremony the *batsira'pe,* or power animal living in the dancer, would come out and the dancer's canine teeth would grow to the size of a bear's. On some occasions red paint would spew from the mouths of the dancers, and they would fall into a deep trance. An incense from bear root was needed to restore them. Therianthropic combinations of humans and bears, as these dancers must have seemed, are replicated by paintings and engravings and highlight the relationships between visionary and religious experience and the imagery found on stone.

Solid-Painted Rectangular-Body Anthropomorphs
This figure type was initially recognized at three Montana sites to the north and east of our study area by Conner and Conner (1971:19) and at Elk Creek Cave in the Pryor Mountains about 25 km north of the Wyoming border (Loendorf 1967, 1974). Additional figures of this type have been recognized in a rockshelter in the Cook's Canyon area on the western flank of the Bighorn Mountains.

The Elk Creek Cave figure is painted in a red pigment and was originally associated with other figures that are now eroded or exfoliated and are no longer identifiable. The remaining human figure has an egg-shaped head on top of a short neck, upraised arms, a phallus, and straight legs that have feet pointing in the same direction, making it appear to be in profile (Figure 7.28). It has been AMS radiocarbon dated (Table 7.1) using the low-temperature oxygen plasma method to an age of 840 ± 50 B.P. (Chaffee, Loendorf et al. 1994).

The similarity between the Elk Creek Cave and the Cook's Canyon figures (Figure 7.29) is striking. The Cook's Canyon figures are painted in a dull red pigment and are about 21 cm in height. All are profile views with short pointed feet oriented to the left; they have bent arms and wear

7.28. Solid, red-painted anthropomorphic figure from Elk Creek Cave in the Pryor Mountains. This figure has been dated by AMS to about 850 years ago.

7.29. Solid, red-painted figures from Cook's Canyon in the southern Bighorn Mountains.

body-length garments and lack headdresses. One of the Cook's Canyon figures holds a box-like object in one hand. Notably, the Cook's Canyon site contains other pictographs executed in the same pigment which apparently represent the same time period. These figures include a human handprint, a row of solid-painted quadrupeds with rectangular bodies and swept-back horns that appear to represent bighorn sheep, a row of outline-painted quadrupeds, and a single animal with a boat-shaped body that is also apparently a bighorn sheep. This group is a rare example of possible sheep images on the eastern side of the Bighorn Basin and represents the largest number of bighorn sheep depicted at a pictograph site in the study area.

Mack (1971:49) conducted test excavations in Cook's Canyon rock-shelter and recovered retouched flake tools, side scrapers, a single corner-notched projectile point, and charred bighorn sheep bone. It is unknown if the sheep bone and the projectile point were associated. These deposits were also not radiocarbon dated. Thus, it is impossible to determine whether the occupation or occupations overlap the date from Elk Creek and are possibly associated with the solid-painted figures.

Headdress Anthropomorphs

A significant type of painted human figures is identified by their distinctive flat headdresses. Figures of this type are found at the Tyrrell and Red Buffalo sites in the Pryor Mountains (Loendorf and Porsche 1985) and at Frozen Leg Cave on the western side of Bighorn Canyon (Loendorf 1994b). They are tied to paintings in the southern Bighorn Mountains by the occurrence of distinctive plant motifs.

The human figures are generally painted in red, yellow, or black and range in height from 30 to 80 cm. The headdresses are either radiating lines from the top or flat bars over the head (Figure 7.30). The flat bar headdresses occasionally have a circle or a circle enclosing a cross on one end and an angular or oblong form on the other. The figures usually display horns beneath the flat bars that sit atop a rounded head, which sometimes has eyes but no mouth. There is considerable variation in the form of the figures. In some the outer lines of the bodies are depicted by straight vertical sides that angle inward at the base and continue downward to form the legs. Others have solid-painted rectangular-shaped bodies and legs that protrude straight down from the base. When arms are depicted, they extend downward. Elbows are shown both bent and straight. Fingers are shown on some figures but not to scale with the rest of the figure and seldom in the correct number.

7.30. Red-painted headdress anthropomorphs at the Tyrrell site in the Pryor Mountains. The headdresses are identical to those used by members of the Crow Tobacco Society. Drawing by Terri Wolfgram.

The flat-headdress figures are associated with other human forms that have large round heads enclosing big round eyes. Some of the eyes have lines radiating from them; others are simple circles. The headgear of these latter figures consists of radiating lines that project upward, giving an antenna-like or rabbit-ear appearance. The bodies of these figures are poorly formed, and frequently only the shoulders are depicted by two downward-oriented side lines.

Bison images or bison tracks and occasionally therianthropic forms occur with the flat-headdress figures. At the Red Buffalo site in the Pryors human/bird/bison conflations are superimposed on a bison. One figure has bird wings for arms and a bison horn on the head. The bison, in turn, has talons for front hooves. As is typical throughout Plains Indian art in all media, star images, made by crossing vertical and horizontal lines, also occur at these sites.

Frozen Leg Cave consists of a series of interconnected limestone caves some 500 m above the bottom of Bighorn Canyon. Two of the three main chambers contain paintings of flat-headdress anthropomorphs and several plants. The plants are represented in two ways: some are painted with straight leaves angled sharply upward at the stem and decreasing in size from bottom to top. Others have horizontal leaves bent downward at the tips.

The latter representations are strikingly similar to icons of the tobacco plant on moccasins and medicine bags of the Crow Tobacco Society (Nabokov 1988). In order to test the possibility that the image could represent a tobacco plant, pollen samples from Frozen Leg Cave, along with samples from other caves not containing paintings, were collected and analyzed by two different laboratories (Loendorf 1994b:100–105). The samples from Frozen Leg Cave contained a far richer variety of pollen than the control samples, and pollen from a variety of medicinal plants was found only in the Frozen Leg Cave samples. They included members of the Campanulaceae (bellflower), Caryophyllaceae (pink), Labiatae (mint), Leguminosae (legume), Onagraceae (evening primrose), and Solanaceae (potato/tomato) families, as well as *Gaur* (gaur), *Phlox* (phlox), and *Nicotiana* (tobacco). Local and wind-transported sources for these plants were also ruled out, strongly indicating that they had been introduced into the cave deposits by humans and that the plant image indeed represents tobacco.

Similar plant images are found in a cavern on Nature Conservancy property in the southern Bighorns. Known locally as Powwow Cavern, or the Amphitheater, this rockshelter measures 62 m front to back and 215 m side to side. At its maximum this large cavern is nearly 50 m in height. Intensive recording of the paintings in the cave is only now underway, but the work of Mack (1971) indicates that pictographs are found along the back wall and are concentrated at one end, where they are partially protected by a large mound of rockfall.

A series of reddish-brown painted figures that resemble a tobacco seed pod is positioned along the back wall (Figure 7.31). Other pictographs in this area include two human figures, solidly painted in red pigment, that have erect rabbit-like ears. Plant forms painted near these figures (Figure 7.32) are much like those from the Montana sites. Two of these plants sit on a table-like form that is enclosed in an arc of parallel dashed lines. Other figures in the rockshelter include a frontal view of a bison and bison tracks, also similar to images in the Montana sites.

Tobacco was and is an extremely important plant among the region's Indian tribes. The Shoshone, Blackfoot, Flathead, Kutenai, and Crow, who formerly had close ties to the Bighorn Basin and nearby regions, all used tobacco for ceremonial purposes. Of these groups, the Crow Indians stand out for their ceremonial association with tobacco (Figure 7.33). The Crow formerly grew two species—*Nicotiania multivalvis* and *Nicotiania quadravalvis*—recognizing the *multivalvis* variety as their sacred tobacco. It is through this tobacco that the various chapters of the Crow Tobacco Society were formed. Stars are an important element of the Crow Sacred

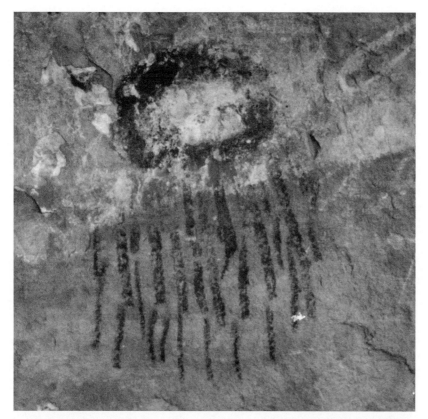

7.31. Red-painted tobacco seed pod from the Amphitheater in the southern Bighorn Mountains.

7.32. Red-painted plant image from the Amphitheater. This image is similar to ones in Frozen Leg Cave, Montana, and to paintings found on ceremonial items of the Crow Tobacco Society.

7.33. Two Crow Indians on their way to a Tobacco Society meeting, ca. 1900. Note the tobacco plant headdress worn by the woman. Photo courtesy of Peter Nabokov.

Tobacco: they gave the sacred tobacco to the Crow and subsequently became the tobacco seeds. The Crow received their first sacred tobacco seeds through a vision that No Intestines had in the Bighorn Mountains on Cloud Peak, known to the Crow as *Awaxaawakussawishe*, or the "Extended Mountain" (McCleary 1997:18). In the vision he was instructed to search for tobacco seeds at the base of the mountain. Looking down for the seeds, he saw "twinkling stars," and an association was made between the stars and the seeds of the Crow sacred tobacco (McCleary 1997:18). The importance of the stars to the Sacred Tobacco Society is reflected in the star images on the headdresses of the anthropomorphs that hold the tobacco plants.

Other Unusual Anthropomorphic Figures
As noted earlier, simple rectangular-bodied anthropomorphs are extremely common throughout the Bighorn and Wind River Basins. They can be incised or outline-painted, and their torsos rarely show a decoration. Two unusual examples of rectangular-bodied human figures occur in the Red Canyon area in the southern Wind River Basin: they have herringbone designs on their chests and deserve special mention because of their possible connection to Plains Indian mythology. Anatomical details of these figures are also quite realistic, suggesting that the artist was attempting to show them as "x-rayed" examples of humans.

7.34. Human image thought to represent one of the Crow/Hidatsa Twin Heroes, Spring Boy, from the Red Canyon area, Wind River Basin. Note the stars at the base of the figure.

One of these figures (Figure 7.34) was made by incising and abrading its form into the sandstone wall; it sports upraised arms with hands and fingers, and a bulbous head that has eyes and a mouth with what appear to be teeth set atop its shoulders. The ears are shown as half-circles attached to the sides of the head. The herringbone pattern shows 16 ribs on each side beneath the clavicle and a bulbous area at the bottom of the ribs which may be its stomach. The legs and feet are shown in realistic fashion, as are testicles and a penis. This figure is set within and on top of more than a dozen deeply incised stars, represented as crossed vertical and horizontal lines.

A second figure displays many of the same attributes except that it is not among a group of stars. The outline and many interior attributes are made by incising. It has a more realistic face with eyes, mouth, and two holes for nostrils. The navel was rendered by drilling a hole into the sandstone. The ears are shown as semicircles attached to the head, and they have earrings dangling from them. Hair or head decoration is shown as a series of vertical lines protruding upward. The figure, which appears to be phallic, has incised feet that look as much like bear claws as feet. The herringbone pattern down its chest, 10 ribs to a side, meets at an area that looks like a sternum.

These figures bear an uncanny resemblance to the human representation on the shield of Arapoosh, or Rotten Belly, a well-known Mountain Crow chief in the 1830s (Schuster 1987:37). The human figure on Rotten Belly's shield exhibits a similar herringbone design on the chest, along with a ferocious face showing a mouth full of teeth and round ears. Based on the recent discovery of a Hidatsa ledger book with pictures of the twin heroes Spring Boy (or "Thrown into the Spring") and Lodge Boy (or "Thrown Behind the Tipi Lining"), specifically identified by the original artist, Cowdrey (1995) identifies the human figure on Rotten Belly's shield as Spring Boy. Additional likenesses of both twin heroes occur on other Crow shields (Cowdrey 1995).

Many of the exploits of these heroes take place among the stars. In his pioneering research McCleary (1997:49–62) describes the Crow constellation known as the Hand Star and its origin as related to the twin heroes. The Hand Star, recognized as such by several Plains tribes, is "part of the Euro-American constellation Orion. The belt of Orion is seen as the wrist, his sword as the thumb, and the stars Cursa, Rigel, and SAO 132067 as the finger tips" (McCleary 1997:49). In one narrative Thrown into the Spring saves his brother by cutting off the hand of Long Arm, which is placed in the sky by the moon (Lowie 1918:93; McCleary 1997). In other versions Thrown into the Spring is said to be the Evening Star and Thrown Behind the Tipi Lining is the last star in the Dipper (Lowie 1918:85). There are several variants of this story, but the twin heroes always travel to the heavens, and the severed hand of the antagonist becomes the Hand Star constellation.

We believe the association of stars with figures bearing a striking resemblance to the Crow twin heroes in the Red Canyon area is significant. This combination is not repeated at other sites in the Bighorn and Wind River Basins and provides strong evidence to connect these figures with the

Crow. The positions of all the stars associated with the human figures at Red Canyon have not yet been thoroughly documented. Additional recording and research might permit the identification of specific Crow constellations in the star arrangements.

Inanimate and Abstract Designs

Images of inanimate objects are common throughout the region. Numerous tipi images are found throughout the Bighorn and Wind River Basins and surrounding areas, for example. Tipi depictions are deeply incised, finely incised, or painted and are represented by various designs and motifs: two crossed poles, individual poles, skin coverings, stakes, doorways, and the lacing that fastens the edges of the lodge covering together (Conner and Conner 1971:23).

Incised tipis (Figure 7.35) are decidedly more common than painted examples and occur along the eastern edge of the Bighorn Basin, at Castle Gardens (Gebhard et al. 1987a:73), and in the Red Canyon area at the southern margin of the Wind River Basin. They are also found to the southwest of the study area at several sites in the Green River Basin, such as the Calpet Rockshelter (Francis et al. 1987) and at Names Hill on the Green River. The Names Hill example is particularly ornate (Figure 7.36). This small tipi, 25 cm tall, has an incised outline with the smoke flaps open to show the upper ends of seven poles poking out. The view is apparently from the back or side because the artist has shown the cover partially open along one side. The back cover is decorated with a vertical zigzag line down its left side and a circle on its right side. A smaller set of two concentric circles is attached to the zigzag line at about midpoint in the tipi, and short horizontal fringe lines decorate the right incised line. The tipi also has a horizontal line that sets off the upper fourth of the lodge, suggesting a painted lodge cover. A horse and other indistinct figures occur nearby. Unfortunately, Euro-Americans traveling the Oregon Trail during the middle of the nineteenth century carved their names and initials across the entire scene.

Painted tipis range from 5 to 50 cm in height and are frequently found in groups of two or three. Pictograph Cave has a single example with the conical walls outlined in black pigment and the smoke flap in solid black. A bright yellow-orange example at the Provinse Pictograph site in the Weatherman Draw area of Montana is solidly painted with the smoke flap shown open (see Davis 1983 for a color illustration). Near the tipi are painted outlines of shields. Both Mulloy (1958:125) and Conner and Conner (1971:23) conclude that painted tipis are relatively more recent,

7.35. Deeply incised panel from the Red Canyon site at the southwestern margin of the Wind River Basin.

7.36. Finely incised tipi from Names Hill, Wyoming. Note the design details, which suggest this was a painted tipi.

based on the frequent depiction of tipis in historic Plains Indian art, the lack of erosion, and the brightness of the paint in many examples.

Perhaps the most elaborate set of painted tipis occurs in the southern Bighorn Basin at the Mahogany Buttes site. Many of the images at this site clearly date to the Historic period, but the tipis may be older because they are more faded than the horses and guns. Two tipis, painted in red, bluish-black, and white, occur under an alcove created by the spalling of a large chunk of Chugwater sandstone from the cliff face. One tipi was made by outlining its conical shape in red. This figure, standing about 45 cm tall, has three bands around its cover that are outlined in red stripes. The lower and upper bands are filled in with a bluish-black pigment, and the middle band has a dot pattern in the same color. The other tipi is smaller and more faded. It appears to have been outlined in white, and its cover has black bands interlayered with red and white pigment.

Lodge covers among Plains Indians were painted with several repetitive arrangements. Ewers (1978:51) places them in four categories: solid-color; three horizontal bands or zones with the narrow top and bottom zones in a dark color and the lighter central area as the background for geometric or life forms; a series of parallel, horizontal stripes in varying colors; and a vertical line dividing the tipi in half with one half solidly painted and the other decorated with life scenes. The second category was used by both the Blackfoot and Kiowa. The few painted tipi covers used by the Crow during the early 1900s included one decorated with a bird set on a lighter background between two painted bands or zones (Lowie 1922:317–319). Ewers (1978:8) points out that Kiowa painted tipis constituted only about 20 percent of the total number in a camp and that the prominent ones were always owned by chiefs, leaders of war parties, or medicine men. Thus, the painted tipis at Mahogany Buttes are almost certainly representations of tipis belonging to important individuals.

Unidentifiable abstract designs are also ubiquitous throughout the Bighorn and Wind River Basins. Many may be representations of entoptic phenomena perceived during altered states of consciousness. These figures are generally incised and are directly associated with shield-bearing warriors, V-shouldered anthropomorphs, and the other human figure types defined for the region, as illustrated by the star designs discussed earlier. None of these figures has yet been directly dated. By virtue of their association with dated anthropomorphic figures, they were assuredly manufactured throughout the Late Prehistoric, Protohistoric, and Historic periods.

Abstract figures also sometimes comprise the dominant design elements on individual panels, forming a bewildering array of seemingly randomly oriented lines, slashes, circles, squares, triangles, and other geometric

7.37. Deeply incised chevrons from the Trapper Canyon site in the Bighorn Mountains. These figures resemble plant images.

forms, with complex patterns of superimposition. One common figure is a series of V or chevron designs bisected by a vertical line (Figure 7.37). These figures are not readily interpretable. They are similar to the herringbone breastplate design seen on some human figures. They also resemble plant images, and some renditions give the appearance of a series of interconnected bird tracks.

One group of abstract figures may be utilitarian and related to tool manufacture and sharpening (Feyhl 1980). Tool grooves, as they are known, consist of elliptical or banana-shaped grooves and may have been produced by rubbing an implement, such as bone or antler, on a sandstone rock face. They occur at many sites in the Bighorn and Pryor Mountains. Perhaps the best example of possible tool grooves in the Bighorn Basin is the Trapper Creek site, where hundreds of grooves and lines have been engraved under a long, low sandstone overhang. Some of them form the familiar geometric shapes of entoptic phenomena. Others are what Conner (1988:58) has called helter-skelter lines that go every which way. Mixed among these lines one finds V-necked human figures and animals that appear to be deer or other cervids. It is extremely difficult to determine which of these lines represent tool manufacture and which are parts of petroglyph designs. It is possible that the individuals using the sandstone wall for shaping tools oriented the grooves into patterns as they worked.

Tool grooves should not be confused with what are identified as tally marks or counter lines. Tally marks are short vertical lines arranged in a series, usually associated with other human and animal figures. They have often been interpreted as representing some sort of enumeration: the number of days marking an event or the number of horses stolen in a raid. This interpretation is based on analogous examples in historic Plains Indian art (Conner and Conner 1971:28; Wellmann 1979:127). Stuart Conner was told by George Bull Tail, a member of the Crow Nation, that tally marks were made "by the Little People to keep track of numbers or something" (Conner and Conner 1971:34).

Historic Period Imagery

Horses reached the Wind River and Bighorn Basins sometime between A.D. 1700 and 1740. According to Shimkin (1986b:517), few horses were noted among the Shoshone in the 1720s, but by the 1740s they were using horse-mounted warriors in full-scale attacks on villages. These horses were obtained from the Spanish in New Mexico after the Great Pueblo Revolt of 1680, and most were traded into southern Wyoming by Utes or Comanches. In particular, the Comanche, who separated from the Wyoming Shoshone after they obtained horses, were a constant source of horses for their kinsmen. The Shoshone in turn traded horses to the Crow and other Northern Plains tribes (Secoy 1953:33–38; Shimkin 1986b:517).

The Spanish were unable to keep horses away from the Indians, but they tightly restricted access to firearms, powder, and bullets. As a result, there was a century or so when horses were in general use by Native Americans in the Wind River and Bighorn Basins but guns were nonexistent or in extremely short supply. In contrast, the French, primarily in Canada, had little compunction regarding the distribution of firearms and initially armed the Cree and other tribes in the northern Great Lakes region. In turn, these tribes traded their guns to the Gros Ventre and the Blackfoot to the west. Thus, by 1800 these tribes enjoyed a tremendous imbalance of power in their favor because they had both the horse and the gun (Secoy 1953:51–52). It was during this time that these tribes, particularly the Blackfoot, started raiding on a regular basis, beginning from their homeland near the Canadian border and extending southward into the Wind River and Bighorn Basins.

The introduction of the horse and the gun, social changes engendered by participation in the capitalist economic system (Klein 1980), and the ravaging effects of disease and conquest wreaked havoc on all Native American cultures, resulting in vast population reductions if not elimination of some groups. These changes are reflected in the petroglyphs and pictographs of the region. Whereas the imagery of the Late Prehistoric period is clearly passive and has unquestionable associations with vision quests, altered states of consciousness, and spiritual beliefs—what Keyser (1987) has termed the "Ceremonial" style—images of the Historic period are active and in many cases appear to depict specific events. Scenes include combat, horse raiding, sexual exploits, treaty signings, and encounters with white men. Keyser (1977, 1987, 1996) has termed such images "biographical art," and by using keys for the interpretation of ledger drawings (Peterson 1971), he explains how these panels can be understood as rudimentary "picture-writing" with "story-lines" (Keyser 1987:44).

Just as the content of Historic period art changes, so does the manner in which images are depicted. Keyser (1987) outlines an evolutionary sequence from the Late Prehistoric period through the late nineteenth century in which scenes tend to be increasingly representational, with humans, animals, and associated objects drawn in a great detail, often with a high degree of realism. Native artists began to use Euro-American stylistic conventions, resulting in images that have a more "standard" appearance in petroglyphs, pictographs, robe art, and ledgers.

Ewers (1957b, 1968) has pointed out that native artists were strongly influenced by Euro-American artists such as Bodmer and Catlin and were exposed to Euro-American views of writing and art in boarding schools. Scenes on tipi covers and hides were commissioned by successful Indians to commemorate exploits and raids. Ledger drawings, accompanied by notes explaining what the scenes represented, were solicited and purchased by Euro-American art patrons, teachers, and others interested in native cultures, thus starting the modern Native American art tradition.

These changes are reflected in the Protohistoric and Historic period imagery of the Bighorn and Wind River Basins, which was executed using both fine-line incising and painting techniques. Change is most apparent in the depictions of horses, with and without riders. Native Americans did not know what horses were when first exposed to them during the early eighteenth century. The Crow, for example, thought the horse was a "strange animal that stood as high as an elk but looked very different" (Medicine Crow 1992:100), and the Blackfoot referred to them as "big dogs" (Ewers 1955:19). The role of the horse in Native American cultures was clearly much different from that of many other animals. Few equines are shown pierced by arrows or spears (Conner 1984:124), for example, a radical departure from the Late Prehistoric illustrations of elk, bison, and other animals.

Early horses are nondescript quadrupedal creatures with long bodies, necks, and heads, regardless of whether they are painted or incised. This awkwardness and unfamiliarity, as well as the difficulty of illustrating a rider's shield (Conner and Conner 1971:20), are evident in the few examples of mounted shield-bearing warriors known from Montana, in which the riders are depicted standing on top of the horses rather than astride them.

One occurrence of mounted shield-bearing warriors is known from the Bighorn Basin. This site, which is located in the lower Military Creek vicinity and has not been completely documented, contains incised, pedestrian shield-bearing warriors, as indicated by the large size of the shield, and one group of three mounted shield-bearing warriors (Figure 7.38). The humans are represented as stick figures showing through the shield, essentially a frontal view, set atop crude horses. The horses are shown in profile and have ovoid or rectangular bodies with straight lines for heads and blank areas for necks. The awkwardness results from the combination of a frontal-view human and a profile-view animal.

Both painted and incised horses and riders are depicted in a more representational manner at other sites in the Wind River and Bighorn Basins, as illustrated by a painting from the Mahogany Buttes area in the southern Bighorn Basin (Figure 7.39). Executed in white, this horse has a long arched neck, a small head, and a long lean body. It legs are shown in perspective with muscular thighs but in a manner that also imparts a sense of motion. The rider is shown in perspective as well and clearly sits astride rather than on top of the horse.

Exceptionally realistic examples of fine-line incised horses in action scenes occur at the Joliet site (Keyser 1996). The horses are shown in perspective with arching necks and small heads. Bridles, headstall decorations, and reins are illustrated, as well as a saddle, cinch, and stirrups. Two horses appear to be branded; one appears to be wounded. Details of the tails are shown, and the hooves are clearly depicted. The humans are also realistic, with detailed clothing and hair and holding quirts and weapons.

The biographical element of Historic period imagery in the Wind River and Bighorn Basins is undeniable. Nevertheless, some Historic images may also be associated with altered states of consciousness. An unusual incised horse in the Red Canyon area, for example, has a rectangular body with a series of three vertical bird tracks above and pointing toward the horse's back (Figure 7.40), perhaps suggesting mystical qualities for this animal.

Illustrations of Historic period weaponry are less common than those of horses. Perhaps the best known are the guns painted in red at Pictograph Cave. This row of seven guns, barrels pointed upward with puffs of smoke, are almost certainly examples of flintlocks, the initial and most widely used firearm among Indians on the Northwestern Plains. The examples in

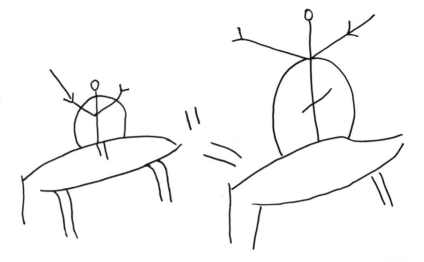

7.38. Sketch of finely incised, mounted shield-bearing warriors from the Military Creek area in the Bighorn Mountains.

7.39. White-painted horse and rider from the Mahogany Buttes area south of Tensleep. White-painted finger dots and a horizontal linear figure hover above the rider.

7.40. Incised rectangular horse from the Red Canyon area in the southwestern extreme of the Wind River Basin.

Pictograph Cave are nearly 50 cm in height, and the weapons are superimposed on several other figures in the panel.

THE INCISED AND painted figures found throughout the Bighorn and Wind River Basins constitute a tradition of imagery that was made and used by a variety of cultural groups, most likely of general Great Plains affiliation. A wide range of ethnographic data clearly associates most of this imagery with religious practices and the visionary experience. Although the vast majority of available chronometric ages fall into the Late Prehistoric period, a much greater antiquity is hinted at by the AMS-dated painted turtle at Pictograph Cave, which has a Late Archaic age. The skewed age distribution may be a factor of differential preservation, that is, of the fragility of paint and the exposure and softness of the surfaces on which images were made, rather than a true indicator of the antiquity and intensity of petroglyph and pictograph manufacture through time. At the same time, the incised and painted images of the region provide a positive link to the Historic period and the irrevocable changes imposed on Native American cultures by the intrusion of Euro-Americans.

The incised and painted figures of the eastern Bighorn and Wind River Basins present a stark contrast to the Dinwoody and en toto pecked figures found throughout the western portion of the area. The differences include temporal distributions, general site location attributes, and the relationships of sites to other archaeological remains. We explore these contrasts in the following chapter to offer some new interpretations of the region's prehistory.

EIGHT

Contrasting Pictures and New Views of the Past

WHEN JUXTAPOSED, THE PETROGLYPHS AND PICTOGRAPHS from the western and eastern sides of the Bighorn and Wind River Basins offer new insights into the area's prehistory. It is apparent that the Dinwoody tradition and the incised and painted classes share little in the way of descriptive figure types or symbols. The elaborate, surreal Dinwoody anthropomorphic images stand in stark contrast to the relatively simple shield-bearing warriors and V-shouldered and rectangular-bodied human figures rendered by painting and incising. Among Dinwoody, especially the more recent Late Prehistoric panels, human images overshadow zoomorphic figures. Yet at sites such as Medicine Lodge Creek small, possibly subservient human figures stand next to animals several meters tall. Images of the same general species of animals occur throughout the Bighorn and Wind River Basins, but medium-sized artiodactyls and canids are common characters on Dinwoody panels whereas elk, bear, and bison, along with paws and tracks, more frequently appear among the incised and painted classes. These differences are easily recognizable by the modern observer, and they suggest that different religious systems were in operation for much of the prehistory of the Bighorn and Wind River Basins.

Chronological Comparisons

One of the major goals of the research in the Bighorn and Wind River Basins has been to collect chronological data using a variety of techniques. The petroglyphs and pictographs of these basins must be considered among the best-dated in the world. All told, 53 figures at 17 sites now have chronometric age estimates of some type.

These studies have yielded some surprising and complex results. First, of course, are the three Paleoindian ages from panel 35 at the Legend Rock site. Though we specifically sampled this panel because of the heavy varnish development and the "old" appearance of the figures, we had expected Early Archaic ages at the oldest. We were quite surprised that both the AMS ages and varnish microlaminations point to Paleoindian ages for three of the sampled figures. Given the uncertain effects of weathering rind organics (WROS) on AMS ages, we view these ages with caution. Nevertheless, we emphasize that the more recent AMS ages are consistent with other chronological data, that the CR data provide a firm relative sequence that can be tied to other chronological information, and that the scheme of inferred Archaic, Late Prehistoric, and Protohistoric ages for the Dinwoody tradition and incised and painted descriptive figure types is generally accurate (Figure 8.1).

The second unexpected finding was the degree of overlap of chronometric ages among all different types of images. Based on our early excavations at the Legend Rock and Petroglyph Canyon sites and unschooled observations of differences in varnish development between these localities, we originally expected to find a fairly simple chronological sequence that included, from oldest to youngest, Dinwoody figures replaced by en toto pecked figures, replaced by outline-pecked shield-bearing warriors and V-shouldered figures, replaced by finely incised Historic period images (Francis et al. 1993:715, 731). The results of the dating studies instead suggest a complex pattern of concurrent manufacture of all different kinds of images and figure types in the Bighorn and Wind River Basins for extensive periods of prehistory.

The available dates suggest that pecked figures not readily classifiable within the Dinwoody tradition are the most ancient, with ages possibly extending to Paleoindian times. The roots of the Dinwoody tradition are identifiable in the Early Archaic period, perhaps as long as 6,800 years ago, in the manufacture of fairly elaborate zoomorphic figures. The Dinwoody tradition comprises several zoomorphic and anthropomorphic figure types, including small, solidly pecked human and animal images originally termed "en toto pecked." The tradition reaches its full-blown expression with the manufacture of the elaborate interior-lined anthropomorphic images during the Late Archaic and Late Prehistoric periods and continues through the Protohistoric and into the Historic period. Ethnographic evidence suggests that Dinwoody tradition figures were still being made as recently as 100 years ago.

Far fewer ages are available for incised and painted imagery; almost all current data suggest that the majority of these figures are less than 1,000

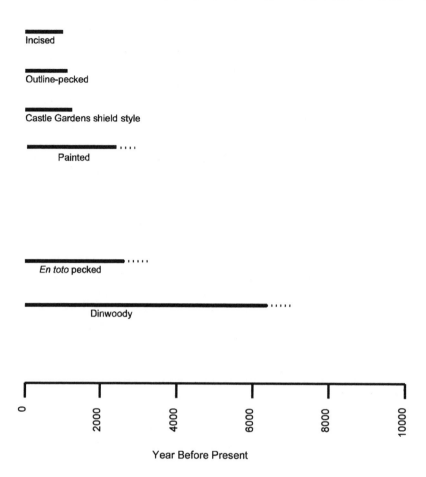

8.1. Chronology of petroglyph and pictograph traditions and classes in the Bighorn and Wind River Basins.

Incised

Outline-pecked

Castle Gardens shield style

Painted

En toto pecked

Dinwoody

Year Before Present

years old. Archaeological evidence from the Valley of the Shields site indicates manufacture of the distinctive Castle Gardens shield style by about 900 years ago. Castle Gardens–style shields and other large polychrome shield-bearing warriors, which may be closely related to the Castle Gardens shield style, appear to be slightly older than smaller, monochrome shield-bearing warriors. The relatively rare, oversized images of outline-pecked animals appear to be less than 1,000 years old, and one solid red-painted figure also has an age of less than 1,000 years. Continuity of manufacture into the Historic period for all these general classes is clearly indicated by the co-occurrence of Historic period items with shield-bearing warriors and V-shouldered figure types, which crosscut all the manufacturing techniques. Simple, V-shouldered, and rectangular-bodied human figures appear to increase in frequency, compared with shield-bearing warriors, during the Historic period.

The three replicate AMS ages from the black-painted turtle at Pictograph Cave, which average slightly older than 2,000 years, hint at a much greater antiquity for painted imagery. Paintings and incised engravings in the Bighorn Basin often occur on fairly soft, unvarnished sandstones that are subject to exfoliation, and they appear to be much less durable than many pecked engravings. Thus, the apparent increased frequency of incised and painted figures during the last 1,000 years may be due in part to differential preservation.

This is a much more complex picture than the simple developmental sequence we originally envisioned. It is clear that Dinwoody and a variety of incised and painted shield-bearing warriors and V-shouldered figures and associated imagery were concurrently manufactured for at least the last 1,000 years, and possibly the last 2,000 years, in the Bighorn and Wind River Basins. This conclusion does not fit the traditional models of the culture history of these basins, which emphasize a very late Late Prehistoric entry into the area by the Shoshone from the Great Basin and several different groups from the Great Plains.

The Dinwoody tradition, which is unquestionably related to the Great Basin culture area and for which there is documented usage by Shoshonean groups, has a much greater antiquity than the postulated Shoshonean entry of just a few hundred years ago. In fact, the Dinwoody tradition points toward long-term occupation of the area by ancestors of the modern Shoshone since at least Early Archaic times, as hypothesized by Husted (1969; Husted and Edgar n.d). Our findings challenge the model of the Numic expansion (Bettinger and Baumhoff 1982, 1983; Young and Bettinger 1992) out of southeastern California beginning less than 1,000 years ago and the replacement of non-Numic peoples in the Great Basin and western Wyoming, a model that has dominated reconstructions of Great Basin and western Wyoming prehistory. The long duration of the Dinwoody tradition is entirely consistent with the archaeological record of northwestern Wyoming, which reflects continuity in cultural adaptation (Husted and Edgar n.d.).

The association of painted and incised imagery with numerous Great Plains groups is also well documented. Although the majority of ages reflect a "sudden" appearance of new figure types affiliated with Great Plains cultural traditions sometime around 1,000 years ago, the Pictograph Cave dates suggest much more ancient roots. Taken as a whole, the chronological evidence indicates that concurrent traditions, affiliated with both Great Basin and Great Plains cultural and religious systems, coexisted in the Bighorn and Wind River Basins for at least the last 1,000 and perhaps 2,000 years.

Spatial Distributions and Boundaries

Clear differences in the spatial distributions of the Dinwoody tradition and incised/painted imagery are also strikingly apparent in the Bighorn and Wind River Basins. These contrasts are evident on two levels: the occurrence of major classes within individual sites and the occurrence of sites within the region.

First, incised/painted figures rarely occur at the same site as en toto pecked and Dinwoody imagery. Shield-bearing warriors and associated figures occur with en toto pecked at fewer than five sites and are almost never found on the same panels or within the same sites as Dinwoody petroglyphs. We are aware of only one panel at the Legend Rock site where a finely incised V-neck figure has been superimposed between two Dinwoody pecked anthropomorphs. Furthermore, the opposite relationship also holds. Elaborate Dinwoody anthropomorphic figures do not occur at sites containing shield-bearing warriors, V-neck figures, and other types of incised or painted images. Very rarely, a few en toto pecked figures can be found with shield-bearing warriors and the like. For example, there are two or three en toto pecked figures among the hundreds of other images at the Medicine Lodge Creek site. The predominance of one class of images at any given site permits classification of the site as a whole, however.

Figure 8.2 illustrates the disparity in spatial distribution of sites according to general class. Incised and painted sites occur in the same general area as pecked images at both the northern and southern extremes of the Bighorn and Wind River Basins, but pecked imagery generally predominates on the west side of the Wind/Bighorn River in both basins. Furthermore, pecked figures are not extremely common south of the Wind River Basin and extend into Montana only slightly north of the Wyoming/Montana state line, occurring along the southern front of the Pryor Mountains (see Loendorf and Porsche 1985).

West of the Wind/Bighorn River the elaborate Dinwoody anthropomorphic figure types have a much more restricted spatial distribution than en toto pecked human figures. Gebhard (1969) first documented the spatial distribution of Dinwoody images along the creek valleys north and south of Dinwoody Canyon in the Wind River Mountains. Numerous sites are also found downstream along the Wind River and its tributaries to Boysen Reservoir (Stewart 1989; Tipps and Schroedl 1985; Wheeler 1957). After the Wind River turns north and emerges through Wind River Canyon as the Bighorn River, Dinwoody anthropomorphs occur in the southern Bighorn Basin along several tributaries of the Bighorn River, all of which

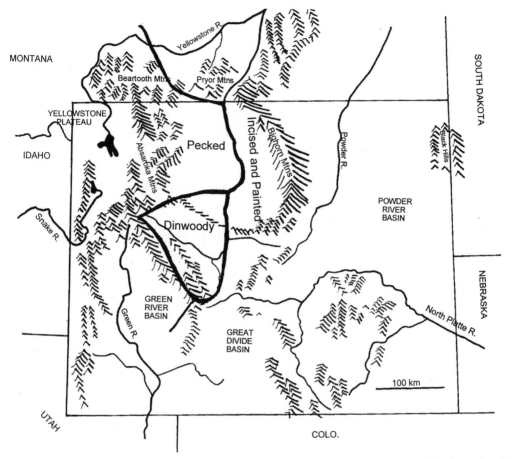

8.2. General spatial distributions of petroglyph and pictograph traditions and classes in the Bighorn and Wind River Basins.

drain the eastern side of the Absaroka Mountains and flow into the Bighorn River from the west (Gebhard 1969). Dinwoody anthropomorphs are extremely rare east of the Bighorn River and quite rare north of Gooseberry Creek. This circumscribed area corresponds to the valley system of the Wind River and the western portion of the upper Bighorn River (Gebhard 1969:20). It can be viewed as a core area of the classic Dinwoody anthropomorphic figure types, surrounded by sites containing smaller and simpler en toto pecked human and animal figures.

In contrast, shield-bearing warriors and associated incised and painted sites occur east of the Bighorn River and Boysen Reservoir, with numerous sites concentrated along north-flowing tributaries of the Clark's Fork of the Yellowstone and the Yellowstone River (Loendorf and Porsche 1985).

Within the Bighorn Basin many of the documented sites occur at the mouths of canyons along streams that drain the west slope of the Bighorn Mountains and flow east into the Bighorn River. Incised/painted imagery is also common on the east slope of the Bighorn Mountains and in the eastern portion of the Wind River Basin and has a broad north-south distribution extending beyond the study area.

These disparities in the distribution of pecked versus incised/painted imagery cannot be explained by natural factors alone. Rock surfaces east of the Bighorn River are plentiful and are just as well suited for the manufacture of pecked as incised or painted figures. The disparate spatial distributions suggest a distinct boundary between Great Plains versus Great Basin religious systems in the Wind River and Bighorn Basins. When combined with the chronological data, this boundary is most apparent during the Late Prehistoric period, but it may well extend into the Archaic. This evidence again diverges from models of the area's prehistory that emphasize the recent entry of Shoshonean people.

Relationships with Other Archaeological Materials
As noted in Chapter 2, the eastern and western sides of the Bighorn Basin have very different bedrock geology. The Bighorn and Wind River Mountains are Laramide uplifts with massive exposures of Paleozoic and Mesozoic rocks whereas the Absarokas on the west side of the Bighorn Basin are formed by Tertiary volcanic rocks. These geological differences have direct implications for the types of siliceous toolstone available to and used by the prehistoric people of the area.

High-quality chipped-stone raw materials, which were extensively exploited by prehistoric people for thousands of years, occur in several of the Paleozoic and Mesozoic formations on the flanks of the Bighorns (Francis 1983). Best known are distinctive cherts in the Mississippian Madison and Permian Phosphoria formations and high-quality orthoquartzites and cherts from the Jurassic Morrison formation. These materials do not occur on the west side of the basin, owing to the volcanic activity that buried older rocks. Here raw materials consist of a variety of cherts, quartzites, and igneous materials from the volcanic deposits, many of which have been redeposited as gravels along drainages by Pleistocene glaciation.

Two suites of nonlocal or exotic lithic raw materials are also fairly common in the Bighorn Basin. The first includes volcanic glasses derived from the Yellowstone Plateau, the southwestern Absarokas, and the Tetons. There are several known sources: Obsidian Cliff in Yellowstone Park, the

Fish Creek area in the Tetons (Kunselman 1994), Bear Gulch on the Targhee National Forest, and Malad in southeastern Idaho (Cannon and Hughes 1993; Kunselman 1994; Smith 1999; Wright and Chaya 1985). A second suite of nonlocal materials is derived from the Powder River Basin east of the study area. These materials include porcellanite, or clinker, and nonvolcanic glass (Fredlund 1976), which occur in the Paleocene Fort Union formation and were formed as a result of burning coal seams.

Francis and Larson (1995) examined the distribution of these different raw materials from a sample of archaeological sites across the Bighorn Basin. In general, they found that the inhabitants of the Bighorn Basin used raw materials that were immediately available. Surface sites on the east side of the Bighorn River contain raw materials from the eastern Paleozoic (Madison and Phosphoria) and Mesozoic (Morrison) materials, with small quantities of local cobble sources (Figure 8.3). Obsidian from northwest Wyoming and porcellanite and nonvolcanic glass comprise the very small amounts of nonlocal raw materials. Sites on the west side of the river are dominated by local cobble quartzites and cherts (Eckles 1990; Francis 1990; Reiss 1987), with only very small quantities of eastern Bighorn Basin raw materials. Thus, raw materials from the east side of the Bighorn Basin were not transported in any significant quantities to the west side and vice versa.

Francis and Larson (1995) noted a similar pattern for excavated assemblages in the Bighorn Basin. Prehistoric people on both sides of the river primarily used raw materials that were close at hand. On the west side of the river, obsidian is the only nonlocal material; on the east side of the river, nonlocal materials include obsidian and Powder River Basin materials. As indicated by excavated assemblages from the Legend Rock site (Walker and Francis 1989) and the Grass Creek house pit site (Reiss 1991) on the west side of the river and from the Laddie Creek site (Larson 1990) on the east side, this same pattern may extend to the Middle Archaic and possibly the Early Archaic.

The distribution of raw materials from the west side of the river coincides with en toto pecked and Dinwoody tradition figures, and the distribution of raw materials from the east side of the river coincides with incised/painted images. The implication is that religious and ideological boundaries may coincide with settlement system boundaries and that concurrent systems have been in place since Archaic times. These findings provide substantial support for Conkey's (1984) suggestion that the distribution of petroglyphs and pictographs reflects the social geography of the past.

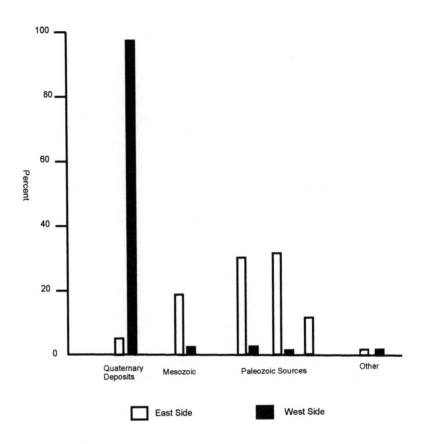

8.3. Comparison of lithic raw materials from surface collections across the Bighorn Basin.

Patterns of Site Use

The spatial distributions of Dinwoody tradition and the incised/painted classes are clearly very different. More subtle differences also occur with respect to site locational attributes and association with other archaeological remains.

At present the Dinwoody tradition is not known to occur in direct association with major habitation or residential sites. Certainly, other types of archaeological sites can be found in the same general area as Dinwoody sites, but our investigations indicate that people were not necessarily living and making Dinwoody imagery in the same places. This conclusion is clearly demonstrated by the 1988 archaeological investigations at the Legend Rock site (Walker and Francis 1989), which included documentation of the imagery and archaeological testing along the terraces of Cottonwood Creek and colluvial deposits along the cliff face before proposed site development. From one perspective, the results of the excavation of seven test units and six backhoe trenches were "disappointing in that no major, extensive prehistoric cultural occupations were located, either near the cliff or in the terrace deposits" (Walker and Francis 1989:279). Instead, only a small number of isolated activity areas containing a hearth, a few pieces of chipped stone, and limited faunal remains were found along the creek, despite the occurrence of over 4 m of alluvium and conditions conducive to preservation. Similarly, the excavation at the base of the partially buried Dinwoody figure yielded datable remains in the form of charcoal but relatively few artifacts.

A similar pattern may also obtain for Dinwoody sites in the Boysen Reservoir area and at Ring Lake Ranch. Numerous occupation sites were documented throughout what is now Boysen Reservoir, and test excavations were conducted at at least two Dinwoody sites (Walker 1994b; Wheeler 1957). These revealed a few burned areas or perhaps the remains of a hearth at the base of a few panels but no extensive occupation debris. Up the Wind River from Boysen Reservoir at Ring Lake Ranch, numerous lithic scatters and stone circle sites occur around the glacial lakes and in the same valley as Dinwoody panels (Francis 1980; Swenson and Chapman 1992), but they are not directly associated with the Dinwoody imagery.

This is not to say that artifactual remains do not occur in direct association with Dinwoody imagery. On the contrary, projectile points, bifaces, ground stone, and debitage were found at several sites in the Boysen Reservoir area by the original investigators (see Walker 1994b for a summary). As part of a recent recording project Loendorf located several projectile points on the surface close to one panel immediately above Ring Lake. Local residents also reported a nearby burial. At Legend Rock a few small pieces of debitage and a possible pecking stone, perhaps related to petroglyph manufacture, were found in test excavations beneath a Dinwoody anthropomorphic figure (Walker and Francis 1989). Most notable, of course, are the carved steatite and sandstone tubes found at the base of a Dinwoody interior-lined anthropomorph at 48HO469 in the Bighorn Basin (Frison and Van Norman 1993). These items have been inferred to be shaman's sucking tubes, used in healing rituals to exorcise illness and evil spirits from the practitioner's patients.

Several sites containing incised and painted imagery on the east side of the Bighorn present a dramatic contrast to Dinwoody sites, with the most striking example being the Medicine Lodge Creek site. Here a record of nearly 10,000 years of human occupation has been preserved at the base of a sandstone cliff containing hundreds of outline-pecked, incised, and painted images (Frison 1978). Late Archaic, Late Prehistoric, and perhaps Protohistoric occupations (possibly related to the Crow) are extensive at Medicine Lodge Creek and are undoubtedly contemporaneous with much of the imagery. Little Canyon Creek Cave contained Paleoindian, Early Archaic, and Protohistoric occupation levels along with elaborate painted imagery. Shaw and Frison (1979) speculated that the paintings were contemporaneous with the Protohistoric occupation of the cave, which was also inferred to be Crow. Recent results of AMS dating at Little Canyon Creek Cave indicate that at least some of the figures are from the end of the Late Prehistoric. Although the Trapper Creek site has not been archaeologically investigated, thick charcoal levels and occupational debris are apparent in exposures at the mouth of the cave. The temporal relationships between these levels and the hundreds of deeply incised figures on the cave walls are unknown.

Nevertheless, incised and painted images on the east side of the Bighorn Basin do not always occur in association with residential sites: many panels here are isolated from other types of archaeological sites and do not contain associated cultural materials. Sites such as the Valley of the Shields (Loendorf 1990) are more like Dinwoody sites and contain limited remains that are directly related to the manufacture and use of the imagery.

Conclusions

The ethnographic record clearly indicates that as a whole the engravings and paintings of the Bighorn and Wind River Basins originated in visionary experiences. But contrasts between Dinwoody and the incised/painted imagery also point to differences in the dynamics of the associated religious systems and worldviews of the prehistoric inhabitants of the area.

Dinwoody sites are isolated: they occur within a highly circumscribed portion of the Wind River and Bighorn Basins. And even within that region they are often isolated from residential areas and other types of archaeological sites. This pattern apparently endured for thousands of years, implying that the ethnographic observations of such sites as portals to supernatural realms and as locations where shamans acquired specialized and esoteric knowledge have great antiquity. From this viewpoint the distribution of Dinwoody imagery likely reflects significant aspects of the sacred geography of the broader Numic realm in the Great Basin. The upper Wind River Basin and southwestern third of the Bighorn Basin should be viewed as a location in which supernatural power is more highly concentrated than in other areas and a place of great spiritual importance to Shoshonean peoples.

This should not be taken to mean that the Numic shamanistic complex was monolithic or unchanging. The Dinwoody tradition lasted thousands of years, and there are clear changes in the relative frequencies of the different descriptive figure types over time. The large, elaborate interior-lined figures—"classic" Dinwoody—seem to be most common during the Late Prehistoric and Protohistoric periods. We suggest, as a point of departure for future research, that the appearance and dominance of these figure types could correspond to the emergence and increasing importance of the shaman in the social and political spheres of Shoshonean life (see Whitley 1994c).

In contrast, incised and painted imagery has a much wider regional distribution and occurs within a variety of archaeological contexts, ranging from small isolated panels with one or two figures to thousands of representations that are integral elements of major residential sites. This variety of distribution suggests that the acquisition of sacred imagery through vision quests and the reproduction of those images on stone were not solely the purview of religious specialists. Instead, the manufacture of the imagery appears to have a much more public role in day-to-day domestic life and may be the product of many different individuals, not just shamans. The dramatic addition of biographic qualities to incised and painted imagery during the Historic period (something not seen in Dinwoody) also suggests a much wider, and nonesoteric, social context for rock images among Great Plains groups than among those of the Great Basin.

The differences between Dinwoody and the incised/painted classes in imagery and symbols, spatial distribution, site location attributes, and association with other types of archaeological materials provide strong evidence that two separate religious systems existed among hunting and gathering people living in the Bighorn and Wind River Basins. The chronological overlap of these two traditions also suggests that this duality has been in place since well into the Archaic period, continuing into Late Prehistoric and Historic times.

These findings offer a much more diverse and complex picture of the area's prehistoric people than one based primarily on our traditional archaeological chronologies and culture historical sequences, which emphasize changes in technological and subsistence systems over time. The paintings and engravings suggest that the historic boundary between Great Plains and Great Basin peoples has been in place for at least two thousand years and may be replicated by general patterns of land use. This possibility offers an exciting point of departure for future research into the ancient history of the region.

NINE

Sacred and Scientific Places for the Future

THE DIVERSE PETROGLYPHS AND PICTOGRAPHS OF THE
Bighorn and Wind River Basins hold a great deal of significance
for different groups of people. For many Native Americans, such localities
are spiritual and religious places. For archaeologists such as ourselves,
these sites often contain a wealth of scientific information from which we
can learn about the people and cultures of the past. And for many members of the general public, the imagery has artistic and commercial value.

Despite their value, which we are only now beginning to understand,
such sites are often in extremely poor condition. Both natural and human
factors have contributed to extensive damage, and visitors to these mysteri-
ous and wondrous places are left with a profound sense of sadness. The
ever-increasing use of public lands and the growing fascination with the
imagery on the part of the public will continue to take a toll on these sites.

The deleterious effects of wind and water erosion, exfoliation caused by
freeze-thaw cycles, nesting birds, and abrasion from plants and shrubs,
along with acts of vandalism, including carved and painted graffiti, bullet
holes, and outright theft of images, are obvious. Indeed, there is probably
not one site we visited as we carried out research for this book that has not
suffered some type of damage from natural forces and human actions. Far
more subtle, however, are the long-term ill effects caused by attempts to
document or record an image, including rubbings, castings, chalking, and
other methods to "enhance" an image for photography. Casting with
materials such as latex can severely damage figures when portions of the
rock and petroglyph adhere to the casting material on its removal from the
rock surface. We observed pieces of casting material that remained on the
rock surface and in and around petroglyphs years after casting had been

undertaken, and damage from latex casting and charcoal outlining of figures at Medicine Lodge Creek severely limited the use of AMS dating at this site.

Rubbings can result not only in physical damage to the rock surface but also in changes to the chemistry of the rock varnish caused by application of the cloth or paper rubbing materials to the rock surface. In a series of before-and-after experiments (Loendorf 1989:161–164), rubbings resulted in significant changes to cation ratios of rock varnish and widely varying age estimates for several pecked images in the Pinon Canyon region of southeastern Colorado.

We are also beginning to better understand the deleterious effects of chalking. Chalk can remain in petroglyphs for decades (Francis et al. 1993) and has been shown to physically damage the rock surface (Bednarik 1988; Grant 1967). Grant (1967) recommended against its use because it is so difficult to remove and because inaccurate chalking can lead to alteration and misinterpretation of specific images. Our own studies (Francis et al. 1993) demonstrate that chalking significantly alters the chemistry of the rock varnish by adding calcium, resulting in artificially high cation ratios and rendering many figures undatable by cation-ratio methods. As a result of years of chalking at well-known sites in the Bighorn Basin, several figures at the Legend Rock site and 11 out of 20 figures at the Medicine Lodge Creek site proved to be undatable.

Whether lands are privately held or in the public domain, modern land use and management can have a profound effect on petroglyph and pictograph sites. Castle Gardens provides an example. This site was opened to the public without any supervision by the Bureau of Land Management in the 1960s, and it has been promoted through the Wyoming State Highway Map, tourist brochures, and directional signs. As reflected by dates defacing the petroglyphs (Figure 9.1), vandalism increased throughout the 1960s, and foot traffic has been so heavy that areas in front of fenced-off panels are now severely eroded, exposing cultural deposits and redirecting vandals to other panels in the site. By the time Gebhard et al. (1987a) investigated the site in the 1980s, at least half the figures had been stolen, initials and dates had been carved on top of almost every readily visible panel, many of the striking shields had been used for target practice, and residue from latex castings and other materials for rubbings covered many other faces (Figure 9.2).

Throughout the Bighorn and Wind River Basins, and indeed much of the American West, the predominant land use is livestock grazing. Cattle often gather at the southern exposures of cliff faces for shelter and warmth, especially during the winter. At the Legend Rock site, for example, many

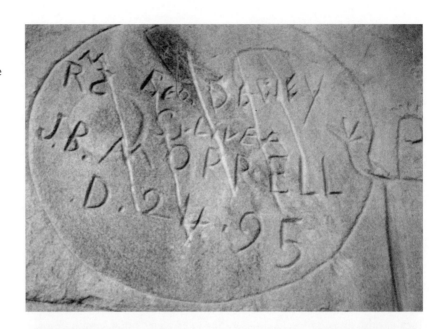

9.1. Vandalism at the Castle Gardens site, Wind River Basin.

9.2. Residue from rubbings and other vandalism at the Castle Gardens site, Wind River Basin.

of the figures on the lower portion of the cliff face have been abraded by cows milling against the cliff face, causing irreparable damage. Fortunately, this problem was remedied after the site was purchased by the state of Wyoming. Through the cooperative efforts of the state, the Bureau of Land Management, and private property owners, cattle were restricted from the site area.

Pictograph Cave provides an example of the benefits of multidisciplinary conservation studies. After the completion of Mulloy's excavations, the site was never backfilled. In 1941 the state of Montana constructed a small museum in the valley below the cave, established a walking trail through the cave complex, and opened the site to the public. Management of the site was difficult during World War II, and when the site caretaker could no longer be employed, the artifacts were removed from the museum and the facility was closed. With no institutional presence, Pictograph Cave turned into the local party spot for young people, who vandalized the site throughout the 1950s, burning the museum building and defacing the back of the cave wall with graffiti.

Through the leadership of Mayor Willard Fraser, the city of Billings took over management of the site in the 1960s. The graffiti was sandblasted off the back wall of the cave, and the area was opened as a park. In the 1970s the Montana Fish, Wildlife, and Parks Department assumed management of the park. Currently, Pictograph Cave is open to the public with controlled access. It has a paved walkway, a viewing area, interpretive signs, and a self-guided tour booklet. Access is controlled through a gated road that stops vehicles more than a mile from the site. Parking and picnic areas are also some distance away. Pictograph Cave is a fee area, and it has a full-time caretaker during the hours it is open.

In recent years two problems became painfully apparent at the site. First, the back wall of the cave started to exfoliate, resulting in destruction of many of the paintings. Second, the remaining paintings were fading rapidly. This deterioration prompted a conservation study of the site and surrounding area.

The fact that the site was never backfilled explains the exfoliation. Before excavation, deposits resting against the back wall served to wick moisture away from it. Once the deposits were removed in the course of the excavation, moisture seeping through the sandstone adhered to the wall, resulting in increased erosion and instability.

The second problem was somewhat more complex. Loendorf and Dean (1993) determined that the paintings, rather than fading, were being covered by a coating of mineral salts caused by water weeping out of the sandstone and evaporating on the surface of the rock. An inspection of the surrounding area to determine the source of the water led to the discovery of a stock pond, built in the 1960s to impound water in an intermittent drainage above the cave. After additional studies by a team of hydrologists and discussions with the property owner, the dam was breached. There has been an obvious decrease in moisture coming through the cave wall, and a conservation program to remove some of the salts covering the paintings is now under way. Nevertheless, the preservation of the paintings in Pictograph Cave presents formidable obstacles for the future.

We are slowly learning more effective management practices. Some agencies, such as the Bureau of Land Management in Worland, have specifically addressed management of petroglyph and pictograph sites on public lands through the land use planning process (Bureau of Land Management 1996). Site-specific plans, including conservation assessments (Dean 1997), detailed documentation procedures using state-of-the-art technology for mapping and photography (Billo and Mark 1999; Loendorf 1999), visitor use policies, permitting procedures, and interpretive needs, have also been developed by other agencies, both federal and state. Many of these programs incorporate Native American perspectives in their long-term management policies and interpretive and educational programs. All these activities hold great promise for the long-term preservation of these sites, which are significant to so many different individuals.

IN MANY WAYS THE research and writing of this book has been a journey. We started fairly simply with a desire to learn the age of some of the images and to examine some of our assumptions about them. We certainly do not have all the answers with respect to chronology, but we know far more about the antiquity of the imagery in the Bighorn and Wind River Basins than when we began. Most important, we have vastly different perspectives on the petroglyphs, pictographs, and prehistory of the Bighorn and Wind River Basins, on the people who made these images, and on the present.

Our findings with respect to chronology led us in other directions, and we discovered that the ancient paintings and engravings that grace the walls of canyons and outcrops throughout this portion of Wyoming provide one small window on past social, religious, and ideological systems. We also began to realize that when viewed from these perspectives the prehistory of the Bighorn and Wind River Basins is far more complex and dynamic than is indicated by other archaeological phenomena such as projectile points, firehearths, or subsistence strategies. We cannot emphasize strongly enough that the insights and understanding we have gained through this research are products of the integration of cultural anthropology, ethnography, and Native American perspectives with standard archaeological method and theory.

As we grew more familiar with the ethnographic record and visited several sites with elders, tribal representatives, and ethnographers, we became keenly aware of the deeply rooted traditional belief systems that continue to be a vibrant and central element of life for many Indian people. We hope we have gained some small amount of understanding about how modern Indian people view the landscape, the sacred, and the secular.

For us, the images—whether spectacular or simple, a single figure or thousands, painted or engraved—have given life to the stones and the bones so commonly described in reports and books, bringing together the archaeological record and the people whose ancestors left that record behind. This new perspective has reunited the science of archaeology with the humanistic aspects of anthropology, which are often lost in the cultural materialist paradigm that dominates our discipline. With stronger legal mandates for consultation with Native American tribal governments on the identification and treatment of places of religious or cultural significance (Advisory Council on Historic Preservation 1999), incorporation of cultural anthropology and Native American viewpoints into the practice of American archaeology will become far more commonplace. We hope this book is a first step toward demonstrating the wisdom of that practice.

REFERENCES

Adams, James
1974   A Photographic Study of the Trail Lake
        Petroglyph Site. *Wyoming Archaeologist*
        17(4):2–27.

Adovasio, James M., and David R. Pedler
1994   A Tisket, a Tasket: Looking at Numic
        Speakers through the "Lens" of a Basket.
        In *Across the West: Human Population
        Movement and the Expansion of the
        Numa,* edited by David B. Madsen and
        David Rhode, pp. 114–123. University
        of Utah Press, Salt Lake City.

Advisory Council on Historic Preservation
1999   36CFR800: Final Rule and Notice. *Fed-
        eral Register* 64(95):27044–27084.

Aikens, C. Melvin
1966   *Fremont-Promontory-Plains Relation-
        ships, Including a Report of Excavations
        at the Injun Creek and Bear River No. 1
        Sites, Northern Utah.* University of Utah
        Anthropological Papers No. 82. Univer-
        sity of Utah Press, Salt Lake City.
1967   Plains Relationships of the Fremont Cul-
        ture: A Hypothesis. *American Antiquity*
        32:198–209.

Aikens, C. Melvin, and Y. T. Witherspoon
1986   Great Basin Numic Prehistory: Linguis-
        tics, Archeology, and Environment. In
        *Anthropology of the Desert West: Essays
        in Honor of Jesse D. Jennings,* edited by
        C. J. Condie and D. D. Fowler, pp. 7–20.
        University of Utah Anthropological
        Papers No. 110. University of Utah Press,
        Salt Lake City.

Antevs, Ernst
1955   Geologic-Climatic Dating in the West.
        American Antiquity 20(4):317–335.

Applegate, Richard B.
1978   *?Atishwin: The Dream-Helper in South-
        Central California.* Ballena Press,
        Socorro, New Mexico.

Arrowsmith, J. Ramon, Glen E. Rice, and J. C.
Hower
1998   Documentation of Carbon-Rich Frag-
        ments in Varnish Covered Rocks from
        Central Arizona Using Electron
        Microscopy and Coal Petrography. Ms.
        on file, Arizona State University.

Bard, J. C., and C. I. Busby
1974   The Manufacture of a Petroglyph: A
        Replicative Experiment. *Contributions of*

the University of California Archaeological Research Facility 20:83–102.

Barnes, F. A.
1982   Canyon Country Prehistoric Rock Art. Wasatch Publishers, Salt Lake City, Utah.

Barnier, Cecil
1969   Lookout Cave (24BH402): A Preliminary Report on Surface Materials. Archaeology in Montana 10(3):13–33.

Basedow, H.
1914   Aboriginal Rock Carvings of Great Antiquity in South Australia. Journal of the Royal Anthropological Institute 44:195–211.

Beck, W., D. J. Donahue, A. J. T. Jull, G. Burr, W. S. Broecker, G. Bonani, I. Hajdas, and E. Malotki
1998   Ambiguities in Direct Dating of Rock Surfaces Using Radiocarbon Measurements. Science 280(5372):2132–2139.

Becker, C. F., and J. D. Alyea
1964   Precipitation Probabilities in Wyoming. Wyoming Agricultural Experiment Station Bulletin No. 416.

Bednarik, R. G.
1988   The Chalking of Petroglyphs: A Response. La Pintura 15(2–3):12–13.

Benson, L., D. Currey, Y. Lao, and S. Hostetler
1992   Lake-Size Variations in the Lahontan and Bonneville Basins between 13,000 and 9,000 ^{14}C Years B.P. Palaeogeography, Palaeoclimatology, Palaeoecology 95:18–32.

Bettinger, R. L., and M. A. Baumhoff
1982   The Numic Spread: Great Basin Cultures in Competition. American Antiquity 47:485–503.
1983   Return Rates and Intensity of Resource Use in Numic and Prenumic Adaptive Strategies. American Antiquity 48:830–834.

Bierman, P., and A. Gillespie
1991   Accuracy of Rock-Varnish Chemical Analyses: Implications for Cation-Ratio Dating. Geology 19:196–199.
1992a   Reply to T. A. Cahill's Comment on Accuracy of Rock-Varnish Chemical Analysis: Implications for Cation-Ratio Dating. Geology 20:471–472.
1992b   Reply to R. I. Dorn's Comment on Accuracy of Rock-Varnish Chemical Analyses: Implications for CR Dating. Geology 20:471–472.

Bierman, P., A. Gillespie, and S. Kuehner
1991   Precision of Rock-Varnish Chemical Analyses and Cation-Ratio Ages. Geology 19:135–138.

Billo, Evelyn, and Robert Mark
1999   Wind River Petroglyph GIS Project. Paper presented at the Fourth Biennial Rocky Mountain Anthropological Conference, Glenwood Springs, Colorado.

Bliss, Wesley L.
1948   Supplementary Appraisal of the Archeological and Paleontological Resources of Boysen Reservoir, Fremont County, Wyoming. Missouri Valley Project, River Basin Surveys, Smithsonian Institution. Submitted to the Missouri River Basin Recreation Survey, Region 2, National Park Service.

Bliss, Wesley L., and Jack T. Hughes
1947   Preliminary Appraisal of the Archaeological and Paleontological Resources of Boysen Reservoir, Fremont County, Wyoming. Missouri Valley Project, River Basin Surveys, Smithsonian Institution. Submitted to the Missouri River Basin Recreation Survey, Region 2, National Park Service.

Boreson, Keo
1998   Rock Art. In Handbook of North American Indians, vol. 12, Plateau, edited by

Deward E. Walker, Jr., pp. 611–619. Smithsonian Institution, Washington, D.C.

Bowers, Alfred
1965   *Hidatsa Social and Ceremonial Organiza-tion.* Bureau of American Ethnology Bulletin No. 194. Smithsonian Institu-tion, Washington, D.C.

Boyd, C. E., and J. P. Dering
1996   Medicinal and Hallucinogenic Plants Identified in the Pictographs and Sedi-ments of the Lower Pecos, Texas, Archaic. *Antiquity* 70:256–275.

Bradley, James H.
1961   *The March of the Montana Column.* Uni-versity of Oklahoma Press, Norman.

Buckles, William G.
1964   *An Analysis of Primitive Rock Art at Medicine Creek Cave, Wyoming, and Its Cultural and Chronological Relationships to the Prehistory of the Plains.* Unpub-lished Master's thesis, Department of Anthropology, University of Colorado, Boulder.

Bull, W. B.
1991   *Geomorphic Responses to Climatic Change.* Oxford University Press, Oxford.

Bureau of Land Management
1996   *Final Environmental Impact Statement, Grass Creek, and Proposed Resource Management Plans for the Grass Creek Planning Area in the Bighorn Basin Resource Areas, Worland District, Wor-land, Wyoming.* U.S. Department of the Interior, Bureau of Land Management, Worland District Office.

Butler, B. Robert
1981   *When Did the Shoshoni Begin to Occupy Southern Idaho? Essays on the Late Pre-historic Cultural Remains from the Upper Snake and Salmon River Country.* Occa-sional Papers of the Idaho State Museum of Natural History No. 32. Pocatello.
1986   The Pottery of Eastern Idaho. In *Pottery of the Great Basin and Adjacent Areas,* edited by Suzanne Griset, pp. 37–57. University of Utah Anthropological Papers No. 111. University of Utah Press, Salt Lake City.

Cahill, T. A.
1992   Comment on "Accuracy of Rock-Varnish Chemical Analyses: Implications for Cation-Ratio Dating." *Geology* 20:469.

Cannon, K. P., and R. E. Hughes
1993   Obsidian Source Characterization of Paleoindian Projectile Points from Yel-lowstone National Park, Wyoming. *Current Research in the Pleistocene* 10:54–56.

Cerling, T. E., R. J. Poreda, and S. L. Rathbun
1994   Cosmogenic ^{3}He and ^{21}Ne Age of the Big Lost River Flood, Snake River Plain, Idaho. *Geology* 22:227–230.

Chaffee, S. D., M. Hyman, and M. W. Rowe
1993   Vandalism of Rock Art for Enhanced Photography. *Studies in Conservation* 39:161–168.
1994   Radiocarbon Dating of Rock Paintings. In *New Light on Old Art: Recent Advances in Hunter-Gatherer Rock Art Research,* edited by David S. Whitley and Lawrence L. Loendorf, pp. 9–12. Mono-graph No. 36. Institute of Archaeology, University of California, Los Angeles.

Chaffee, Scott D., Marian Hyman, Marvin W. Rowe, Nancy J. Coulam, Alan Schroedl, and Kathleen Hogue
1994   Radiocarbon Dates on the All American Man Pictograph. *American Antiquity* 59:769–781.

Chaffee, Scott D., Lawrence Loendorf, Marian Hyman, and Marvin W. Rowe

1994   Dating a Pictograph in the Pryor Mountains, Montana. *Plains Anthropologist* 39(148):195–201.

Childers, Beverly Booth

1984   Petroglyphs of the Ring Lake Ranch, Fremont County, Wyoming. *Journal of New World Archaeology* 6(3):1–18.

1991   Ring Lake Ranch Petroglyph Site: Conservation Efforts and Dating. Ms. on file, Wind River Historical Center, Dubois, Wyoming.

1994   Long-Term Lichen-Removal Experiments and Petroglyph Conservation: Fremont County, Wyoming, Ranch Petroglyph Site. *Rock Art Research* 11(2): 101–112.

Clark, William P.

1885   *The Indian Sign Language, with Brief Explanatory Notes of the Gestures Taught Deaf-Mutes in Our Institutions for Their Instruction, and a Description of Some Peculiar Laws, Customs, Myths, Superstitions, Ways of Living, Code of Peace, and War Signals of Our Aborigines.* Hamersly, Philadelphia.

Clemmer, Richard O., and Omer C. Stewart

1986   Treaties, Reservations, and Claims. In *Handbook of North American Indians,* vol. 11, *Great Basin,* edited by Warren L. D'Azevedo, pp. 525–558. Smithsonian Institution, Washington, D.C.

Clottes, Jean

1994   Who Painted What in Upper Paleolithic European Caves. In *New Light on Old Art: Recent Advances in Hunter-Gatherer Rock Art Research,* edited by David S. Whitley and Lawrence L. Loendorf, pp. 1–8. Monograph No. 36. Institute of Archaeology, University of California, Los Angeles.

Clottes, Jean, and Jean Courtin

1996   *The Cave beneath the Sea: Paleolithic Images at Cosquer.* Harry N. Abrams, New York.

Clottes, Jean, and J. David Lewis-Williams

1998   *The Shamans of Prehistory: Trance and Magic in the Painted Caves.* Harry N. Abrams, New York.

COHMAP

1988   Climatic Changes in the Last 18,000 Years: Observations and Model Simulations. *Science* 241:1043–1052.

Cole, Sally J.

1990   *Legacy on Stone: Rock Art of the Colorado Plateau and Four Corners Region.* Johnson Books, Boulder, Colorado.

Colman, S. M., K. L. Pierce, and P. W. Birkeland

1987   Suggested Terminology for Quaternary Dating Methods. *Quaternary Research* 28:314–319.

Conkey, Margaret W.

1984   To Find Ourselves: Art and Social Geography of Prehistoric Hunters and Gatherers. In *Past and Present Hunter Gatherer Studies,* edited by Carmel Schrire, pp. 253–276. Academic Press, Orlando, Florida.

Conner, Stuart W.

1962   *A Preliminary Survey of Prehistoric Picture Writing on Rock Surfaces in Central and South Central Montana.* Anthropological Paper No. 2. Billings Archaeological Society, Billings, Montana.

1980   Historic Period Indicators in the Rock Art of the Yellowstone. *Archaeology in Montana* 21(2):1–13.

1984   The Petroglyphs of Ellison's Rock. *Archaeology in Montana* 25(2–3):123–145.

1988   Comments Concerning the Petroglyphs at Sites 24RB1153, 24RB1171,

24RB1176, and 24RB1181. In *Archeological Investigations at Sites 24RB1153, 24RB1171, 24RB1176, and 24RB1181,* by Gene Munson. Report on file, Montana State Historic Preservation Office, Helena.

1995   Indian Paint Pigment Sources. Memorandum dated November 18.

Conner, Stuart W., and Betty Lou Conner
1971   *Rock Art in the Montana High Plains.* The Art Galleries, University of California, Santa Barbara.

Cooper, John M.
1957   *The Gros Ventres of Montana: Religion and Ritual.* Catholic University of America Press, Washington, D.C.

Cowdrey, Mike
1995   Spring Boy Rides the Moon: Celestial Patterns in Crow Shield Design. Ms. in possession of L. L. Loendorf.

Cremaschi, M.
1996   The Desert Varnish in the Messak Sattafet (Fezzan, Libyan Sahara): Age, Archaeological Context, and Paleo-Environmental Implication. *Geoarchaeology* 11: 393–421.

Culin, Stewart
1901   *A Summer Trip among Western Indians: The Wanmaker Expedition.* Bulletin of the Free Museum of Science and Art of the University of Pennsylvania 3(1–3). Philadelphia.

Danin, A.
1983   Weathering of Limestone in Jerusalem by Cyanobacteria. *Zeitschrift für Geomorphologie* 27:413–421.

Davis, Carl, James D. Keyser, and Cynthia D. Craven
1994   Coyote House: Prehistoric Butte Top Occupation in the Pine Parklands. Ms. on file, Custer National Forest, Billings, Montana.

Davis, Leslie B. (editor)
1983   *From Microcosm to Macrocosm: Advances in Tipi Ring Investigation and Research.* Plains Anthropologist Memoir No. 19.

Dean, J. Claire
1997   Ten Things to Think About That Might Generally Help Rock Art Conservation Efforts and Rock Art Research as a Whole. Paper presented at the 62nd Annual Meeting of the Society for American Archaeology, Nashville.

Dodd, W.
1979   The Wear and Use of Battered Tools at Armijo Rockshelter. In *Lithic Use Wear Analysis,* edited by Brian Hayden, pp. 231–242. Academic Press, New York.

Dorn, Ronald I.
1986   Rock Varnish as an Indicator of Aeolian Environmental Change. In *Aeolian Geomorphology,* edited by W. G. Nickling, pp. 291–307. Allen and Unwin, London.

1989   Cation-Ratio Dating of Rock Varnish: A Geographical Perspective. *Progress in Physical Geography* 13:559–596.

1990   Quaternary Alkalinity Fluctuations Recorded in Rock Varnish Microlaminations on Western U.S.A. Volcanics. *Palaeogeography, Palaeoclimatology, Palaeoecology* 76:291–310.

1992   Comment on "Accuracy of Rock-Varnish Chemical Analyses: Implications for Cation-Ratio Dating." *Geology* 20:470–471.

1994   Dating Petroglyphs with a Three-Tier Rock Varnish Approach. In *New Light on Old Art: Recent Advances in Hunter-Gatherer Rock Art Research,* edited by David S. Whitley and Lawrence L. Loendorf, pp. 13–36. Monograph No. 36.

Institute of Archaeology, University of California, Los Angeles.

1997 Constraining the Age of the Côa Valley (Portugal) Engravings with ^{14}C and ^{36}Cl. *Antiquity* 71:105–115.

1998a Age Determination of the Coso Rock Art. In *Coso Rock Art: A New Perspective,* edited by Elva Younkin, pp. 67–96. Maturango Press, Ridgecrest, California.

1998b Response to Beck et al. *Science* 280(5372):2132–2139.

Dorn, Ronald I., T. Cahill, R. Eldred, T. E. Gill, B. H. Husko, A. J. Bach, and D. Elliot-Fisk

1990 Dating Rock Varnishes by the Cation-Ratio Method with PIXE, ICP, and the Electron Microprobe. *International Journal of PIXE* 1:157–195.

Dorn, Ronald I., P. Clarkson, M. F. Nobbs, L. L. Loendorf, and D. S. Whitley

1992 Radiocarbon Dating Inclusions of Organic Matter in Rock Varnish, with Examples for Drylands. *Annals of the Association of American Geographers* 82:136–151.

Dorn, Ronald I., and M. J. DeNiro

1985 First Paleoenvironmental Interpretation of a Pre-Quaternary Rock Varnish Site, Davidson Canyon, Southern Arizona. *Geology* 17:1029–1031.

Dorn, Ronald I., A. J. T. Hull, D. J. Donahue, T. W. Linick, and L. T. Toolin

1989 Accelerator Mass Spectrometry Radiocarbon Dating of Rock Varnish. *Geological Society of American Bulletin* 101:1363–1372.

Dorn, Ronald I., and D. H. Krinsley

1991 Cation-Leaching Sites in Rock Varnish. *Geology* 19:1077–1080.

Dorn, Ronald I., and T. M. Oberlander

1981 Microbial Origin of Desert Varnish. *Science* 213:1245–1247.

1982 Rock Varnish. *Progress in Physical Geography* 6:317–367.

Dorsey, George A.

1906 *The Pawnee Mythology.* Pt. 1. Carnegie Institution of Washington, Washington, D.C.

Dorsey, James O.

1890 *A Study of Siouan Cults.* Bureau of American Ethnology Annual Report No. 11. Smithsonian Institution, Washington, D.C.

Dowson, Thomas A.

1989 Dots and Dashes: Cracking the Entoptic Code in Bushman Rock Paintings. *South African Archaeological Society Goodwin Series* 6:84–94.

1992 *The Rock Engravings of Southern Africa.* Witwatersrand University Press, Johannesburg.

Dragovich, D.

2000 Rock Engraving Chronologies and Accelerator Mass Spectrometry Radiocarbon Age of Desert Varnish. *Journal of Archaeological Science* 27:871–876.

Drake, N. A., M. T. Heydeman, and K. J. White

1993 Distribution and Formation of Rock Varnish in Southern Tunisia. *Earth Surface Processes and Landforms* 18:31–41.

Eakin, Daniel. H.

1987 *Final Report of Salvage Investigations at the Split Rock Ranch Site (48FR1484), Highway Project SCPF-020-2(19), Fremont County, Wyoming.* Office of the Wyoming State Archaeologist. Report prepared for the Wyoming Highway Department, Cheyenne. Copies available from the SHPO Cultural Records Office, Laramie.

1989 *Report of Archaeological Test Excavations at the Pagoda Creek Site, 48PA853, Wyoming Project SCPF-031-1(21).*

Office of the Wyoming State Archaeologist. Report prepared for the Wyoming Highway Department, Cheyenne. Copies available from the SHPO Cultural Records Office, Laramie.

1993   *Cultural Resource Investigations Along U.S. Highway 14-16-20, Mileposts 0.0–27.5, Wyoming Project SCPF-031-1(21), North Fork of the Shoshone River Valley, 1984–1993.* Office of the Wyoming State Archaeologist. Report prepared for the Wyoming Department of Transportation, Cheyenne. Copies available from the SHPO Cultural Records Office, Laramie.

Eakin, Daniel H., Julie. E. Francis, and Mary Lou Larson

1997   The Split Rock Ranch Site: An Early Archaic Housepit Site in Central Wyoming. In *New Perspectives on the Archaic of the Northwestern High Plains and Rocky Mountains,* edited by Mary Lou Larson and Julie E. Francis, pp. 394–435. University of South Dakota Press, Vermillion.

Eckles, David G.

1990   *Results of a Class III Cultural Resource Inventory, Wyoming Project PREB-033-1(11), Thermopolis-Meeteetse Road, Hot Springs County, Wyoming.* Office of the Wyoming State Archaeologist, Laramie. Submitted to the Wyoming Highway Department, Cheyenne. Copies available from the Office of the Wyoming State Archaeologist, Laramie.

Eichmeier, J., and O. Höfer

1974   *Endogene Bildmuster.* Urban and Schwarzenberg, Munich.

Elliott-Fisk, D. L.

1987   Glacial Geomorphology of the White Mountains, California and Nevada: Establishment of a Glacial Chronology. *Physical Geography* 8:299–323.

Epperson, S.

1936   Photographs Relating to Wyoming Archaeology, Including View of Pictographs. Archives and Manuscript Collection, Smithsonian Institution, Washington, D.C.

Ewers, John C.

1955   *The Horse in Blackfoot Indian Culture, with Comparative Material from Other Western Tribes.* Bureau of American Ethnology Bulletin No. 159. Smithsonian Institution, Washington, D.C.

1957a *Hair Pipes in Plains Indian Adornment: A Study in Indian and White Ingenuity.* Bureau of American Ethnology Bulletin No. 159. Smithsonian Institution, Washington, D.C.

1957b *Early White Influence upon Plains Indian Painting: George Catlin and Carl Bodmer among the Mandan, 1832–34.* Smithsonian Institution Miscellaneous Collections 134(7).

1958   *The Blackfeet: Raiders of the Northwestern Plains.* University of Oklahoma Press, Norman.

1967   *Indian Life on the Upper Missouri.* University of Oklahoma Press, Norman.

1968   Plains Indian Painting: The History and Development of an American Art Form. Introduction to *Howling Wolf: A Cheyenne Warrior's Graphic Interpretation of His People,* by Karen Daniels Peterson. American West, Palo Alto, California.

1978   *Murals in the Round: Painted Tipis of the Kiowa and Kiowa-Apache Indians.* Smithsonian Institution Press, Washington, D.C.

Feyhl, Kenneth

1980   Tool Grooves: A Challenge. *Archaeology in Montana* 21(1):1–31.

Fleischer, M., T. Liu, W. S. Broecker, and W. Moore

1999   A Clue Regarding the Origin of Rock Varnish. *Geophysical Research Letters* 26:103–106.

Fletcher, Alice C., and Francis La Flesche

1911   *The Omaha Tribe.* Bureau of American Ethnology Annual Report No. 27. Smithsonian Institution, Washington, D.C.

Flood, Josephine

⭐1997   *Rock Art of the Dreamtime: Images of Ancient Australia.* Harper Collins, Sydney.

Ford, Bruce, Ian MacLeod, and Phil Haydock

1994   Rock Art Pigments from Kimberley Region of Western Australia: Identification of the Minerals and Conversion Mechanisms. *Studies in Conservation* 39:57–69.

Ford, Bruce, and Alan Watchman

1990   Art on the Rocks. *New Scientist* 127:33–37.

Fowler, Catherine S. (editor)

1989   *Willard Z. Park's Ethnographic Notes on the Northern Paiute of Western Nevada, 1933–1934,* vol. 1. University of Utah Anthropological Papers No. 114. University of Utah Press, Salt Lake City.

Francis, Julie E.

1980   *A Cultural Resource Inventory of the Proposed Torrey Creek Road.* Office of the Wyoming State Archaeologist. Submitted to the USDA Shoshone National Forest. Copies available from the Office of the Wyoming State Archaeologist, Laramie.

1983   *Procurement and Utilization of Chipped Stone Raw Materials: A Case Study from the Bighorn Mountains and Basin of North-Central Wyoming.* Unpublished Ph.D. dissertation, Department of Anthropology, Arizona State University, Tempe.

1989   Rock Art at Legend Rock. In *Legend Rock Petroglyph Site (48HO4), Wyoming: 1988 Archaeological Investigation,* edited by Danny N. Walker and Julie E. Francis, pp. 151–208. Office of the Wyoming State Archaeologist, Laramie. Submitted to the Wyoming Recreation Commission, Cheyenne.

1990   *Class III Cultural Resource Inventory of WHD Thermopolis-Meeteetse Road, Gooseberry Creek Section, Wyoming Project PREB-033-1(11), Hot Springs County, Wyoming.* Office of the Wyoming State Archaeologist. Submitted to the Wyoming Highway Department, Cheyenne. Copies available from the Office of the Wyoming State Archaeologist, Laramie.

1991   An Overview of Wyoming Rock Art. In *Prehistoric Hunters of the High Plains,* 2nd ed., by George C. Frison, pp. 397–430. Academic Press, New York.

1994   Cation-Ratio Dating and Chronological Variation within Dinwoody Tradition Rock Art in Northwestern Wyoming. In *New Light on Old Art: Recent Advances in Hunter-Gatherer Rock Art Research,* edited by David S. Whitley and Lawrence L. Loendorf, pp. 37–50. Monograph No. 36. Institute of Archaeology, University of California, Los Angeles.

2000   Root Procurement in the Upper Green River Basin: Archaeological Investigations at 48SU1002. In *Intermountain Archaeology,* edited by David B. Madsen and Michael D. Metcalf, pp. 166–175. University of Utah Anthropological Papers No. 122. University of Utah Press, Salt Lake City.

Francis, Julie E., and Mary Lou Larson

1995   Petroglyphs, Points, and Pots: The Numic Expansion and Prehistoric Boundary Conditions in Northwestern Wyoming. Paper presented at the 60th Annual Meeting of the Society for American Archaeology, Minneapolis.

Francis, Julie E., Lawrence L. Loendorf, and Ronald I. Dorn

1993   AMS Radiocarbon and Cation-Ratio Dating of Rock Art in the Bighorn Basin of Wyoming and Montana. *American Antiquity* 58:711–737.

Francis, Julie E., Danny N. Walker, Kyle Baber, and Karin Guernsey

1987   *Archaeological Investigations at 48SU354, Calpet Rockshelter: Fremont Occupation in the Northern Green River Basin, Wyoming.* Office of the Wyoming State Archaeologist, Laramie. Report prepared for the Sublette County Certified Local Government Board, Pinedale. Copies available from the Office of the Wyoming State Archaeologist, Laramie.

Fredlund, D. E.

1976   Fort Union Porcellanite and Fused Glass: Distinctive Lithic Materials of Coal Burn Origin in the Northern Plains. *Plains Anthropologist* 21(73):207–212.

Fredlund, Lynn

1988   Distribution and Characteristics of Avonlea South of the Yellowstone River in Montana. In *Avonlea Yesterday and Today: Archaeology and Prehistory,* edited by Leslie B. Davis, pp. 171–182. Saskatchewan Archaeological Society, Saskatoon.

Frison, George C.

1976   The Chronology of Paleo-Indian and Altithermal Period Groups in the Bighorn Basin, Wyoming. In *Cultural Change and Continuity: Essays in Honor of James Bennett Griffin,* edited by Charles E. Cleland, pp. 147–173. Academic Press, New York.

1978   *Prehistoric Hunters of the High Plains.* Academic Press, New York.

1979   The Crow Indian Occupation of the High Plains: The Archaeological Evidence. *Archaeology in Montana* 20(3):3–16.

1983   The Helen Lookingbill Site, Wyoming 48FR308. *Tebiwa* 20:1–16.

1988   Avonlea Contemporaries in Wyoming. In *Avonlea Yesterday and Today: Archaeology and Prehistory,* edited by Leslie B. Davis, pp. 155–170. Saskatchewan Archaeological Society, Saskatoon.

1991   *Prehistoric Hunters of the High Plains.* 2nd ed. Academic Press, New York.

1997   The Foothill-Mountain Late Paleoindian and Early Plains Archaic Chronology and Subsistence. In *Changing Perspectives on the Archaic of the Northwest Plains and Rocky Mountains,* edited by Mary Lou Larson and Julie E. Francis, pp. 84–105. University of South Dakota Press, Vermillion.

Frison, George C., James M. Adovasio, and Ronald C. Carlisle

1986   Coiled Basketry from Northern Wyoming. *Plains Anthropologist* 31(112):163–167.

Frison, George C., Rhonda L. Andrews, J. M. Adovasio, Ronald C. Carlisle, and Robert Edgar

1986   A Late Paleoindian Animal Trapping Net from Northern Wyoming. *American Antiquity* 51:352–361.

Frison, George C., and Bruce Bradley

1980   *Folsom Tools and Technology at the Hanson Site, Wyoming.* University of New Mexico Press, Albuquerque.

Frison, George C., and Marion Huseas

1968   Leigh Cave, Wyoming, Site 48WA304. *Wyoming Archaeologist* 11(3):20–33.

Frison, George C., and Larry C. Todd

1986   *The Colby Mammoth Site: Taphonomy and Archaeology of a Clovis Kill in Northern Wyoming.* University of New Mexico Press, Albuquerque.

1987   *The Horner Site: The Type Site of the Cody Cultural Complex* Academic Press, New York.

Frison, George C., and Zola Van Norman

1993   Carved Steatite and Sandstone Tubes: Pipes for Smoking or Shaman's Paraphernalia? *Plains Anthropologist* 38(143):163–176.

Gayton, Anna H.

1948   Yokuts and Western Mono Ethnography. *Anthropological Records* 10:12–90.

Gebhard, David S.

1951   The Petroglyphs of Wyoming: A Preliminary Paper. *El Palacio* 58:67–81.

1954   Petroglyphs in the Boysen Reservoir Area. In *Archaeological Investigations in the Shoshone Basin of Wyoming,* by William T. Mulloy, pp. 66–70. University of Wyoming Publications 18(1).

1966   The Shield Motif in Plains Rock Art. *American Antiquity* 31:721–732.

1969   *The Rock Art of Dinwoody, Wyoming.* The Art Galleries, University of California, Santa Barbara.

1972   Rock Art. In *American Indian Art: Form and Tradition,* pp. 26–33. E. P. Dutton, New York.

Gebhard, David S., and Harold A. Cahn

1950   The Petroglyphs of Dinwoody, Wyoming. *American Antiquity* 15:219–228.

Gebhard, David S., Fred Heaton, and Jonathan Laitone

1987a   *The Rock Drawings of Castle Gardens, Wyoming.* Stanley and Associates, Lafayette, California. Report submitted to the Bureau of Land Management, Cheyenne, Contract No. YA-512-CT9-283. On file at the SHPO Cultural Records Office, Laramie.

1987b   *The Rock Drawings of Cedar Canyon, Wyoming.* Stanley and Associates, Lafayette, California. Report submitted to the Bureau of Land Management, Cheyenne, Contract No. YA-512-CT9-283. On file at the SHPO Cultural Records Office, Laramie.

1987c   *The Rock Drawings of Whoopup Canyon, Wyoming.* Stanley and Associates, Lafayette, California. Report submitted to the Bureau of Land Management, Cheyenne, Contract No. YA-512-CT9-283. On file at the SHPO Cultural Records Office, Laramie.

Gillespie, R.

1991   Charcoal Dating-Oxidation Is Necessary for Complete Humic Removal. *Radiocarbon* 33(2):199.

Glazovskiy, A. F.

1985   Rock Varnish in the Glacierized Regions of the Pamirs. *Data of the Glaciological Studies* 54:136–141.

Gosse, J. C., E. Evenson, J. Klein, B. Lawn, and R. Middleton

1995b   Precise Cosmogenic ^{10}Be Measurements in Western North America: Support for a Global Younger Dryas Cooling Event. *Geology* 23:877–880.

Gosse. J. C., J. Klein, E. B. Evenson, B. Lawn, and R. Middleton

1995a   Beryllium-10 Dating of the Duration and Retreat of the Last Pinedale Glacial Sequence. *Science* 268:1329–1333.

Grant, Campbell

1967   *Rock Art of the American Indian.* Crowell, New York.

Grant, Campbell, James W. Baird, and J. Kenneth Pringle

1968   *Rock Drawings of the Coso Range.* Maturango Museum Publication No. 4. China Lake, California.

Greiser, Sally T.

1994   Late Prehistoric Cultures on the Montana Plains. In *Plains Indians, A.D. 500 to 1500,* edited by Karl H. Schlesier, pp. 34–55. University of Oklahoma Press, Norman.

Grinnell, George Bird
1923   *The Cheyenne Indians: Their History and Ways of Life.* 2 vols. University of Nebraska Press, Lincoln.

Hale, Kenneth, and David Harris
1979   Historical Linguistics and Archaeology. In *Handbook of North American Indians, vol. 9, The Southwest,* edited by Alfonso Ortiz, pp. 170–177. Smithsonian Institution, Washington, D.C.

Hallowell, A. Irving
1975   Ojibwa Ontology, Behavior, and World View. In *Teachings from the American Earth: Indian Religion and Philosophy,* edited by D. Tedlock and B. Tedlock. Liverwright, New York.

Harrell, Lynn L., Ted Hoefer III, and Scott T. McKern
1997   Archaic Housepits in the Wyoming Basin. In *Changing Perspectives on the Archaic of the Northwestern Plains and Rocky Mountains,* edited by Mary Lou Larson and Julie E. Francis, pp. 334–367. University of South Dakota Press, Vermillion.

Hedges, Ken
1982a   Phosphenes in the Context of Native American Rock Art. *American Indian Rock Art* 7–8:1–10. American Rock Art Research Association, El Toro, California.
1982b   Great Basin Rock Art Styles: A Revisionist View. *American Indian Rock Art* 7–8:205–211. American Rock Art Research Association, El Toro, California.

Heizer, Robert F., and Martin A. Baumhoff
1962   *Prehistoric Rock Art of Nevada and Eastern California.* University of California Press, Berkeley.

Hendry, Mary Helen
1983   *Indian Rock Art of Wyoming.* Privately published. Augstums Printing Service, Lincoln, Nebraska.

Herbort, Dale P., and Gene Munson
1984   Archaeological Investigations at the Ellison's Rock Site. *Archaeology in Montana* 25(2–3): 65–122.

Hill, James N., and R. K. Evans
1972   A Model for Classification and Typology. In *Models in Archaeology,* edited by David L. Clark, pp. 231–273. Methuen, London.

Hobson, J. Allan
1994   *The Chemistry of Conscious States: How the Brain Changes Its Mind.* Little, Brown, Boston.

Hoffman, G. R., and R. R. Alexander
1976   *Forest Vegetation of the Bighorn Mountains, Wyoming: A Habitat Type Classification.* U.S.D.A. Forest Service Research Paper No. 170.

Holmer, Richard N.
1994   In Search of Ancestral Northern Shoshone. In *Across the West: Human Population Movement and Expansion of the Numa,* edited by David B. Madsen and David Rhode, pp. 179–187. University of Utah Press, Salt Lake City.

Holmer, Richard N., and Dennis G. Weder
1980   Common Post-Archaic Projectile Points of the Fremont Area. In *Fremont Perspectives,* edited by David B. Madsen, pp. 55–68. Antiquities Section Selected Papers No. 16. Utah State Historical Society, Salt Lake City.

Hooke, R. L., H. Yang, and P. W. Weiblen
1969   Desert Varnish: An Electron Probe Study. *Journal of Geology* 77:275–288.

Horowitz, M. J.
1964   The Imagery of Visual Hallucinations. *Journal of Nervous and Mental Disease* 138:513–523.

Horse Capture, George
1980   *The Seven Visions of Bull Lodge.* Bear Claw Press, Ann Arbor, Michigan.

Howard, James H.
1965 *The Ponca Tribe.* Bureau of American Ethnology Bulletin No. 195. Smithsonian Institution, Washington, D.C.

Hultkrantz, Åke
n.d. The Sheepeaters of Wyoming: Culture History and Religion among Some Shoshoni Mountain Indians. 2 vols. Handwritten ms. in possession of L. L. Loendorf.
1958 Tribal Divisions with the Eastern Shoshoni of Wyoming. *Proceedings of the 32nd International Congress of Americanists.* Copenhagen, 1956,148–154.
1960 Religious Aspects of the Wind River Shoshone Folklore Literature. In *Culture and History: Essays in Honor of Paul Radin,* edited by Stanley Diamond, pp. 552–569. Columbia University Press, New York.
1961 The Masters of the Animals among the Wind River Shoshone. *Ethnos* 26(4):198–218.
1966 An Ecological Approach to Religion. *Ethnos* 31(1–4):131–150.
1966–67 The Ethnological Position of the Sheepeater Indians in Wyoming. *Folk* 8–9: 155–163.
1970 Attitudes towards Animals in Shoshone Indian Religion. *Temenos: Studies in Comparative Religion* 4(2):70–79.
1974a The Shoshones in the Rocky Mountains. In *American Indian Ethnohistory: California and Basin Plateau Indians,* pp. 173–214. Garland Press, New York.
1974b A Definition of Shamanism. *Temenos: Studies in Comparative Religion* 9:25–37.
1981 Accommodations and Persistence: Ecological Analysis of the Religion of the Sheepeater Indians in Wyoming, U.S.A. *Temenos: Studies in Comparative Religion* 17:35–44.
1986 Mythology and Religious Concepts. In *Handbook of North American Indians,* vol. 11, *Great Basin,* edited by Warren L. D'Azevedo, pp. 630–640. Smithsonian Institution, Washington, D.C.
1987 *Native Religions of North America: The Power of Visions and Fertility.* Harper and Row, San Francisco.

Husted, Wilfred M.
1969 *Bighorn Canyon Archaeology.* Smithsonian Institution River Basin Surveys Publications in Salvage Archaeology No. 12. Washington D.C.

Husted, Wilfred M., and Robert Edgar
n.d. The Archaeology of Mummy Cave, Wyoming: An Introduction to Shoshonean Prehistory. Ms. on file, Buffalo Bill Historical Center, Cody, Wyoming.

Hyman, Marian, and Marvin W. Rowe
1992 Direct ^{14}C Dating of Rock Paintings. Paper presented at the 57th Annual Meeting of the Society for American Archaeology, Pittsburgh.

Irwin, Lee
1996 *The Dream Seekers: Native American Visionary Traditions of the Great Plains.* University of Oklahoma Press, Norman.

Johnson, O.
1969 *Flathead and Kootenay: The Rivers, the Tribes, and the Region's Traders.* Arthur H. Clark, Glendale, California.

Jones, B., and P. Goodbody
1982 The Geological Significance of Endolithic Algae in Glass. *Canadian Journal of Earth Science* 19:671–678.

Jones, C. E.
1991 Characteristics and Origin of Rock Varnish from the Hyper Arid Coastal Deserts of Northern Peru. *Quaternary Research* 35:116–129.

Jones, William A.
1875 *Report on the Reconnaissance of Northwestern Wyoming including Yellowstone*

Park Made in the Summer of 1873. U.S. Government Printing Office, Washington, D.C.

Jorgensen, Joseph G.
1964   *The Ethnohistory and Acculturation of the Northern Ute.* Unpublished Ph.D. dissertation, Department of Anthropology, Indiana University, Bloomington.

Kehoe, Alice Beck
2000   *Shamans and Religion: An Anthropological Exploration in Critical Thinking.* Waveland Press, Prospect Heights, Illinois.

Kehoe, Thomas B.
1966   The Small Side-Notched Point System of the Northern Plains. *American Antiquity* 31:827–841.
1968   Saskatchewan. In *The Northwestern Plains: A Symposium,* edited by Warren Caldwell and Stuart W. Conner, pp. 21–35. Occasional Papers No. 1. Center for Indian Studies, Rocky Mountain College, Billings, Montana.

Kelly, Isabel T.
1932   Ethnography of the Surprise Valley Paiutes. *University of California Publications in American Archaeology and Ethnology* 31(3):67–210.
1939   Southern Paiute Shamanism. *Anthropological Records* 2(4):151–167.

Keyser, James D.
1975   A Shoshonean Origin for the Plains Shield Bearing Warrior Motif. *Plains Anthropologist* 20(69):207–216.
1977   Writing-on-Stone: Rock Art on the Northwestern Plains. *Canadian Journal of Archaeology* 1:15–80.
1984   *Rock Art of Western North Dakota and the North Cave Hills, South Dakota.* Special Publication of the South Dakota Archaeological Society No. 9. Augustana College, Sioux Falls, South Dakota.

1987   A Lexicon for Historic Plains Indian Rock Art: Increasing Interpretive Potential. *Plains Anthropologist* 32(115):43–71.
1996   Painted Bison Robes: The Missing Link in the Biographic Art Style Lexicon. *Plains Anthropologist* 41(155):29–52.
1997   *Indian Rock Art of the Columbia Plateau.* University of Washington Press, Seattle.

Keyser, James D., and George C. Knight
1976   Rock Art of Western Montana. *Plains Anthropologist* 21(71):1–12.

Keyser, James D., and Phillip Minthorn
1998   Columbia Plateau Biographic Art: An Expansion of a Plains Tradition. Paper presented at the 63rd Annual Meeting of the Society for American Archaeology, Seattle.

King, P. B.
1977   *The Evolution of North America.* Rev. ed. Princeton University Press, Princeton.

Kirkland, F., and W. W. Newcomb Jr.
1967   *The Rock Art of Texas Indians.* University of Texas, Austin.

Klein, Alan M.
1980   Plains Economic Analysis: The Marxist Complement. In *Anthropology on the Great Plains,* edited by W. Raymond Wood and Margot Liberty, pp. 129–140. University of Nebraska Press, Lincoln.

Klüver, H.
1942   Mechanism of Hallucinations. In *Studies in Personality,* edited by Q. McNemar and M. A. Merrill, pp. 175–207. McGraw-Hill, New York.

Knight, D. H., R. J. Hill, and A. T. Harrison
1976   *Potential Natural Landmarks in the Wyoming Basin: Terrestrial and Aquatic Ecosystems.* Department of Botany, University of Wyoming, Laramie.

Koski, Randolph, Edwin McKee, and David Hurst Thomas

1973   Pigment Composition of Prehistoric Pictographs of Gatecliff Shelter, Central Nevada. *American Museum Novitiates* 2521:1–9.

Krieger, Alex D.

1944   The Typological Concept. *American Antiquity* 9:271–288.

1960   Archaeological Typology in Theory and Practice. In *Selected Papers of the Fifth International Congress of Anthropology and Ethnological Sciences,* pp. 141–151. Philadelphia.

Krinsley, D. H., and Ronald I. Dorn

1991   New Eyes on Eastern California Rock Varnish. *California Geology* 44(5): 107–114.

Krinsley, D. H., R. I. Dorn, and S. Anderson

1990   Factors That May Interfere with the Dating of Rock Varnish. *Physical Geography* 11:97–119.

Krinsley, D. H., and C. R. Manley

1989   Backscattered Electron Microscopy as an Advanced Technique in Petrography. *Journal of Geological Education* 37:202–209.

Krumbein, W. E., and K. Jens

1981   Biogenic Rock Varnishes of the Negev Desert (Israel): An Ecological Study of Iron and Manganese Transformation by Cyanobacteria and Fungi. *Oecologia* 50:25–38.

Kunselman, Ray

1994   Prehistoric Obsidian Usage in the Central Rocky Mountains: The Lookingbill Site, 48FR308. *Wyoming Archaeologist* 38(1–2):1–17.

Lamb, Sydney M.

1958   Linguistic Prehistory in the Great Basin. *International Journal of American Linguistics* 24:95–100.

Lanteigne, M.

1991   Cation-Ratio Dating of Rock Engravings: A Critical Appraisal. *Antiquity* 65:292–295.

Larocque, François

1910   *Journal of Larocque from the Assinboine to the Yellowstone, 1805.* Publications of the Canadian Archives No. 3.

Larson, Mary Lou

1990   *Early Plains Archaic Technological Organization: The Laddie Creek Example.* Unpublished Ph.D. dissertation, Department of Anthropology, University of California, Santa Barbara.

1997   Rethinking the Early Plains Archaic. In *Changing Perspectives on the Archaic of the Northwestern Plains and Rocky Mountains,* edited by Mary Lou Larson and Julie E. Francis, pp. 106–136. University of South Dakota Press, Vermillion.

Lewis-Williams, J. David

1981   *Believing and Seeing: Symbolic Meaning in Southern San Rock Paintings.* Academic Press, London.

1982   The Economic and Social Context of Southern San Rock Art. *Current Anthropology* 23:429–438.

1983   *The Rock Art of Southern Africa.* Cambridge University Press, Cambridge.

1984   Ideological Continuities in Prehistoric Southern Africa: The Evidence of Rock Art. In *Past and Present in Hunter Gatherer Studies,* edited by C. Schrire, pp. 225–252. Academic Press, Orlando, Florida.

Lewis-Williams, J. David, and Thomas A. Dowson

1988   The Signs of the Times: Entoptic Phenomena in Upper Paleolithic Art. *Current Anthropology* 29:201–245.

1989   *Images of Power: Understanding Bushman Rock Art.* Southern Books, Johannesburg.

Lewis-Williams, J. David, and Johannes H. N. Loubser

1986   Deceptive Appearances: A Critique of Southern African Rock Art Studies. *Advances in World Archaeology* 5:253–289.

Liljeblad, Sven

1986   Oral Tradition: Content and Style of Verbal Arts. In *Handbook of North American Indians, vol. 11, Great Basin,* edited by Warren L. D'Azevedo, pp. 641–659. Smithsonian Institution, Washington, D.C.

Liu, Tanzhuo

1994   *Visual Microlaminations in Rock Varnish: A New Paleoenvironmental and Geomorphic Tool in Drylands.* Unpublished Ph.D. dissertation, Department of Geography, Arizona State University, Tempe.

Liu, Tanzhuo, and Wallace S. Broecker

2000   How Fast Does Rock Varnish Grow? *Geology* 28(2):183–186.

Liu, Tanzhuo, and Ronald I. Dorn

1996   Understanding the Spatial Variability of Environmental Change in Drylands with Rock Varnish Microlaminations. *Annals of the Association of American Geographers* 86(2):187–212.

Loendorf, Lawrence L.

1967   *A Preliminary Archaeological Survey of the Clark Fork River, Carbon County, Montana.* Unpublished master's thesis, Department of Anthropology, University of Montana, Missoula.

1974   *Archaeological Survey in the Pryor Mountain Bighorn Canyon Area: 1970 Field Season.* Report prepared for the National Park Service, Midwest Region, Lincoln, Nebraska.

1984   *Documentation of Rock Art, Petroglyph Canyon, Montana, 24CB601.* Contribution No. 207. Department of Anthropology, University of North Dakota, Grand Forks.

1988   Rock Art Chronology in Carbon County, Montana, and the Valley of the Shields Site, 24CB1094. *Archaeology in Montana* 29(2):11–24.

1989   *Nine Rock Art Sites in the Pinon Canyon Maneuver Site, Southeastern Colorado.* Contribution No. 248. Department of Anthropology, University of North Dakota, Grand Forks.

1990   A Dated Rock Art Panel of Shield Bearing Warriors in South Central Montana. *Plains Anthropologist* 35(127):45–54.

1991a   The Chilling Effects of the Little Ice Age on North Dakota. *North Dakota Quarterly* 59(4):192–199.

1991b   Cation-Ratio Varnish Dating and Petroglyph Chronology in Southeastern Colorado. *Antiquity* 65(247):247–255.

1994a   Finnegan Cave: A Rock Art Vision Quest Site in Montana. In *Shamanism and Rock Art in North America,* edited by Solveig A. Turpin, pp. 125–137. Special Publication No. 1. Rock Art Foundation, San Antonio, Texas.

1994b   Traditional Archaeological Methods and Their Applications at Rock Art Sites. In *New Light on Old Art: Recent Advances in Hunter-Gatherer Rock Art Research,* edited by David S. Whitley and Lawrence L. Loendorf, pp. 95–103. Monograph No. 36. Institute of Archaeology, University of California, Los Angeles.

1995   *The Great Turtle Shield, Castle Gardens Site, Wyoming.* Loendorf and Associates, Las Cruces, New Mexico. Report prepared for the Bureau of Land Management, Wyoming State Office, Cheyenne. On file at the Bureau of Land Management, Cheyenne.

1999   Planning for the Visitors in the Torrey Valley, Wyoming. Paper presented at the

64th Annual Meeting of the Society for American Archaeology, Chicago.

Loendorf, Lawrence L., and J. Claire Dean
1993   *Rock Art Research in Pictograph Cave (24YL1), Yellowstone County, Montana.* Loendorf and Associates, Las Cruces, New Mexico. Report prepared for the Montana Department of Fish, Wildlife, and Parks, Billings.

Loendorf, Lawrence L., Cynthia Kordecki, and Michael L. Gregg
1988   Preliminary Report, Pinon Canyon Maneuver Site Rock Art Project. Ms. on file, Department of Anthropology, University of North Dakota, Grand Forks.

Loendorf, Lawrence L., and David D. Kuehn
1991   *1989 Rock Art Research, Pinon Canyon Maneuver Site, Southeastern Colorado.* Contribution No. 258. Department of Anthropology, University of North Dakota, Grand Forks.

Loendorf, Lawrence L., and Audrey Porsche
1985   *The Rock Art Sites in Carbon County, Montana.* Contribution No. 224. Department of Anthropology, University of North Dakota, Grand Forks.

Love, J. D.
1932   Petroglyphs of Central Wyoming. *Annals of Wyoming* 9(2):690–723.

Lowie, Robert B.
1909a   *The Assinboine.* Anthropological Papers of the American Museum of Natural History 4. New York.
1909b   *The Northern Shoshone.* Anthropological Papers of the American Museum of Natural History 2(2):165–306. New York.
1916   *Societies of the Kiowa.* Anthropological Papers of the American Museum of Natural History 11 (Pt. 11). New York.
1918   *Myths and Traditions of the Crow Indians.* Anthropological Papers of the

American Museum of Natural History 25:1–308. New York.
1922   *Crow Indian Art.* Anthropological Papers of the American Museum of Natural History 21:271–322. New York.
1924   *Notes on Shoshonean Ethnography.* Anthropological Papers of the American Museum of Natural History 20:185–314. New York.
1956   *The Crow Indians.* Reprinted. Holt, Rinehart, and Winston, New York. Originally published 1935.

Loy, T. H., R. Jones, D. E. Nelson, N. Meehan, J. Vogel, J. Southon, and R. Cosgrove
1990   Accelerator Radiocarbon Dating of Human Blood Proteins in Pigments from Late Pleistocene Art Sites in Australia. *Antiquity* 64:110–116.

Mack, Joanne
1971   *Archaeological Investigations in the Bighorn Basin, Wyoming.* Unpublished master's thesis, Department of Anthropology, University of Wyoming, Laramie.

Madsen, David B.
1975   Dating Paiute-Shoshoni Expansion in the Great Basin. *American Antiquity* 40: 82–86.
1986   Prehistoric Ceramics. In *Handbook of North American Indians, vol. 11, Great Basin,* edited by Warren L. D'Azevedo, pp. 206–214. Smithsonian Institution, Washington, D.C.

Madsen, David B., and David Rhode
1994   *Across the West: Human Population Movement and Expansion of the Numa.* University of Utah Press, Salt Lake City.

Magne, Martin P. R., and Michael A. Klassen
1991   A Multivariate Study of Rock Art Anthropomorphs at Writing-on-Stone, Southern Alberta. *American Antiquity* 56:389–418.

Malefijt, Annemarie de Waal
1968   *Religion and Culture: An Introduction to Anthropology of Religion.* Macmillan, New York.

Mallery, Garrick
1886   *Pictographs of the North American Indians: A Preliminary Paper.* Fourth Annual Report of the Bureau of American Ethnology, pp. 3–256. Smithsonian Institution, Washington, D.C.
1893   *Picture-Writing of the American Indians.* Tenth Annual Report of the Bureau of American Ethnology, Pt. 1. Smithsonian Institution, Washington, D.C.

Malouf, Carling
1961   Pictographs and Petroglyphs. *Archaeology in Montana* 3(1):1–13.
1967   Historic Tribes and Archaeology. *Archaeology in Montana* 8(1):1–16.
1968   The Shoshonean Migrations Northward. *Archaeology in Montana* 9(3):1–19.

Malouf, Richard T.
1979   *Camas and the Flathead Indians of Montana.* Contributions to Anthropology No. 7. University of Montana, Missoula.

Mandelbaum, David G.
1940   The Plains Cree. *Anthropological Papers of the American Museum of Natural History 37.*

Mariategui, J., and M. Zambrano
1959   Acerco del empleo de drogas alucinogenas en el Perú. *Revista de NeuroPsiquitria* 2.

Markley, E., and B. Crofts
1997   *Walk Softly, This Is God's Country: Sixty Six Years on the Wind River Indian Reservation.* Mortimore Publishing, Lander, Wyoming.

Marquis, T. B.
1928   *Memoirs of a White Crow Indian.* Century, New York.

Martin, William
1999   Contributions to Archaeology. In *Archaeological Investigations along the Wyoming Segment of the Express Pipeline: Project Synthesis,* edited by William Martin and Craig S. Smith, pp. 4.1–4.22. TRC Mariah Associates, Inc., Laramie, Wyoming. Submitted to Express Pipeline Company. Copies available from the Bureau of Land Management, Worland Field Office, Worland, Wyoming.

Martineau, LeVan
1973   *The Rocks Begin to Speak.* KC Publications, Las Vegas.

McCleary, Timothy P.
1997   *The Stars We Know: Crow Indian Astronomy and Lifeways.* Waveland Press, Prospect Heights, Illinois.

McCracken, Harold (editor)
1978   *The Mummy Cave Project in Northwestern Wyoming.* Buffalo Bill Historical Center, Cody, Wyoming.

McKee, Edwin, and David Hurst Thomas
1973   X-Ray Diffraction Analysis of Pictograph Pigments from Toquima Cave, Central Nevada. *American Antiquity* 38(1): 112–113.

McNees, Lance M., William H. Harding, and Cynthia D. Webb
1995   *Data Recovery Investigations at Sites 48HO550 and 48HO558, Buffalo Creek Section Project (PREB-033-1[14]), Hot Springs County, Wyoming.* TRC Mariah Associates, Inc., Laramie, Wyoming. Report prepared for the Wyoming Department of Transportation, Cheyenne. Copies available from the SHPO Cultural Records Office, Laramie.

Medicine Crow, Joseph
1962   Panel Discussion on Buffalo Jumps. In *Symposium on Buffalo Jumps,* pp.

40–56. Montana Archaeological Society Memoir No.1.

1992 *From the Heart of Crow County: The Crow Indians' Own Stories.* Library of the American Indian. Orion Books, New York.

Metcalf, Michael D.

1987 Contributions to the Prehistoric Chronology of the Wyoming Basin. In *Archaeological Resources Management on the Great Plains,* edited by Alan J. Osborn and Robert C. Hassler, pp. 233–261. I and O Publishing, Omaha.

Miller, Jay

1985 Shamans and Power in Western North America: The Numic, Salish, and Keres. In *Woman, Poet, and Scientist: Essays in New World Anthropology, Honoring Dr. Emma Lou Davis,* edited by the Great Basin Foundation, pp. 55–66. Ballena Press, Los Altos, California.

Mooney, James

1897 Kiowa Heraldry Notebook. Ms. No. 2531, vol. 1. National Anthropological Archives, Smithsonian Institution, Washington, D.C.

1898 *Calendar History of the Kiowa Indians.* Seventeenth Annual Report of the Bureau of American Ethnology (1895–1896), Pt. 1, pp. 129–445. Smithsonian Institution, Washington, D.C.

Moore, C. B., and C. D. Elvidge

1982 Desert Varnish. In *Reference Handbook on the Deserts of North America,* edited by G. L. Bender, pp. 527–536. Greenwood Press, Westport, Connecticut.

Moore, Roger A.

1994 The Lithic Assemblage from a Pueblo Petroglyph Site: Artifacts, Shrines, and Pueblos: Papers in Honor of Gordon Page. *The Archaeological Society of New Mexico* 20:167–182.

Morss, Noel

1931 *The Ancient Culture of the Fremont River in Utah.* Papers of the Peabody Museum of American Archaeology and Ethnology 12(3). Harvard University, Cambridge.

Mulloy, William. T.

1954 Archaeological Investigations in the Shoshone Basin of Wyoming. *University of Wyoming Publications* 18(1): 1–70.

1958 A Preliminary Historical Outline for the Northwestern Plains. *University of Wyoming Publications* 22(1):1–235.

1965 Archaeological Investigations along the North Platte River in Eastern Wyoming. *University of Wyoming Publications* 31(2):24–51.

Nabokov, Peter

1988 *Cultivating Themselves: The Inter-play of Crow Indian Religion and History.* Unpublished Ph.D. dissertation, Department of Anthropology, University of California, Berkeley.

Nabokov, Peter, and Lawrence L. Loendorf

1994 *Every Morning of the World: Ethnographic Resources Study, Bighorn Canyon National Recreation Area.* Loendorf and Associates, Red Lodge, Montana. Report prepared for the Department of the Interior, National Park Service, Rocky Mountain Region.

2000 *American Indians and Yellowstone National Park.* Loendorf and Associates, Red Lodge, Montana. Report prepared for the Department of the Interior, National Park Service, Yellowstone National Park.

Nagy, B. L., A. Nagy, M. J. Rigali, W. D. Jones, D. H. Krinsley, and N. A. Sinclair

1991 Rock Varnish in the Sonoran Desert: Microbiologically Mediated Accumulation of Manganiferous Sediments. *Sedimentology* 38:1153–1171.

Nobbs, Margaret, and Ronald I. Dorn
1993   New Surface Exposure Ages for Petroglyphs from the Olary Province, South Australia. *Archaeology in Oceania* 28:18–39.

Norris, Philetus W.
1880   *Report upon the Yellowstone National Park to the Secretary of the Interior for the Year 1879.* U.S. Government Printing Office, Washington, D.C.

O'Hara, P., D. H. Krinsley, and S. W. Anderson
1989   Elemental Analysis of Rock Varnish Using the Ion Microprobe. *Geological Society of America Abstracts with Programs* 21:A165.
1990   Microprobe Analysis of Rock Varnish Cation-Ratios and Elemental Variance. *Geological Society of America Abstracts with Programs* 22:271.

Palmer, F. E., J. T. Staley, R. G. E. Murray, T. Counsell, and J. B. Adams
1985   Identification of Manganese-Oxidizing Bacteria from Desert Varnish. *Geomicrobiology Journal* 4:343–360.

Perry, R. S., and J. B. Adams
1978   Desert Varnish: Evidence of Cyclic Deposition of Manganese. *Nature* 276:489–491.

Peterson, Karen Daniels
1971   *Plains Indian Art from Fort Marion.* University of Oklahoma Press, Norman.

Phillips, F. M., M. G. Zreda, S. S. Smith, D. Elmore, P. W. Kubik, and P. Sharma
1990   A Cosmogenic Chlorine-36 Chronology for Glacial Deposits at Bloody Canyon, Eastern Sierra Nevada, California. *Science* 248:1529–1532.

Pineda, C. A., L. Jacobson, and M. Peisach
1988   Ion Beam Analysis for the Determination of Cation-Ratios as a Means of Dating Southern African Rock Varnishes. *Nuclear Instruments and Methods in Physics Research* B35:463–466.

Pineda, C. A., M. Peisach, L. Jacobson, and C. G. Sampson
1990   Cation-Ratio Differences in Rock Patina on Hornfels and Chalcedony Using Thick Target PIXE. *Nuclear Instruments and Methods in Physics Research* B49: 332–335.

Plog, Fred T.
1974   *The Study of Prehistoric Change.* Academic Press, New York.

Porter, C. L.
1962   Vegetation Zones of Wyoming. *University of Wyoming Publications* 27(2):6–12.

Potter, R. M., and G. R. Rossman
1977   Desert Varnish: The Importance of Clay Minerals. *Science* 196:1446–1448.

Powell, John Wesley
1904   Work in Esthetology. *Twenty-Third Annual Report of the Bureau of American Ethnology,* pp. xii–xxv. Smithsonian Institution, Washington, D.C.

Putnam, J. D.
1876   *Hieroglyphics Observed in Summit Canyon, Utah, and on Little Popo Agie River in Wyoming.* Proceedings of the Davenport Academy of Nature Sciences, 1867–1876, vol. 1.

Reed, Verner Z.
1896   The Ute Bear Dance. *American Anthropologist* 9(3):237–244.

Reeve, Stuart A.
1986   *Root Crops and Prehistoric Social Process in the Snake River Headwaters, Northwestern Wyoming.* Unpublished Ph.D. dissertation, Department of Anthropology, State University of New York, Albany.

Reichel-Dolmatoff, G.

1978   The Cultural Context of an Aboriginal Hallucinogen: *Banisteriopsis casapi*. In *Flesh of the Gods: The Ritual Use of Hallucinogens*, edited by P. T. Furst, pp. 84–113. Allen and Unwin, London.

Reiss, David

1987   *Results of a Class III Cultural Resource Inventory of a Proposed Road Widening and Construction Areas along Highway 120, Wyoming Project PREB-033-1(7), Thermopolis-Meeteetse, Grass Creek Section, M.P. 20.7–27.5, Hot Springs County, Wyoming*. Office of the Wyoming State Archaeologist, Laramie. Submitted to the Wyoming Highway Department, Cheyenne. Copies available from the Office of the Wyoming State Archaeologist, Laramie.

1991   *Archaeological Investigations at 48HO120, Wyoming Project F-033-1(7), Thermopolis-Meeteetse Road, Hot Springs County, Wyoming*. Office of the Wyoming State Archaeologist, Laramie. Submitted to the Wyoming Highway Department, Cheyenne. Copies available from the Office of the Wyoming State Archaeologist, Laramie.

Reiss, David, David G. Eckles, Karin M. Guernsey, Michael McFaul, and William R. Doering

1993   The Grass Creek Site (48HO120): A Middle Archaic Period Housepit, Hot Springs County, Wyoming. *Wyoming Archaeologist* 37(1–2):27–48.

Reiss, David, and Robert G. Rosenberg

1998   *A Class III Cultural Resource Survey, Sinks Canyon Road, WYDOT Project PREA-0701(3), Fremont County, Wyoming*. Office of the Wyoming State Archaeologist, Laramie. Submitted to the Wyoming Department of Transportation, Cheyenne. Copies available from the Office of the Wyoming State Archaeologist, Laramie.

Renaud, E. B.

1936   Pictographs and Petroglyphs of the High Western Plains. *Archaeological Survey of the High Western Plains, Eighth Report*. Department of Anthropology, University of Denver.

Reneau, S. L., T. M. Oberlander, and C. D. Harrington

1991   Accelerator Mass Spectrometry Radiocarbon Dating of Rock Varnish: Discussion and Reply. *Geological Society of America Bulletin* 103:310–314.

Reneau, S. L., and R. J. Raymond

1991   Cation-Ratio Dating of Rock Varnish: Why Does It Work? *Geology* 19:937–940.

Rennick, I. C.

n.d.   Photographs in the Glenn A. Connor Papers. Accession No. 1961. American Heritage Center, University of Wyoming, Laramie.

Ritter, Eric W.

1994   Scratched Rock Art Complexes in the Desert West: Symbols for Socio-Religious Communication. In *New Light on Old Art: Recent Advances in Hunter-Gatherer Rock Art Research*, edited by David S. Whitley and Lawrence L. Loendorf, pp. 51–66. Monograph No. 36. Institute of Archaeology, University of California, Los Angeles.

Rockwell, David

1991   *Giving Voice to Bear: North American Indian Myths, Rituals, and Images of the Bear*. Roberts Rinehart, Niwot, Colorado.

Russ, J. M, Marian Hyman, Harry J. Shafer, and Marvin W. Rowe

1990   Direct Radiocarbon Dating of Rock Art. *Nature* 348:710–711.

Sackett, J. R.

1966   Quantitative Analysis of Upper Pale-
        olithic Stone Tools. *American Antiquity*
        25:324–329.

Sacks, O. W.

1970   *Migraine: The Evolution of a Common
        Disorder.* Faber, London.

Schaafsma, Curtis F.

1996   Ethnic Identity and Protohistoric Archae-
        ological Sites in Northwestern New
        Mexico: Implications for Reconstructions
        of Navajo and Ute History. In *The
        Archaeology of Navajo Origins,* edited by
        Ronald H. Towner, pp. 19–46. Univer-
        sity of Utah Press, Salt Lake City.

Schaafsma, Polly

1971   *Rock Art of Utah.* Papers of the Peabody
        Museum of Archaeology and Ethnology
        65. Harvard University, Cambridge.

1980   *Indian Rock Art in the Southwest.* Uni-
        versity of New Mexico Press,
        Albuquerque.

1985   Form, Content, and Function: Theory
        and Method in North American Rock Art
        Studies. In *Advances in Archaeological
        Method and Theory,* edited by Michael B.
        Schiffer, pp. 237–277. Academic Press,
        New York.

1994   Trance and Transformation in the
        Canyons: Shamanism and Early Rock Art
        on the Colorado Plateau. In *Shamanism
        and Rock Art in North America,* edited
        by Solveig A. Turpin, pp. 45–72. Special
        Publication No. 1. Rock Art Foundation,
        San Antonio, Texas.

Schapiro, M.

1953   Style. In *Anthropology Today,* edited by
        A. L. Kroeber, pp. 287–312. University
        of Chicago Press, Chicago.

Schlesier, Karl H.

1994   *Plains Indians, A.D. 500–1500.* Univer-
        sity of Oklahoma Press, Norman.

Schuster, Helen H.

1987   Tribal Identification of Wyoming Rock
        Art: Some Problematic Considerations.
        Archaeology in Montana 28(2):25–43.

Scott, David, and William Hyder

1993   A Study of Some California Indian Rock
        Art Pigments. *Studies in Conservation*
        38(3):155.

Secoy, Frank R.

1953   *Changing Military Patterns on the Great
        Plains (Seventeenth Century through
        Early Nineteenth Century).* Monographs
        of the American Ethnological Society No.
        21. J. J. Augustin, Locust Valley, New
        York.

Shaw, Leslie C., and George C. Frison

1979   A Possible Pre-Clovis Occupation at Lit-
        tle Canyon Creek Cave, Wyoming. Paper
        presented at the 44th Annual Meeting of
        the Society for American Archaeology,
        Vancouver, British Columbia.

Shimkin, Demitri B.

1947a   *Wind River Shoshone Ethnogeography.*
        University of California Anthropological
        Records 5(4). Berkeley.

1947b   Childhood and Development among the
        Wind River Shoshone. *University of Cali-
        fornia Anthropological Records* 5(5):
        289–325. Berkeley.

1947c   Wind River Shoshone Literary Forms: An
        Introduction. *Journal of the Washington
        Academy of Sciences* 37(10):329–376.

1953   *The Wind River Shoshone Sun Dance.*
        Anthropological Papers No. 41. Bureau
        of American Ethnology Bulletin No. 151,
        pp. 397–484. Smithsonian Institution,
        Washington, D. C.

1986a   Eastern Shoshone. In *Handbook of North
        American Indians, vol. 11, Great Basin,*
        edited by Warren L. D'Azevedo, pp.
        308–335. Smithsonian Institution, Wash-
        ington, D.C.

1986b Introduction of the Horse. In *Handbook of North American Indians, vol. 11, Great Basin,* edited by Warren L. D'Azevedo, pp. 517–524. Smithsonian Institution, Washington, D.C.

Siegel, R. K., and M. E. Jarvik
1975 Drug-Induced Hallucinations in Animals and Man. In *Hallucinations: Behaviour, Experience, and Theory,* edited by R. K. Siegel and L. J. West, pp. 81–161. John Wiley and Sons, New York.

Skinner, Alanson
1914 Ceremonies of the Plains Cree. *Anthropological Papers of the American Museum of Natural History* 11:513–542.

Smith, Craig S.
1988 Seeds, Weeds, and Prehistoric Hunters and Gatherers: The Plant Macrofossil Evidence from Southwest Wyoming. *Plains Anthropologist* 33(120):141–158.
1999 Obsidian Use in Wyoming and the Concept of Curation. *Plains Anthropologist* 44(169):271–291.

Sowers, Ted C.
1939 *Petroglyphs and Pictographs of Dinwoody.* Federal Works Progress Administration, Archaeological Project Report, Casper, Wyoming. Original on file at the Coe Library, University of Wyoming, Laramie.
1940 *Petroglyphs of West Central Wyoming: Eight Sites.* Federal Works Progress Administration, Archaeological Project Report, Casper, Wyoming. Original on file at the Coe Library, University of Wyoming, Laramie.
1941a *Petroglyphs of Castle Gardens, Wyoming.* Federal Works Progress Administration, Archaeological Project Report, Casper, Wyoming. Original on file at the Coe Library, University of Wyoming, Laramie.

1941b *The Wyoming Archaeological Survey: A Report.* Federal Works Progress Administration, Archaeological Project Report, Casper, Wyoming. Original on file at the Coe Library, University of Wyoming, Laramie.

Spaulding, Albert C.
1953 Statistical Techniques for the Discovery of Artifact Types. *American Antiquity* 18:305–313.

Steward, Julian H.
1929 *Petroglyphs of California and Adjoining States.* University of California Publications in American Archaeology and Ethnology Vol. 24. Berkeley.
1938 Pantatübiji', an Owens Valley Paiute. *Bureau of American Ethnology Bulletin* 119:183–195. Smithsonian Institution, Washington, D.C.
1943 Culture Element Distributions XXIII. *University of California Anthropological Records* 8(3):263–392. Berkeley.

Stewart, James J.
1989 Distribution Analysis of a Petroglyph Motif from Legend Rock Petroglyph Site (48HO4), Hot Springs County, Wyoming. In *Legend Rock Petroglyph Site (48HO4), Wyoming: 1988 Archaeological Investigations,* edited by Danny N. Walker and Julie E. Francis. Office of the Wyoming State Archaeologist, Laramie. Submitted to the Wyoming Recreation Commission, Cheyenne.

Stone, Eric
1932 *Medicine among the American Indian.* Paul B. Hoeber, New York.

Sundstrom, Linea
1984 *Rock Art of Western South Dakota and the Southern Black Hills.* Special Publication of the South Dakota Archaeological Society No. 9. Augustana College, Sioux Falls, South Dakota.

1989   *Culture History of the Black Hills with Reference to Adjacent Areas of the Northern Great Plains.* J & L. Reprints, Lincoln, Nebraska.

1990   *Rock Art of the Southern Black Hills: A Contextual Approach.* Garland Publishing, New York.

1997   The Sacred Black Hills: An Ethnohistorical Review. *Great Plains Quarterly* 17:185–212.

Swaim, Charles

1975   *A Survey of the Trail Lake Petroglyphs.* Unpublished master's thesis, Department of Anthropology, University of Wyoming, Laramie.

Swanson, Earl H.

1972   *Birch Creek: Human Ecology in the Cool Desert of the Northern Rocky Mountains, 9000 B.C.–A.D. 1850.* Idaho State University Press, Pocatello.

Swenson, Anthony A., and Fred Chapman

1992   *National Register Nomination, Torrey Lake Petroglyph District.* Wyoming State Historic Preservation Office, Cheyenne.

Teit, J. A.

1930   *The Salishan Tribes of the Western Plateau.* Annual Report of the Bureau of American Ethnology for 1927–1928. Smithsonian Institution, Washington, D.C.

Thornbury, William D.

1965   *Regional Geomorphology of the United States.* John Wiley and Sons, New York.

Tipps, Betsy L.

1995   *Holocene Archeology near Squaw Butte, Canyonlands National Park, Utah.* Selections from the Division of Cultural Resources No. 7. Rocky Mountain Region, National Park Service, Lakewood, Colorado.

Tipps, Betsy L., and Alan R. Schroedl

1985   *The Riverton Rock Art Study, Fremont County, Wyoming.* P-III Associates, Inc., Salt Lake City. Submitted to the U.S. Bureau of Reclamation, Great Plains Region Office, Billings, Montana.

Towner, Ronald H. (editor)

1996   *The Archaeology of Navajo Origins.* University of Utah Press, Salt Lake City.

Tratebas, Alice M.

1993   Stylistic Chronology versus Absolute Dates for Early Hunting Style Rock Art on the North American Plains. In *Rock Art Studies: The Post-Stylistic Era*, edited by Michel Lorblanchet and Paul G. Bahn, pp. 164–177. Oxbow Monograph 35. Oxbow Press, London.

Trenholm, Virginia C., and M. Carley

1964   *The Shoshonis: Sentinels of the Rockies.* University of Oklahoma Press, Norman.

Turpin, Solveig A.

1994   On a Wing and a Prayer: Flight Metaphors in Pecos River Art. In *Shamanism and Rock Art in North America*, edited by Solveig A. Turpin. Special Publication No. 1. Rock Art Foundation, San Antonio, Texas.

Vander, Judith

1997   *Shoshone Ghost Dance Religion: Poetry Songs and Great Basin Context.* University of Illinois Press, Urbana.

Walker, Danny N.

1994a   Archaeological Investigations at Boysen Reservoir, Fremont County, Wyoming, Forty Years after the River Basin Survey. In *40 Something: The River Basin Surveys*, edited by Kimball N. Banks, pp. 117–126. North Dakota Archaeology 5. North Dakota Archaeological Association, Department of Anthropology, University of North Dakota, Grand Forks.

1994b   Rock Art at Boysen Reservoir, Fremont
          County, Wyoming. In *40 Something: The
          River Basin Surveys,* edited by Kimball
          N. Banks, pp. 127–176. North Dakota
          Archaeology 5. North Dakota Archaeo-
          logical Association, Department of
          Anthropology, University of North
          Dakota, Grand Forks.

1999   *1997 Archaeological Investigations at the
          Sand Draw Dump Site, 48FR3123, Fre-
          mont County, Wyoming.* Occasional
          Papers on Wyoming Archaeology No. 6.
          Office of the Wyoming State Archaeolo-
          gist, Laramie.

Walker, Danny N., and Julie E. Francis
1989   *Legend Rock Petroglyph Site (48HO4),
          Wyoming: 1988 Archaeological Investi-
          gations.* Office of the Wyoming State
          Archaeologist, Laramie. Submitted to
          the Wyoming Recreation Commission,
          Cheyenne.

Walker, Danny N., and Lawrence C. Todd (editors)
1984   *Archaeological Salvage at 48FR1398:
          The Castle Gardens Access Road Site,
          Fremont County, Wyoming.* Occasional
          Papers on Wyoming Archaeology No. 2.
          Wyoming Recreation Commission,
          Cheyenne.

Wallace, Ernest, and E. Adamson Hoebel
1952   *The Comanches: Lords of the Southern
          Plains.* University of Oklahoma Press,
          Norman.

Walsh, Roger
1990   *The Spirit of Shamanism.* Jeremy P.
          Tarcher, New York.

Watchman, Alan
1992   Potential Methods for Dating Rock Paint-
          ings. *American Indian Rock Art*
          18:465–473.
1995   Recent Petroglyphs, Foz Côa, Portugal.
          Rock Art Research 12(2):104–108.

Wellmann, Klaus F.
1979   *A Survey of North American Indian Rock
          Art.* Akademische Druck-u. Ver-
          lagsanstalt, Graz, Austria.

Welsh, P. H., and R. I. Dorn
1997   Critical Analysis of Petroglyph ^{14}C Ages
          from Côa, Portugal, and Deer Valley, Ari-
          zona. *American Indian Rock Art*
          21:11–24.

Whalley, W. B.
1983   Desert Varnish. In *Chemical Sediments
          and Geomorphology: Precipitates and
          Residue in the Near Surface Environ-
          ment,* edited by A. S. Goudi and K. Pye,
          pp. 197–226. Academic Press, London.

Wheeler, Richard P.
1957   *Archaeological Remains in Three Reser-
          voir Areas in South Dakota and
          Wyoming.* Report on file, National Park
          Service, Midwest Archaeological Center,
          Lincoln, Nebraska.

Whitley, David S.
1982   *The Study of North American Rock Art:
          A Case Study from South-Central Cali-
          fornia.* Unpublished Ph.D. dissertation,
          Department of Anthropology, University
          of California, Los Angeles.
1988   Reply. *Current Anthropology* 29:238.
1992   Shamanism and Rock Art in Far Western
          North America. *Cambridge Archaeologi-
          cal Journal* 2:89–113.
1994a   Ethnography and Rock Art in the Far
          West: Some Archaeological Implications.
          In *New Light on Old Art: Recent
          Advances in Hunter-Gatherer Rock Art
          Research,* edited by D. S. Whitley and
          L. L. Loendorf, pp. 81–94. Monograph
          No. 36. Institute of Archaeology, Univer-
          sity of California, Los Angeles.
1994b   Shamanism, Natural Modeling, and Rock
          Art of Far Western North American
          Hunter-Gatherers. In *Shamanism and*

Rock Art in North America, edited by Solveig A. Turpin, pp. 1–44. Special Publication No. 2. Rock Art Foundation, San Antonio, Texas.

1994c   By the Hunter, for the Gatherer: Art, Social Relations, and Subsistence Change in the Prehistoric Great Basin. *World Archaeology* 25(3):356–373.

1998a   Finding Rain in the Desert: Landscape, Gender, and Far Western North American Rock Art. In *The Archaeology of Rock Art,* edited by Christopher Chippendale and Paul S. Taçon, pp. 11–29. Cambridge University Press, Cambridge.

1998b   Cognitive Neuroscience, Shamanism, and the Rock Art of Native California. *Anthropology of Consciousness* 9(1):22–37.

1998c   Meaning and Metaphor in the Coso Petroglyphs: Understanding Great Basin Rock Art. In *Coso Rock Art: A New Perspective,* edited by Elva Younkin, pp. 109–174. Maturango Press, Ridgecrest, California.

Whitley, D. S., and H. J. Annegarn

1994   Cation-Ratio Dating of Rock Engravings from Klipfontein, North Cap Province, South Africa. In *Contested Images: Diversity in Southern African Rock Art Research,* edited by Thomas A. Dowson and J. David Lewis-Williams, pp. 189–197. University of Witwatersrand Press, Johannesburg.

Whitley, David S., and Lawrence L. Loendorf (editors)

1994   *New Light on Old Art: Recent Advances in Hunter-Gatherer Rock Art Research.* Monograph No. 36. Institute of Archaeology, University of California, Los Angeles.

Whitney, J. W., and C. D. Harrington

1993   Relict Colluvial Boulder Deposits as Paleoclimatic Indicators in the Yucca Mountain Region, Southern Nevada. *Geological Society of America Bulletin* 105:1007–1018.

Wilcox, David R.

1988   Avonlea and Southern Athapaskan Migrations. In *Avonlea Yesterday and Today: Archaeology and Prehistory,* edited by Leslie B. Davis, pp. 273–280. Saskatchewan Archaeological Society, Saskatoon.

Wildschut, W.

1975   *Crow Indian Medicine Bundles.* Contributions from the Museum of the American Indian Vol. 17. Heye Foundation, New York.

Willey, Gordon R., and Philip Phillips

1958   *Method and Theory in American Archaeology.* University of Chicago Press, Chicago.

Willey, Gordon R., and Jeremy A. Sabloff

1974   *A History of American Archaeology.* W. H. Freeman, San Francisco.

Wissler, Clark

1905   The Whirlwind and the Elk in the Mythology of the Dakota. *Journal of American Folklore* 18(71):257–268.

1907   *Some Protective Designs of the Dakota.* Anthropological Papers of the American Museum of Natural History 1(2):19–56. New York.

1912   *Ceremonial Bundles of the Blackfoot Indians.* Anthropological Papers of the American Museum of Natural History 12 (Pt. 2). New York.

Wood, C. E.

1985   The Plains-Lakes Connection: Reflections from a Western Perspective. In *Archaeology, Ecology, and Ethnohistory of the Prairie-Forest Border Zone of Minnesota and Manitoba,* edited by Janet Spector and Elden Johnson, pp. 1–8. J & L Reprints, Lincoln, Nebraska.

Wormington, H. Marie

1955   *Ancient Man in North America.* Popular
        Series No. 4. Denver Museum of Natural
        History, Denver.

Wright, Gary A.

1978   The Shoshonean Migration Problem.
        Plains Anthropologist 23(80):113–137.

Wright, Gary A., and Henry J. Chaya

1985   Obsidian Source Analysis in Northwest-
        ern Wyoming: Problems and Prospects.
        Plains Anthropologist
        30(109):237–242.

Young, David A., and Robert L. Bettinger

1992   The Numic Spread: A Computer Simula-
        tion. *American Antiquity* 57:85–98.

Younkin, Elva (editor)

1998   *Coso Rock Art: A New Perspective.* Mat-
        urango Press, Ridgecrest, California.

Zhang, Y., T. Lie, and S. Li

1990   Establishment of a Cation-Leaching
        Curve of Rock Varnish and Its Appli-
        cation to the Boundary Region of
        Gansu and Xinjiang, Western China.
        Seismology and Geology 12:
        251–261.

Zigmond, Maurice

1977   The Supernatural World of the Kawaiisu.
        In *Flowers of the Wind: Papers on Ritual,
        Myth, and Symbolism in California and
        the Southwest,* edited by Thomas C.
        Blackburn, pp. 59–95. Ballena Press,
        Socorro, New Mexico.

1980   *Kawaiisu Mythology: An Oral Tradition
        of South-Central California.* Ballena
        Press, Socorro, New Mexico.

1981   *Kawaiisu Ethnobotany.* University of
        Utah Press, Salt Lake City.

carbon: biological processes and accumulation of, 53–54; organic materials in paint and dating methods, 51, 52, 55. *See also* radiocarbon dating

Carbon County (Montana), 44, 50

casting, and damage to petroglyphs, 196–97

Castle Gardens shield style, 46, 136–39, 186

Castle Gardens site, 35, 39–40, 42, 126, 145, 147, 150, *151f*, 152, 158, 160, *162f*, 163, 175, 197, *198f*

cation-ratio (CR) dating: and advances in dating methods for petroglyphs, 57–63, 66–67; and Bear Shield site, 155; and Dinwoody tradition, 97, *98t*, 99, 105, *107t*, 185; and en toto pecked figures, 79, *80–81t*; outline-pecked and painted figures, *134t*. *See also* chronology; dating techniques

Cedar Buttes, 112

Cedar Canyon, 42

Ceremonial style, 39

chalk and chalking: and damage to petroglyphs, 197; and dating of petroglyphs, 61, *106f*

Chapman, F., 37

Cheyenne, 136

Childers, B. B., 37, 110

chronology: and analysis of style, 39–43; of Castle Gardens shield style, 141–42; of Dinwoody tradition, 94–105, *106f*, *107t*, 122–23, 184–87, 195; of en toto pecked figures, 78–79, *80–81t*, 82; of incised/painted imagery, 183, 184–87, 195; and inference of

relative ages, 48–50; interdisciplinary approach to, 66–67; of outline-pecked and painted figures, *134f*; of shield-bearing warrior images, *146f*, 147; of solid-painted rectangular-body anthropomorphs, 166; of V-shouldered anthropomorphs, 148, 150. *See also* accelerator mass spectrometry; cation-ratio dating; dating techniques; radiocarbon dating

Clark, W. P., 33

Clark's Fork, of Yellowstone River, 189

class, and analytical groupings for classification, 45–46

classification, and approaches to style and tradition, 43–46

climate: and cultural history of Early Archaic period, 12–13; and correlative methods of dating, 64–66; and physical environment of Bighorn and Wind River Basins, 5–6

clothing, and V-shouldered anthropomorphs, 152. *See also* headdresses and hairstyles

Clovis projectile points, 11

Coal Draw area, 88, 103

Cody Complex, 11

Cole, S. J., 16

colors, of paints, 129–30

Columbia Plateau, 1, 26

Comanche, 179

composite anthropomorphic type, and Dinwoody tradition, 91, 103, 110

Conkey, M. W., 191

Conner, B. L., 154–55, 161, 166, 175, 177

Conner, S. W., 38, 154–55, 161, 166, 175, 177, 178, 179

Cook's Canyon area, 166–68

Corbusier, Dr. William H., 34

correlative methods, of dating, 50, 63–66

cosmography, of Shoshone and Numic-speaking groups, 120–22

cosmology, and visionary experiences of Great Plains groups, 25

Coso Range (California), 28, 59, 112

Cowdrey, M., 174

Coyote House, 14

Cree, 179

Crocker Nuclear Laboratory, University of California at Davis, 59

Crooked Creek site, 76, 145

Crow: and bear images, 166; and Castle Gardens shield style, 142; and cultural history of Bighorn and Wind River Basins, 16–17, 18; and ethnography as interpretive tool, 2–3; and images of twin heroes, 174–75; and introduction of horses, 179, 180; and painted tipi covers, 177; and supernatural meaning of paint colors, 129; and tally marks, 179; and tobacco, 170, 172. *See also* ethnography; Native Americans

Crowheart Butte, 112

Culin, S., 120, 121

cultural history: and archaeological record of Bighorn and Wind River Basins, 9–18; and boundary between Great Basin and Great Plains religious systems in Bighorn and Wind River Basins, 190;

cultural history *(continued):* and
chronological sequence of
petroglyphs and pictographs,
187; and diversity in prehistoric and historic periods
of Bighorn and Wind River
Basins, 2; petroglyphs and
perspective on in Bighorn and
Wind River Basins, 200–201.
See also material culture;
social change

dating techniques, advances in
methods of, 50–66. *See also*
accelerator mass spectrometry;
cation-ratio dating; chronology; radiocarbon dating
Dead Indian Creek site, 13
Dean, J. C., 199–200
death, as metaphor for trance
state, 27–28
deep-line incising, 128
deer, images of, 154, 157–58.
See also animals and animal
images
descriptive types: and
classification of images, 45;
and Dinwoody tradition,
82–94, 104t
design elements, and
classification of images,
44–45
diffusionist-migration models,
for images of shield-bearing
warriors, 133
Dinwoody Camp site, 36
Dinwoody Canyon, 112
Dinwoody Cave, 36
Dinwoody Lake, 6, 110
Dinwoody tradition: and bird
images, 30; chronology of,
63, 184–87, 195; definition
of, 69; and descriptive figure

types, 82–94; distinctiveness
and internal cohesion of,
46–47; and en toto pecked
figure types, 74; and ethnography, 110–23; incised/
painted imagery compared to,
183, 184–87, 194–95; and
manufacturing techniques,
73–74; and painted images,
36; and settings of sites,
70–72; spatial distributions
of, 107–10; and symbolism
of turtles, 32; temporal
parameters of, 94–105, *106f,
107t,* 123; and water images,
30, *31f;* and Wind River
Shoshone, 16. *See also*
petroglyphs and pictographs;
tradition
Dorn, R. I., 49, 53, 54–55,
56–57, 58–60, 63, 64–65,
66, *75f,* 94, 96
Dowson, T. A., 21–22
Dragovitch, D., 55–56
dreaming, and visionary
experiences, 26
drowning, and metaphors of
water, 30

Early Archaic period: and
cultural history of Bighorn
and Wind River Basins,
12–13, 187; and Dinwoody
tradition, 97, 99, 104, 105,
106f, 185; and evolutionary
trends in development of
anthropomorphic and
zoomorphic figures, 122,
123. *See also* Archaic period
Early Hunting style, 41, 42, 43
elk, images of, 154, 157–58,
159f, 160f. See also animals
and animal images

Elk Creek Cave, 52, 166–68
Ellison's Rock site, 139, 147,
148
elongate interior-lined
anthropomorphic type, and
Dinwoody tradition,
91–93
entopics, and neuropsychological
model, 22
en toto pecked figure types: and
chronology, 78–82, 185; co-
occurrence with Dinwoody
images, 74, 78; and
distribution of lithic raw
materials, 191; and human
forms, 74–76, *77f;* incised/
painted imagery compared to,
183; and site settings, 76, 78;
and spatial distribution, 188;
zoomorphic figures of
Dinwoody traditional
compared to, 86, 87
Epperson, S., 35
erosion: and inference of relative
ages of petroglyphs, 49–50; of
rock varnish and cation-ratio
dating, 60
ethnography: and Dinwoody
tradition, 110–23, 185;
incised/painted imagery and
religious practices or visionary
experiences, 183; and
interpretation of petroglyphs
and pictographs, 2–3, 21,
194–95; and perspective on
prehistory of Bighorn and
Wind River Basins, 201; and
power of bears, 156; and
shield-bearing warrior figures,
136; and studies of Crow, 17;
and studies of Wind River
Shoshone, 15–16. *See also*
Crow; Native Americans;
Shoshone

etic frameworks, and interpretation of petroglyphs and pictographs, 20–21

Euro-Americans, and trade goods in Protohistoric and Historic periods, 14. *See also* French; guns; Historic period; horses; Spanish

Ewers, J. C., 135, 180

faunal assemblages, and Paleoindian period, 10, 11. *See also* animals and animal images

Feyhl, K., 38

fine-line incised figures, 128

Finnegan Cave, 130

firearms. *See* guns

fish, as source of food in Paleoindian period, 10

Flathead, 130

flight: as metaphor for visionary experiences, 29–30; Shoshone traditions and anthropomorphic figures in Upper Wind River area, 113–14. *See also* birds

flotation analyses, and usage of plants in Paleoindian period, 10

Folsom sites, 11

Francis, J. E., 66, 83, 88, 96, 97, 104, 191

Fraser, W., 199

French, and distribution of firearms, 179. *See also* Euro-Americans

Fremont culture, and shield-bearing warrior images, 133

Frison, G. C., 9, 11–12, 12–13, 16, 118, 194

Frozen Leg Cave, 131, 168, 169, 170

Gebhard, D., 37, 40–42, 43, 45, 69, 82, 133, 141, 150, 154, 197

gender, and images of elk, 158, *160f*

geography, of Bighorn and Wind River Basins, 1–2, *4m*, 5

geology: minerals and pigments of paints, 129–30; and physical environment of Bighorn and Wind River Basins, 5, 6, *7f*; and sources of lithic raw materials, 190–91. *See also* rock varnish

geometric designs. *See* abstract and geometric designs; herringbone designs

ghost beings, and Shoshone oral tradition, 112–13

Ghost Dance religion, 42

Gillespie, A., 59

glaciation, and geology of Bighorn and Wind River Basins, 5, 6, *7f*

Gobernador style, and shield images, 143–44

Gooseberry Creek, 189

Grant, C., 133, 197

Grass Creek house pit site, 191

Great Basin: and Great Plains religious systems, 190; and shield-bearing warriors, 133, 135. *See also* Numic expansion

Great Hot Springs, 9

Great Plains cultural groups: and bear ceremonialism, 166; and Dinwoody tradition, 187; and Great Basin religious systems, 190; and images of shield-bearing warriors and V-shouldered anthropomorphs, 132, 135–36; and incised/painted imagery, 183, 187,

195; mythology of and rectangular-bodied anthropomorphs, 172–75; and painted lodge covers, 177; and tally marks, 179; and vision quest, 25; and Wind River Shoshone, 16

Great Pueblo Revolt of 1680, 179

Green River Basin, 175

Green Springs, 131

Greybull North site, 150, *151f*

Greybull River, 107–108

Greybull South site, *146f*, 147, 156

Gros Ventre Indians, 179

guns: and historic period imagery, 179–83; and inference of relative ages of petroglyphs, 48; and Shoshone spiritual beliefs, 115–16

Hanson site, 11

headdresses and hairstyles: and Dinwoody tradition, 91, *101f*; and en toto pecked figures, 76, *77f*; and incised/painted imagery, 168–72

head and head shape: and Castle Gardens style shield, *138f*, 139; and en toto pecked figures, 74, *77f*; and shield-bearing warrior images, 133

Hedgepeth Hills site (Arizona), 55

Hendry, M. H., 34, 37, 42–43, 44

herringbone designs: and rectangular-bodied anthropomorphs, 172, 173, 174; and V-shouldered anthropomorphs, 152. *See also* abstract and geometric designs

Hidatsa Indians, 16, 174
hide paintings, and winter
counts, 19
Hilej site, 144–45
Historic period: and Castle
Gardens shield style, 139,
186; and Dinwoody tradition,
105, 123, 185; and en toto
pecked figures, 81f; and
incised/painted imagery, 126,
128, 179–83, 195; and shield-
bearing warriors, 133, 148;
and subject matter of petro-
glyghs, 48; and V-shouldered
anthropomorphs, 150
Holmer, R. N., 15
Horner site, 9, 11
horses: and Castle Garden shield
style, 144; Crow and introduction of, 16–17; and Dinwoody tradition, 105, 106f;
and Historic period imagery,
179–83; and inference of
relative ages of petroglyphs,
48; and shield types, 135. See
also animals and animal
images
house pits, and Early Archaic
period, 12–13
Hultkrantz, Å., 15, 16, 24, 111,
113, 120
human forms: and en toto
pecked figures, 74–76;
incised/painted imagery and
unusual types of, 163–75. See
also anthropomorphic images;
V-shouldered anthropomorphs
hunter-gatherers: and complexity
of religious ideologies in Bighorn and Wind River Basins,
3; and shamanic basis of
religions, 23, 24
hunting scenes: and death metaphor, 28; shield-bearers and

V-shouldered figures, 154. See
also animals and animal images
Husted, W. M., 187

ideology, and settlement system
boundaries, 191
imagery: and Historic period,
179–83; incised/painted
imagery and tradition of, 183;
metaphors and interpretation
of, 27–32; neuropsychological
model and iconic, 22; visionary experiences and interpretation of, 26–27. See also
animals and animal images;
anthropomorphic images;
human forms; symbols and
symbolism; zoomorphic images
inanimate objects, and incised/
painted imagery, 175–77
incised/painted imagery: and
abstract designs, 177–79;
chronology of, 134t, 184–87,
195; and Dinwoody tradition,
184–87, 194–95; distribution
of in Bighorn and Wind River
Basins, 124m; and Historic
period imagery, 179–83; and
inanimate objects, 175–77;
and manufacturing techniques,
128–32; and settings of sites,
125–27; and shield-bearing
warriors, 132–48, 154–63;
and tradition of imagery, 183;
and unusual human figure
types, 163–75; and V-
shouldered anthropomorphs,
132, 133, 148–63
inductively coupled plasma (ICP)
dating, 58
interior-lined figures, and
Dinwoody tradition, 105,
110, 123

Interior Line style, 41, 42, 43,
45, 69, 82
Irwin, L., 25, 26, 27, 136, 157

Joliet site, 145, 181
Jones, Capt. William A., 33–34,
130–31

Kehoe, T. B., 24
Keyser, J. D., 39, 131, 135,
148, 150, 180
Kiowa: and bear imagery, 157;
and Castle Gardens shield
style, 142–43; and cultural
environment of Bighorn and
Wind River Basins, 18; and
painted tipi covers, 177
Klassen, M. A., 135, 150
Krause site, 145, 147, 156,
157f
Kukundika, 15–16

Laddie Creek site, 191
Lakota: and colors of paints,
129; and winter counts, 19
Lamb, S. M., 15
land use and management, and
preservation of petroglyphs
and pictographs, 197,
199–200
Langstaff site, 155
Larson, M. L., 191
Late Archaic period: and cultural
history of Bighorn and Wind
River Basins, 13; and Dinwoody tradition, 101, 103,
105, 185; and en toto picked
figures, 79, 82; and evolutionary trends in development
of anthropomorphic and
zoomorphic figures, 122. See
also Archaic period

Navajo, 143
neuropsychological model, and shamanistic hypothesis, 21–24
numerical methods, of dating, 50
Numic expansion: and cosmography, 120–22; and Dinwoody tradition, 187; debate on existence, timing, and directionality of, 15

Obsidian Cliff (Yellowstone Park), 190
Oregon Basin, 78
outline-pecked figures: chronometric ages for, *134t*; distribution of in Bighorn and Wind River Basins, *124m*; and Medicine Lodge Creek site, 126; and shield-bearing warriors, 145–47; and V-shouldered anthropomorphs, 150
Owl Creek, 112
Owl Creek Mountains, 9, *71f*, 108
oxygen plasma technique, and dating of pictographs, 52

paints and painted figures: and bear images, 155; and Castle Gardens shield style, 137, *140f*, 144–45; and Dinwoody tradition, 83; and early descriptions of petroglyphs, 35, 38; and elk or deer images, 158; and headdress anthropomorphs, 168; and manufacturing techniques, 129–32; organic materials and dating of, 50, 51–52;

and tipis, 175–77; and V-shouldered anthropomorphs, 150, 152. *See also* incised/painted imagery
Paleoindian period: and cultural environment of Bighorn and Wind River Basins, 9–11; and Dinwoody tradition, 96, 185
Paleolithic paintings, in Europe, 22, 23, 51
particle-induced X-ray emission (PIXE), 58–59
patination. *See* rock varnish
pecking, and manufacturing techniques of Dinwoody tradition, 73–74. *See also* en toto pecked figure types
Pelican Creek, 131
Pelican Lake complex, 143
Petroglyph Canyon, 50, 72, 74, *75f*, 76, *77f*, 78–79, 185
petroglyphs and pictographs: diversity and complexity of in Bighorn and Wind River Basins, 1–3; early drawings and reports of, 33–34; early studies of, 35–38; major paradigms for interpretation of, 19–21; metaphors and interpretation of, 27–32; preservation of and development of management practices, 196–200; and previous treatments of style, 39–43; and shamanistic hypothesis, 21–24; and visionary perspectives, 24–27. *See also* chronology; Dinwoody tradition; en toto pecked figure types; ethnography; imagery; incised/painted imagery; outline-pecked figures; paints and painted figures; religion; super-

imposition; *specific sites and topics*
phallic figures, and sexual symbolism, 30, *32f*
Phillips, P., 46
physical environment, of Bighorn and Wind River Basins, 5–9
Pictograph Cave, 38, 52, 126–27, 132, 139, *140f*, 144, 148, 158, *159f*, 160, 161, *162f*, 164, *165f*, 175, 181, 183, 199–200
pigments, and colors of paints, 129–32, 137
Pinon Canyon (Colorado), 44, 61, 197
Plains Indians. *See* Great Plains cultural groups
plants: and headdress anthropomorphs, 169–72; shamanism and images of, 118; usage of in Paleoindian period, 10. *See also* tobacco; vegetation
polythetic rules, of image classification, 45
Ponca, 26
Popo Agie River, 76, 78
Porsche, A., 69, 74, 155
pottery, and Late Prehistoric period, 13
Powwow Cavern. *See* Amphitheater site
projectile points: and Archaic period, 12; and Dinwoody tradition, *93f*, *119f*, 193; and images of shield-bearing warriors and V-shouldered anthropomorphs, 154; and Late Archaic sites, 13; and Late Prehistoric period, 13–14; and Paleoindian period, 11. *See also* bow and arrow; lithic assemblages